WHAT THE REVIEWERS SAY ABOUT SALLY HOVEY WRIGGINS

Like Grousset [*In the Footsteps of the Buddha*], Wriggins [*Xuanzang: A Buddhist Pilgrim on the Silk Road*] approaches both Buddhism and its several Asian homelands as a sympathetic, but non-Buddhist, outsider. Her account is in some ways superior to that of Grousset, because it synthesizes the scholarly works on both the historical and anthropological-archaeological sides that have appeared since that time. Wriggins also provides detailed, but unobtrusive, endnotes, a bibliography, glossary, index, and a rich supply of illustrations.

Edward H. Kaplan
The Historian

Sally Hovey Wriggins has been a one-woman bridge between America and Asia, with her biography of Xuanzang becoming a classic. ASIA ON MY MIND captures her adventures with Quakerly goodwill heard on every page.

John Major
Author, *China Chic*

Sally Hovey Wriggins' life reflects the globalization of the twentieth century. Readers who enjoyed her standard biography of Xuanzang will be enchanted by the autobiographical journeys of this knowledgeable woman in ASIA ON MY MIND.

Morris Rossabi
Distinguished Professor of History
City University of New York

Table of Contents

Karen Swartfyger

Rosalee STACK pa 26

List of Illustrations

To W. H. W.,
love of my life

PART ONE
AMERICA AND SWITZERLAND
(1922-1949)

Chapter 1

BEGINNINGS

"If we are lucky the places and people that give our lives an aura of magic potential enter our experience at the right moment to sustain our dreams. Invariably the magic is rooted in place."

Jil Ker Conway

I grew up in the shadow of Mount Rainier, "the rough edge of the world," in Seattle. There the mountain ranges come down to the sea, and the giant evergreens are always a presence. My father was in the first party that climbed Mt. Rainier on the south side. He covered his face with a black cream against the sun's glare on the snow. In photo albums, he looks like Freeman Gosden, who played Amos on the popular comedy show. He slept in the crater at the top and climbed down this 14,410-foot mountain the next day. Daddy, then a handsome young man, slight of build, always in khakis, pursued my mother near a rushing stream on that mountain. He offered her fresh clear water from a tin collapsible cup. My mother, also a member of the Mountaineer Club, was a vivacious young woman whose brown hair was so long that, when she unbraided her pigtails, she could sit on it.

Theirs was a swift courtship: they were married in 1916 in the Congregational Church in Tacoma, Washington where Mother was born. After they had been married for thirty-seven years, Daddy—applying for a passport—received a letter from the King County marriage clerk in Seattle saying that the county had no record of their marriage. Daddy wrote the clerk saying that he didn't know he had been living in sin for so long, especially since he had three children and six grandchildren. I was the youngest of his children, with two older brothers, Jim and Win.

We lived on a quiet street in Madison Park, a residential area on Lake Washington. Ours was a roomy wooden house surrounded by a garden with four enormous cherry trees—ninety feet tall—in the back yard. Every summer my parents' good friend, Charlie Clise, would come with his tall fireman's ladders to pick cherries. There was a sprawling apricot tree I could climb, as well as several plum trees. Behind a traditional flower garden were patches of blackberries and loganberries, and then huge vacant lots where we built forts and had secret hiding places. The blackberry brambles were a hiding place for wild birds too, before a back alley was put in.

Our garden went right up to the blackberries. One day Mother called, "Come quickly!" Out from the brambles burst forth two magnificent ring-necked pheasants almost as big as turkeys. These pheasants originated in China and are sometimes called China pheasants. They were introduced in 1881, when thirty birds were released in the Northwest. When I was a child I didn't know the exotic origins of these harbingers of my future, but I was impressed with the awful screeching as they fought over their turf. The males, with their long, pointed tails and iridescent green heads with red eye patches, lunged at each other. They squawked, making fearsome noises. They fought until one of them retreated into the brambles.

Mt. Rainier was part of all our lives. I still remember my puzzlement and excitement with the fact that, although I could see Mt Rainier, along with the Cascade and Olympic ranges, in the distance, we could actually drive up the mountain itself and go skiing down its sides without falling off. At age six I was so taken with this that I wrote this embarrassing piece for my second grade teacher:

I am Mt. Rainier. I am very high. I am covered with snow and ice but flowers grow on me too. When the sun shines on my snow, I have beautiful colors. I look down on the world and see so many things. I see farms, trees, lakes, rivers and people. The people are going fast in automobiles. The people come fast to me and climb my steep sides. They look down from me and see wonderful things. They climb on me with snowshoes and make tracks. They slide on me with skis and go—whiz, whiz through the air. Sometimes they do not like my crevasses because they think I am hard to climb.

A little girl comes to visit me. She slides upon my back with great delight. She has gay trousers. She wears boots and a gay rough neck and kinds of gay clothes.

She is a great sport. She is happier when she has good plans for her sports. *[I always thought the teacher inserted this sentence.]* Her name is beautiful. It is Sally Hovey. She is so gay in the snow. She wears snow shoes and she goes down me on skis. She beats all the boys in the races. Don't you think she is wonderful? I do.

She has a heart of God in her all the time. *[Another sentence from the teacher—I couldn't seem to find the right words for what I wanted to say.]* I call her Queen of the Mountain.

Our family frequently took camping trips with the Clise family at Silver Spring in the Cascade mountains. And of course my brothers, who were older, could ski with their grown-up ski harnesses, while mine had only straps. When the straps came off—as they often did—the ski shot down the hill all by itself. Before the snow came, our two families walked in the forest to see the giant Douglas fir. It took twelve of us to stretch our arms around its massive trunk. Not far from this tree, Mr. Young, the caretaker to the cabin, lived in an open lean-to in front of a fire. People said he actually kept a rifle under his mattress.

In the summer time, we went to Anderson's Point, one of the few sandy beaches on Puget Sound on the west passage between Seattle and Tacoma. It had been in the Anderson family since 1870 and was wonderfully unspoiled. We got to Anderson's Point on the *Old Virginia V*, a pointed ferry that did not carry cars. On Friday evenings, Daddy and Mr. Anderson—in his straw hat—would take the ferry to the Andersons' dock. When the *Virginia V* was put out of commission, we stocked supplies at Olalla and rowed four miles along the shore to get there. Sometimes we slept in tents, other times in a small caretaker's cottage. We pumped our water from a well and used kerosene lanterns for light. We were miles away from any human habitation.

When I was a teenager, Mother and I went out for two weeks alone, and we slept in the cottage. We used to hear animal noises at night near the cooler. We smelled skunk but we didn't dare chase it away. Daytimes, I explored the beach at low tide, watched the log booms go by and smelled the mock orange bushes. Mother and I talked a lot, too. This is when she showed me the old-fashioned root house where people used to store potatoes, turnips and beets to keep them at a steady temperature throughout the cold winter months. She explained to me that when I was a baby, I caught whooping cough. In those days, thousands of American babies died of this respiratory infection, which keeps phlegm in their chests. If the baby is able to cough, it is a tiny little cough followed by a whooping sound. As I began to get well, the doctor recommended exposing me to the "good Puget Sound air." Mother had brought me, along with a nurse, to recuperate at Anderson's Point. They used to put me in this roothouse to sleep!

The beach was always filled with driftwood and long silver-grey logs under Madrona trees. These are distinctive evergreens, native to the northwest, with peeling red bark, a little like Eastern birch trees. The water in Puget Sound was so cold that we dashed in and out. We rarely swam for pleasure. My brothers spear-fished or rowed out to the middle of the sound's deep channel to hitch onto the giant log booms that were going north from Tacoma and Seattle. We gathered huckleberries for pancakes, and driftwood for our huge nighttime fires. We listened to the hermit thrushes singing their ethereal songs in the tops of the trees above the beach.

One of our chores was to gather bark, from the piles left on the beach by the log booms, and to stash it in large gunny sacks to burn in the fireplace in our house in Seattle. In the summer, when we didn't use the fireplace, we stowed our bags of bark in the basement. One day a spark from the furnace landed on the bags of bark. The whole basement caught fire. The flames came up through the register and went roaring up to the second floor. Mother called the Fire Department and then she called Daddy, who was downtown having lunch at the Rainier Club. The family story is that Daddy took a taxi home. When the taxi reached the edge of Madison Park, the taxi driver turned around and said, "Look, there are fire engines at the top of the hill."

Daddy, who hadn't said anything to the driver about hurrying until the driver mentioned the fire trucks, said calmly, "Why yes, it is my house!" This was, the family thought, the quintessence of Daddy's Eastern reserve. Daddy had grown up in New England and had come out West in 1906, the year of the San Francisco earthquake. He found a job right away in a bank in San Francisco because he had a reputation for being able to count checks faster than anyone else. He then went north to Seattle and worked in "commercial paper" —which, until I was about fourteen, I thought was stationery.

When I was ten I became a Girl Scout. Mother was the Girl Scout leader. She taught us the names of plants and birds. She had taken botany courses from Professor Fry at the University of Washington. She knew the area well from having grown up there. Once she had stood up in Professor Fry's class and announced, "The real name of Mt. Rainier should be Mt. Takoma, the Indian name of the mountain." Mother took our Scout troop on day trips that included such delicious excursions as running for a mile down the steep hill of the Seattle Sand and Gravel Pit, just for the fun of it.

We had been comfortably off until, in 1932, Daddy's investment banking firm went bankrupt. That's when Mother started a knitting business, teaching young and old how to knit. Our friend Charlie Clise paid the mortgage on the house, and we gave up our car. We continued my membership in the Seattle Tennis Club. One Sunday, *The Seattle Times* ran a full-page color spread about me. This caused a lot of problems for my father, because all his creditors then knew where to find him. They called him up, wanting him to pay our bills.

Daddy loved to walk in the rain, so Mother used to send the two of us on Sunday afternoon walks "to get him out of the house." In the course of these excursions, he used to pull out from his vest pocket an old envelope that had notations as to how much he had to pay on the light bill, the telephone bill, the heating bill, to keep them from being shut off. One time we were so poor that we couldn't charge any more at the local grocery store, so Mother walked five miles to her sister's house in Madrona to pick up a huge fresh fish for supper. My brothers each had morning paper routes. I was young and was protected from many of the family's money woes. I didn't know the fish story until many years later. Most nights Mother stayed up until two o'clock to finish sweaters for her customers. Daddy fumed because he figured she was making no more than fifteen cents an hour. Gradually the stock market improved, and Mother's knitting business flourished too.

I don't remember my father's sayings, but I do remember Mother's. "Aren't you glad you are living?" Or doing something "just for ducks" like taking her Girl Scouts to the Sand and Gravel Pit. And the lovely one, "to add to the gaiety of nations." Mother's many friends loved this zest for living that was so much a part of her.

The respect in which my father was held came from a different source. One of his clients was "old Fred Everett," a gaunt wealthy man who dressed in an old-fashioned winged collar. He looked like Neville Chamberlain with his scrawny neck. Daddy knew that Old Fred kept his money in cash in a number of banks around Seattle, and that he gave his wife Elizabeth only about twenty dollars a week to live on. Finally Daddy felt that he must do something to help Elizabeth, so he told her how Old Fred had been hoarding his money all these years. She was so grateful that she gave my parents a trip to Honolulu. Some years later, in 1953, because Daddy was a big Anglophile, she gave them a trip to Queen Elizabeth II's Coronation in England.

Our house was always full of people. First, Mother's nephew Norrie joined our household. Later on his mother, Aunt Nona, came to live with us after her husband died. During World War II, refugees from Germany came to stay with us after fleeing their own country to escape Hitler. My brothers' friends used to come and play poker at the dining room table. Mother had wonderful rapport with them; she knew how to kid and how to scold. Once, when she discovered the boys smoking in the basement, she made them all come upstairs and smoke their cigarettes in the living room until they got sick. One thing she couldn't seem to prevent was their delight in teasing me. When Sonny Lewis, Win's friend, came roaring into the house saying, "Where is Sally? I am going to tickle her!," I used to run upstairs and hide.

When I think of all the people in our house I am afraid that I always think of wet sheets hanging in the basement. Washing machines and clothes wringers there were, but no electric dryers. Ditto refrigerators. We had a cooler and an ice box, which was a cabinet-sized wooden cupboard containing a huge chunk of ice. The ice man carried this ice slab on his shoulder, which was protected by a large leather shield. He also carried tongs and a deadly-looking ice pick. I liked to watch him swing the block of ice down off his back and stuff it in the ice box. There was also the grimy-faced coal man who brought sacks of coal to pour down the chute that emptied into the basement. Then one day an organ grinder with a little brown monkey came to our street and stopped in our front yard. It seems so implausible now that I wonder if I imagined it, but I don't think so.

When I was fourteen, I was given a scholarship to the Helen Bush School. At the time I didn't think about where it came from, except I knew my parents had many friends. Whatever the source, the following four years opened up new horizons—especially in music, art, literature, modern dance and foreign languages. It was a new progressive school, started by Helen Bush in her home in 1924; it grew, and later took over the building of the Lakeside School. Mrs. Bush was in favor of co-education, but when I attended the school it was still getting started and was limited to girls. I was in the fifth graduating class and we all felt that we were "shaping the school."

There were no grades on our report cards, only so-called "helpful comments," such as mine in chemistry: "Sally works hard but acts baffled." Which was true: I was afraid of the chemistry equipment—but I admired the chemistry teacher, Dr. Gayley, who had also taught me Latin. She said to me once, "You know, you can do anything you really want to." Another time, I was racing down the hall and I ran into—who else?—Dr. Gayley. She embraced me with a smile, brushing aside my embarrassment by saying, " It is my pleasure." Of course I worshipped her from then on. Mrs. Bush found remarkable teachers. She drew on people connected with the Cornish School, an innovative art and music school in Seattle. Bonnie Bird, a former member of the Martha Graham dance troupe, and John Cage, her accompanist, were on the Helen Bush School faculty.

The school's emphasis on the arts was reflected in many of the girls who attended there. My best friend, also a scholarship student, was Jenness Summers. Her mother had died when she was young and her father, an admiralty lawyer, had married his secretary afterwards. Her mother had been well-known as being rather ethereal, as indeed was Jenness, with her distinctive hushed and rather breathless voice. She had a fey sense of humor and a lilting laugh. Jenness introduced me to exciting new worlds: to symphony music (César Franck's *Fifth Symphony* was one of our favorites); to the Indian philosopher Krishnamurti; and to Asian ideas of dispassion, detachment and discrimination (a typical utterance was: *"What is impossible becomes possible only when you understand there is no tomorrow")*. In music appreciation classes we analyzed Sibelius' *Second Symphony*. Bush sponsored trips to the symphony and I bought my tickets with the sixty dollars I had saved from my allowance on banking day in grade school. I was able to see Stravinsky conduct and to hear George Gershwin play. I still remember what a sad face he had.

Mother used to talk about the Seattle Art Museum. Dr. Richard Fuller, its founder and benefactor, hired Carl Gould, an architect, to build it in the early 1930s. But it wasn't until Jenness and I became such intimate friends that I would often walk from Madison Hill through what we used to call—to my shame now—

Coon Hollow, and up Capitol Hill to the museum. Dudley Pratt, the husband of our art teacher, had made the huge wooden sculpture in the foyer. My favorite pieces were the sandstone Khmer heads with their downcast eyes and secret smiles. Weren't they the embodiment of detachment and dispassion?

In 1938, while we were haunting the Asian Art Museum, Morris Graves, a young Northwest painter, was also going to the museum and drawing inspiration from the Chinese ritual vessels and chalices there. As Graves put it at the time, "I was museuming by day and walking with my heart in my hands by night." Along with Mark Tobey, Kenneth Callahan, and Guy Anderson, he became one of the founders of the Northwest Visionary school of art. They achieved national recognition at the Museum of Modern Art in New York in 1942, not long after my days of hanging out at the museum.

I knew Morris Graves's name, and perhaps that he was a Buddhist painter, because he used to spend time at Enetai where my cousins, the Hatches, had a summer place. Eventually Helen Hatch and her husband Marshall became serious art collectors and bought many of his paintings. I grew to love his work.

Morris Graves had a keen appreciation of Asian art and culture. His charged images of sea birds, fish, small animals represented a fascinating synthesis of Pacific Northwest and Asian cultures across the Pacific. As a young man, Graves had been to Japan, and in later years would go again many times. But when World War II started, everything and everyone Japanese fell into disfavor. It was at this time that the United States government drove the Japanese from their homes on the coast and compelled them to live in detention camps.

In the summers I went for two weeks to Robinswold, the Girl Scout Camp on Hoods Canal. In 1938, I was experienced enough to go on a 45-mile pack trip in the Olympic mountains. This is when I met and became friends with Toto Ohata, a Japanese-American girl. It was also at Robinswold that I became aware that I wasn't just a person but part of a social class. I hadn't thought about this before, but Mother and Daddy's friends were a privileged group. The land for Camp Robinswold had, after all, been given to the Scouts by the Robbins family. And the Girl Scout day camp on Mercer Island had been donated by the Clise family. Mother worked with both Mrs. Robbins and Mrs. Clise in the Scout movement in Seattle. Helena Robbins saw to it that there were blacks in her scout troop and in her home. In Seattle, in those days, this was very unusual among the people we knew.

During my junior year at Bush, clouds of war were gathering. Jenness Summers had a brother, Thane, who volunteered for the International Brigade in the Spanish Civil War. Thane was older than we were, and had taught philosophy at the University of Washington. He was killed March 28, 1938. Jenness persuaded the other girls that instead of the usual class gift of a tree, they should give money to bring a Spanish war orphan to America. Her plan was foiled by the school administrators, who insisted on the tree.

Helen Bush and Marjory Livengood, the Vice Principal, in the summer of 1939 took a group of students—I didn't go—to Fontainebleau in France to study French at the École des Beaux Arts. Just before Labor Day, with the news that war was imminent, the students were hustled onto a boat at Le Havre, along with hundreds of other refugees. Passengers slept on the floors of cabins and in public rooms. They heard the Declaration of War over the ship's radio two days before landing in New York. The grand cruise ships were painted gray to escape detection on the seas, carrying Americans and refugees who stood elbow to elbow waiting to get to America.

A London fireman, who had battled the fires from terrible Nazi bombings of London, talked at our house. And soon after, two German refugees, Eva Bilsten and her young son, George, came to live with us. They were cultivated people and very stoical. We always used to laugh behind their backs when they told us just how many pee-pees their little dachshund made on their walks. Eventually Eva's mother came to live with us too. Eva taught me German composition. I loved German music, especially Beethoven, and admired the novels of Thomas Mann. On the strength of this slender reed, I hoped to give a talk on German culture at my graduation from Bush in 1940. Happily, I didn't do so. I spoke on American culture, which I thought consisted mostly of things made of plastic. It was just as well, since France fell in June of that year, and German culture fell out of favor.

That last year at Bush, our English teacher Will Pre Tyler, who was a vegetarian, brought to Bush a tall exotic Indian wearing a long white tunic. As President of the Student Body, I met him ahead of time for orange juice in Mrs. Bush's office. I introduced him to the student assembly, where he spoke in a clipped English accent about his country's struggle for independence from the British. He told us that since we lived in the land of the freedom of Lincoln and Jefferson, surely we understood Indians' desire for independence. Like all the other girls in my class, I had a crush on him and could hardly wait to tell my parents what he said. Several weeks later the school—which thought we should also hear the British point of view—arranged for a portly British colonel to come and talk to us about the importance of upholding the British empire. Not only was the Colonel middle-aged and tubby, but the times were against him. The Colonel didn't stand a chance of convincing us girls, against such a glamorous Indian.

As a high school senior in 1940, I didn't know that the exotic Indian would represent the wave of the future in Asia and Africa— the rise of newly independent nations. I had even less of an idea that studying the rise of newly independent countries would be the central occupation of my future husband. When the time came to go to college, I wanted to go to a liberal school. I had been disappointed that Bush had chosen the tree for a class present instead of money for a war orphan. At this time, I was also enthusiastic about Indian independence, so I applied to Black Mountain College in North Carolina where geniuses like John Cage, Merce Cunningham, Buckminster Fuller and Josef Albers were teaching in a communal environment.

I was somewhat surprised one day when I came home from school to find on the dining table a newspaper with large black headlines saying **BLACK MOUNTAIN COLLEGE CLOSED: SALLY SORRY**, that my father had mocked up. I got the point, even though Black Mountain College did not, in fact, close until a decade later. I then applied for, and won, a scholarship to Reed College in Portland, Oregon. At that time, Reed College was referred to as "Red College," and my father was convinced the place was Communist. I'm not sure he ever changed his mind. My older brothers had chosen more conventional routes: Jim had gone to Whitman College in eastern Washington, but a visit there convinced me that it was not for me. Because of the Depression, Win didn't go to college at all, much to Mother's disappointment.

Reed held an introductory weekend camping trip on Mt. Hood in Oregon before college started that fall, so the first people I knew were outdoor types. Unfortunately, my reputation as a Seattle socialite had preceded me to Reed, so I had to dress down. First, I tanked up in the Barbey Beer Hall just to show an upper class-mate, Pat Corbley, that I was not a softie. I received the appropriate reprimand from the Dean of Students Maida Bailey, who later became a dear friend. Maida had a ranch in central Oregon, where she had lived before becoming a dean, first at Stanford, then at Reed. Later I would take the bus down to Sisters, Oregon, to see her because I admired her work in the League of Women Voters and in the community.

After my preparation at the Helen Bush School, I found Reed's two-year humanities course a rich encounter with the literature and history of Western Civilization. We read Plato's philosophy, the histories of Herodotus and Thucydides, and the tragedies of Aeschylus and Sophocles. I nearly flunked mathematics. As part of the National Youth Administration Assistance program, I earned money by operating the Capehart machine in the music room. Records in the forties were only three-and-a-half minutes long and it was my job to turn them over. I learned to love many new composers and new-to-me music. Then during spring vacation of my junior year, when many of us came down with measles and couldn't use our eyes, I took all the Beethoven quartets out of the music room and did nothing but listen to them for ten days!

One of the brightest of my fellow students was Pat Beck, several feet taller than I, and forthright with her strong chin, hearty laugh and deep voice. We were in Victor Lovett Oakes Chittick's literature classes together. Chittick was a gaunt, grand figure with a supremely ugly face which was somehow beautiful. Pat came to

14

refer to him as "God," which I could never quite manage. Under his tutelage we read Faulkner, and learned to love Melville and T. S. Eliot. We devoured Eliot's *Four Quartets*, which became part of my mental landscape.

Pat was also from Seattle. Her mother had played the harp for the Seattle Symphony and maintained her glamorous image offstage by wearing a black dress and white gloves with a long cigarette holder in one hand. Her father was the head of Bon Marché, a large department store in Seattle. He died when Pat was thirteen. She missed him the rest of her life. She later developed a close friendship with Clement Atlee, a former prime minister of England, who was sort of a father figure to her.

The isolation of our college world—we called Reed "the orchid in a dunghill" of pre-war Portland (at best a sleepy city, and, in our eyes, a very dull town)—ended when the Japanese bombed Pearl Harbor on December 7, 1941. The boys in my class were called up by their draft boards. Every time one of them departed, we would drink quite a lot as we said goodbye. Bit by bit, Reed became more and more of a female institution. Then Reed began to fill up with men in uniform, the 125 soldiers who were studying meteorology there as part of the war effort. I still remember coming to the Commons for dinner one day and being surrounded by soldiers. The future was uncertain for all the young men in America at that time. My brother Win, who worked in a bank in San Francisco, was drafted into the army; Jim was sent to Officer Training School at Harvard.

The disruption did not stop there. Following the Japanese attack on Pearl Harbor, the United States was gripped by war hysteria. By 1942, President Roosevelt signed Executive Order 9066, exiling 120,000 people of Japanese ancestry to camps in isolated inland areas. My friend Toto Ohata's parents were among those interned, even though, like most of the detainees, they were patriotic citizens of the United States. The conditions in camps for Japanese-Americans were harsh. The last of the camps survived until the war ended. Toto herself was able to go East to study dancing, but the shock of the war and her family's internment were too much for her and she became a schizophrenic. Before she was institutionalized, we went together on a ferry to Staten Island in New York, but it was a scary business. Her behavior was erratic. She kept wandering off and I was afraid that I might not be able to bring her back safely.

Over the summers I earned money for college. After freshman year I worked in a bank (and hated every moment); after sophmore year I was a file clerk at the Headquarters of the Twelfth Naval District. By that time, everyone was contributing to the war effort: Daddy volunteered to work swing shift as a pipefitter in the Todd Shipyard. He would come home from his daytime job at the investment banking firm, Paul Harper & Sons, and change his clothes to go to work at the shipyard. This was truly remarkable because Daddy was not handy with his hands—my brothers would joke that he couldn't change a light bulb. Both brothers were in the armed services. Win was with the Army in Europe, part of the invasion of Sicily in 1943, when his jeep hit a land mine. He was unconscious when the Army shipped him to a hospital in the U.S., where he stayed for nine months. Jim was Lieutenant Commander on a naval destroyer in the Pacific theater. Mother wrote them both all about what had been happening on Puget Sound between Seattle and Tacoma, and the censor had a field day cutting out all her descriptions of our local defenses.

The summer of 1943, after my junior year, Pat Beck and I went to California to work in the shipyards at Moore Dry Dock in Oakland. Pat was in charge of a strap shop and I ran the rack shop where the strips of iron that held up electrical wires on Liberty Ships were created. We persuaded our parents that if we lived at the Anna Head School in Berkeley—a proper girls school—it would be all right. Of course we had the time of our lives. Pat had an introduction to Alexander (Sasha) Schneider, the second violinist of the Budapest String Quartet, so when we went to the San Francisco Opera House to hear them perform at Tuesday evening concerts, we would visit him backstage. With his charming European accent, he used to introduce us: "Zees are my friends from zee shipyard," and we used to roll up our sleeves and show his sophisticated lady friends "zee orange paint" we had acquired during the day.

I loved the shipyard, working with all kinds of people to outfit the Liberty ships. After this exciting summer, it was hard to get back to academic work that last year at Reed. Every Reed senior had to write a thesis. I was veering toward cultural history, the history of ideas, largely because of the inspired teaching of my professor, Richard Jones. I was fascinated by the way ideas changed, how a word like Nature could mean one thing in eighteenth-century France and something entirely different in nineteenth-century Germany. How was it that key words of eighteenth-century France were "reason, nature and progress," and in the early nineteenth, the key words of the century had become "genius, individuality and organic development"? I worked terribly hard at the project. My model was Carl Becker's *The Heavenly City of Eighteenth Century Philosophers*. However, the final product was a flop. I called it "Some Possible Origins of German Scientific History." After handing in the thesis, the Reed senior was subjected to a two-hour oral examination. I didn't do well at that, either. I had bitten off more than I could chew. It may well be this failure that spurred me on finally to write a serious book umpteen years later.

What would I do next? Pat went on to do graduate work in history at Stanford. Mother thought I should join the Waves, but that seemed much too conventional and not very adventuresome. Instead, I found a job on a housing project in West Seattle in Work Project Services, but I was restless.

Chapter 2

NEW DIRECTIONS (1940-1955)

In August, 1944 the ever-enterprising Helen Bush opened up the facilities of her school to the Quakers for a conference on Peace and International Relations. Fred Shorter, whom I had known slightly at Reed, was at the conference. He told me about a graduate program at Haverford College, a venerable Quaker school outside Philadelphia, that was granting master's degrees in Relief and Reconstruction during World War II. Their graduates would assist in rebuilding European villages after the war and help re-create a peaceful world. The Quakers had been active in relief work in Europe after World War I and hoped to do the same after World War II. So who were the Quakers? I wondered. What kind of place was Haverford? I found a book about the college and was amused by a photograph of a "very inward-looking man" named T. Wister Brown, with a caption underneath which said, "Be bold, be bold, everywhere be bold, but not too bold."

That seemed promising to me with my sense of adventure.

I received a small scholarship and was able to cut down my expenses by living with the Comfort family. My good friend Nell Clark in Seattle had known Betty Comfort in Greece when Betty's father had been dentist to the King of Greece. Betty's husband Howard Comfort was the son of the former President of Haverford, William Wister Comfort. Howard taught Latin. I was to stay with them and their children, Wister and Laura, while I was at Haverford. All the other students in the program—five men and twenty-one women—lived at Language House on the campus.

On my train ride east to Philadelphia I lost my typewriter when I changed trains in Chicago. Once I arrived in Philadelphia, I took a taxi all the way out to Haverford, since no one thought to tell me that there was such a thing as a suburban train. I enjoyed my stay with the Comforts. Howard had a sardonic wit and could do a marvelous imitation of Groucho Marx. He loved to sing Gilbert and Sullivan. I had a grand time at Haverford, which was filled with bright young men—especially coming from Reed, which had nearly become a female seminary after America joined the war. There were so many attractive boys around. The only drawback was that Betty Comfort taught French in my program at Haverford. If I had been out with a Haverford boy and didn't do well in French the next day, I was in trouble.

In addition to French class, the Reconstruction and Relief Program at Haverford included area study, accounting, social work, nutrition, public health and, at one time, auto mechanics. Douglas Steere, Professor of Philosophy and Religion, directed the Reconstruction and Relief Program. He also saw to it that we learned about Quaker philosophy as well as about practical matters. The Quaker belief that "there is that of God in every man" underlay the the AFSC (American Friends Service Committee) and their relief work. I also learned the practice of silence in Quaker meeting. We attended Quaker Meeting with the Haverford boys on Thursday mornings.

The course most valuable for me was taught by a large, soft-spoken German woman named Hertha Krauss, who was also teaching at Bryn Mawr. She had been head of the Welfare Services in Frankfurt in her twenties, before coming to America. Her course, International Relief and Social Reconstruction, was very systematic. It illuminated culture patterns so that we would be sensitive to what refugees had been through—the physical exhaustion of the refugees, the hostilities of rival European countries, the shift in values as the war progressed, and impatience with American waste—such things as leaving food on our plates, or leaving the lights on.

In March 1945, two months before the end of our first year, an official from UNRRA (United Nations Relief and Reconstruction Agency) came to recruit students for overseas assignments. Fifteen of us were selected. With the end of the war looming, huge movements of displaced persons were predicted. UNRRA felt it had to move quickly to prepare for this wave of emigration, and by June—just before the war in Europe ended—those of us selected were on the way to the UNRRA training center at the University of Maryland in College Park, outside Washington, D.C. We recruits from Haverford were much younger than other UNRRA employees. The list of our UNRRA field staff equipment included a belt with pistol and revolver, but mercifully we never received these.

The program director was Dr. Frank Munk, who had also been at Reed. Bertram Pickard, an elderly English Quaker from Geneva (whom I knew about because of his travels in the United States), was Munk's assistant. The two of them did a Laurel and Hardy act together, in which slight-of-build Bertram pretended to be afraid of his boss. Munk played the mean, tough-minded bully. It was lots of fun. We all loved it. But other than these two men, I didn't know a soul. This might not have mattered, except that I never got to join my UNRRA Training Center colleagues in Germany. Instead, much to my surprise, I ended up in a hospital in Washington having a kidney removed. In the rush to get started, UNRRA had taken all young graduate students from Haverford without making sure until the last moment that they could pass their physical examinations. I didn't pass mine and, after the six weeks' training, the rest of my UNRRA class took off for Europe without me.

Leaving the UNRRA training center in Maryland and going on a bus into Washington to get to the hospital, I had a feeling of falling, falling and falling, of hitting rock bottom. I didn't think anything more could happen to me. Rather than throwing me into despair, it created a curious sense of freedom.

21

Bertram Pickard came to see me in the hospital. He's one of those articulate Englishmen with a lightness of touch that characterizes many Quakers. (I noticed this characteristic when I first went to Haverford.) Bertram loved word play—in fact, all kinds of play. As a child he had lost the use of one eye, but he was still a great birder—he learned to recognize birds by listening to their calls. Bertram wore a glass eyeball which was scarcely noticeable because of his glasses. I'm told that he used to take it out and toss it up in the air to amuse his grandchildren. So, knowing Bertram's playful nature, I wasn't surprised when he brought me a copy of James Thurber's *Is Sex Necessary?*

Hertha Krauss came down from Bryn Mawr. She informed me that I was very fortunate to lose the one organ of the body of which there were two. "Organizationally speaking," she said, "you don't really need both kidneys." Toni Sender, the Austrian Socialist leader who had been at the UNRRA Training Center, gave me a lovely pink bed jacket. My hospital roommate, whom I had never met before, arranged for me to go stay with her family until I was strong enough to go back to Haverford. Mother knit sweater suits for her two little boys to thank her for this unusual act of kindness.

Back at Haverford, one of my old beaux walked all the way across the campus to ask, "Well, did everything come out all right?" The Comforts took me in again, and I spent the fall finishing course work at Haverford before going back to Washington. Although I was not able to go Europe, I found a job with the Displaced Persons division of UNRRA. I was glad to be working, since I still had debts from college, not to mention doctor bills. I worked on my master's thesis on the Displaced Persons Operation in Germany—at night. I submitted my thesis in June, 1946.

At that time, Congress was debating the Stratton bill, temporary legislation suspending immigration quotas and allowing displaced persons to enter the United States. Of course, all of us relief workers wanted to see it passed. But even with all our concern with international affairs, life still went on. I had been living at the Kingsmith School—so-called because, ostensibly, we took a few language courses in addition to boarding there—and there I met Anne Shipley, who worked at the Friends Committee on National Legislation. I attended Quaker meeting in Washington and, coincidentally, found a nifty basement apartment right across from the Meetinghouse on Florida Avenue. Anne, still at Kingsmith, invited me to her wedding in Philadelphia.

Her Aunt Sally Moore, the family matriarch, gave the wedding reception at her big old Victorian house in Germantown in Philadelphia. She greeted us at the door in a long black dress and black button shoes. Among the people there was a young man who had grown up right across the street from Anne at 470 Locust Avenue. He had just come back from six years' service with the American Friends Service Committee, doing relief work in Portugal, Italy, Egypt and France. We met at the punch bowl. He was tall, slim, with wonderful brown eyes, bushy eyebrows, chestnut-colored hair above a high forehead. His name was Howard Wriggins. I had vague memories of a tall lanky guy I had heard give a talk at AFSC headquarters in Philadelphia, but I wasn't sure whether this was the same man. At the time, Howard was representing the American Friends Service Committee, a leading non-governmental organization (NGO), to plan ways in which NGOs could work constructively with the newly-formed United Nations. If I had gone overseas with all my Haverford friends, I would never have met this marvelous man!

I didn't learn until later that he had gone to Germantown Friends School and Dartmouth College. He had spent his junior year abroad at the Sciences Politiques in Paris. Not that these achievements mattered to me. I loved his sense of humor, the way he talked, the sound of his voice. "I don't think this punch is spiked," one of us said, but we can never remember which of us it was. I was wearing a stylish brown silk shirtwaist dress with buttons up the front. Life has never been the same since that day when I fell madly in love with Howard.

I can still remember each time I saw Howard. He sometimes came to Washington to check on the progress of the Stratton bill, which was finally passed in 1948. We shared many memorable times—our first dinner eating coq au vin together at the Napoleon Restaurant, at which I told every funny story I knew; our walk in

Rock Creek Park where he caught poison ivy; a trip to Massachusetts for the Berkshire Festival; a trip to the Pocono Mountains. Then there was the miserable weekend I went to the Shenandoah Valley where we were not together. Eventually we took a serious trip together, visiting friends around New England. The O'Haras were our hosts at Goose Rocks, Maine. Mrs. O'Hara's elderly father, Herbert Putnam (who was long retired from being head of the Library of Congress), asked his daughter whether ours was a trial marriage, and she didn't know. Howard said later that he thought he had proposed on Sprucehead Island in Maine, but I wasn't sure that his words about being "old shoes together" were really a proposal of marriage.

We returned to 470 Locust Avenue in Germantown, to his family's spacious fieldstone house with its long driveway. At dinner that night, sitting around a large mahogany table, the kind with lion claw feet, we waited as long as we could. We were just starting to tell Howard's mother, a tall gray-haired lady with quiet gray eyes, that we had something important to say when she shushed us, nodding towards the maid. "Katherine is still clearing the table," she advised us. "Perhaps your news can wait." As soon as Katherine had taken away the silver, we shared our exciting news.

That summer Mother and Daddy were touring the Western parks, so they asked us to meet them in Salt Lake City. It was so hot on our arrival that Mother suggested going to the Great Salt Lake to cool off. It was then that Howard formally (or informally) asked Daddy for my hand as we waded in the salty lake. Howard got along famously with my parents as the four of us toured the Grand Canyon, Bryce Canyon, and Glacier National Park. Howard had to leave us to start a fall term studying International Relations at Yale. After bidding him goodbye in the airport, I had dinner with Mother and Daddy. I promptly lost it, choking up over Howard's absence.

Howard, his mother (whom we called Gran), his sister Edith, and her husband, Bob Atmore, came out West for the wedding, December 22, 1947. Gran endeared herself to me ahead of time by saying that she was glad we were going to have an Episcopal wedding with music and flowers, because sometimes Quaker weddings can be a little gloomy. I had no Quaker friends in Seattle and didn't know anyone in the Quaker Meeting there, so we were married in the Episcopal church in Madrona where I had attended as a child.

Everyone was charmed by Gran, and kept saying, "But you are such fun . . ." with the unspoken half of the sentence being, "so much more fun than we thought you would be." The person responsible for her reputation as a dignified, reserved and stoical person could have been no one else but me.

Had I talked about Daddy's Eastern reserve that my mother, my brothers and I had teased him about? Had I suggested that Howard's mother was not spontaneous? Or marveled at her protection of her privacy? Or commented on how people in the East didn't always say what they thought? Had I pointed out her tremendous self-discipline? Probably I had. I am sure I told them that Gran had met Howard's father, Charlie, on an ocean liner going to Europe. They married eight years later. Brothers married sisters (Charlie's sister Helen married Gran's brother John). Howard and his sisters had grown up in a large stone house in Philadelphia and his father's brother, Tom, lived in a similar stone house right behind theirs. Charlie and Tom ran a fashionable ladies' specialty store in downtown Philadelphia called B. F. Dewees. For many years, their mother Lizzie Dewees, who was owner of the store, lived with her son Tom, Howard's uncle. No wonder Gran had learned to be circumspect!

I didn't think about it at the time, but I was marrying an Easterner just as Mother had. My only regret was that Howard's father was not with us. Although I had never met him, I knew from the people who had known him that he was a charming and brilliant man.

After the wedding, we moved to Connecticut so that Howard could work on his PhD at Yale. Three months into the second year at Yale, on December 6, 1948, AFSC asked Howard to serve as their liaison in Geneva with the U.N. program for Palestine refugees. He didn't take long to accept: he knew how great were the problems of Palestinian refugees; he knew that, with his experience from World War II, he could be useful; and he wanted me to have the chance—that I had missed four years earlier because of my health problems—to live in Europe. In less than a week, we were in Switzerland. This all happened so fast that when we stepped out of the airplane in Geneva, Elmore Jackson, the Quaker representative who met us, said, "Oh, I didn't know Sally was coming."

I was pregnant when we arrived in Geneva and I delivered our daughter Diana four months later, on April 2, 1949, *à la* Natural Childbirth. My obstetrician, Doctor Luc Danon, a mysterious-looking man with dark olive skin, told me that there were fashions in childbirth. One year all the American ladies wanted anesthetics, the next year they wanted Natural Childbirth. He was not enthusiastic about my choice of Natural Childbirth, but he was both competent and tolerant.

Howard assisted at the birthing and translated from the French for me. I can still hear the *sage femme* (midwife) shouting, "PLUS FORT, MADAME, PLUS FORT!" The birth of our daughter gave us three honorary grandparents, English Quakers Bertram and Irene Pickard and Rosalie Stack, who said, as she admired Dinny, "You know, Sally, this is the one time in your life when you feel you are wonderful and you really *are* wonderful." The Bois Gentil, the lying-in hospital where Diana was born, was no ordinary nursing home: I stayed two weeks, invited people for tea, had a massage, and one day left the clinique with Howard in a newly purchased decrepit Topolino (a Mickey Mouse Fiat) to take a spin on the Salève to see the burgeoning spring.

This dramatic disruption of our life, taking us to Geneva and bringing Howard's talents to Palestine relief, also brought us new and enduring friends; not this only, but some of our children have also become friends with their children. Howard met Paul Booz at the Palais des Nations, which housed all the agencies connected with the United Nations. He and his wife Elizabeth—always called Ben—would contribute to our lives in significant ways, and we to theirs. Paul and Ben had met when they both worked on the Yugoslav railway in 1947. Ben was taking a degree at the School

The 1940s

Le Bois-Gentil, Geneva

for International Studies in Geneva but she was also an unusually gifted painter and author. Howard was off on his Palestine field trips when they were married in Geneva, but I went to their wedding in the American Church. Just before we left Geneva, we took Dinny in a laundry basket out to the Boozes' newly acquired house in Yvoire on Lake Geneva, where Ben has lived for six months of the year ever since.

Our wonderful Geneva stay lasted only eight months. Howard had written to the Director of International Affairs at Yale (who shall be nameless), who wrote back that "there would be no objections to his return." So after this warm welcome, Howard resumed his courses at Yale. We returned with our three-month-old baby and found housing in East Haven in a large public housing project. Howard continued with his courses and began preparing for his orals, and when that huge hurdle was crossed he started his thesis, working with Gabriel Almond on "The Appeals of Communism." Howard was coming along nicely with his thesis when our son Christopher was born, again by Natural Childbirth, on August 12, 1951. Right away Christopher and I were put into an experimental program at Grace New Haven Hospital called Rooming-In, where his crib was placed right next to my bed and I took care of him without much assistance from the nursing staff.

Howard received his degree from Yale in 1952 and was lured into teaching at Vassar in Poughkeepsie, one hundred miles north of New York City. We bought our first house in Poughkeepsie, and we even found some land on the coast of Maine at Little Cranberry Island, off Mount Desert, at a bargain price. The evergreen trees were smaller than those on Puget Sound, but the sharp salt air was just like that of my childhood. Finally we were putting down roots. Much to our surprise, we had become "people of property."

Just as we were settling down for the first time in our lives, Mother sent a clipping from the *Seattle Times* announcing that Patricia Beck was going out to Ceylon. It turned out that she was traveling with the family of an old Quaker friend of Howard's, Geoffrey Wilson. Geoffrey had moved to Ceylon to head up the Colombo Plan, a cooperative regional agency initiated by the British Commonwealth. With its headquarters in Colombo, it promised innovative aid programs for all of South and Southeast Asia.

I knew that Pat had left Stanford to work for *Life* magazine in New York City. She had then gone on to England to work for Time/Life in London, and had become a British citizen. Why was she leaving London? And why go to Ceylon? Wasn't it somewhere in Asia? What a crazy thing to do! An island in the Indian Ocean? A British colony? Where the tea came from? I was so swamped caring for our small children that the idea of going to the other side of the world was incomprehensible. Why would anyone want to go to Ceylon? It all seemed remote—and, frankly, a little strange.

PART TWO
CEYLON
(1955-1957)

Chapter 3

OUR OLD HOUSE IN CINNAMON GARDENS

What had been unthinkable became a reality. As our British prop jet circled over the cobalt blue Indian Ocean, we could look down on the swaying palm trees of this newly independent country that Howard hoped to write a book about: Ceylon. This is where we would be spending the next two years of our lives. We were a young family with two small children, Dinny and Chris. The year was 1955.

Very early on, when I was making preparations to go, I wrote to Judy Wilson, who had lived in Ceylon when Geoffrey ran the Colombo Plan. I wanted to know whether, in Ceylon, we could have a true evergreen tree with needles, and not just a palm branch, for a Christmas tree. I also talked to Judy in London, for we spent three months in England before going to Ceylon: Howard studied the newspaper clippings of the Royal Institute of International Affairs, reading about Ceylon's peaceful transition from Crown Colony to independent nation.

As we approached the Colombo airport, I wondered about the great unknown that the small island represented. One of Howard's friends in graduate school, Ponna Wignaraja, was from Ceylon. I remember once he gave a party at Yale and the reception room was filled with incense! "What a touch of sophistication!" we said to ourselves. My only other association with Ceylon was the Lipton tea Mother served every afternoon at home when I was growing up in Seattle. Shortly before we left America, she sent us a beautiful two volumes on the art of Indian Asia, just as she had given us a book of Russian folk songs at a time when Howard thought he might become a Soviet specialist. Mother was always able to reach out, to enrich and support us in whatever we did.

Two of Ponna's friends met us at the airport, and his family welcomed us. Not long after our arrival in Colombo, the capital of Ceylon, we went to an Asian diplomats' conference, sponsored by the American Friends Service Committee. Geoffrey Wilson came out from London to run it. We rode on the train together to the University of Ceylon's campus at Peradeniya near Kandy, where the conference was held. Curiously, I am not sure I ever asked him how he had met Pat Beck and how she happened to come to Ceylon with his family. A handsome man with a serious demeanor, Geoffrey's occasional smile revealed wonderful crinkles around his eyes—but he didn't smile very often. I nicknamed him "Cold Geoffrey."

Asian diplomats came from Pakistan, Ceylon, Japan, Indonesia, Malaysia, Singapore, India, and Australia. From the West, representatives of the United Kingdom, France, the Netherlands, Germany, the United States and Canada joined them to discuss national sovereignty and international responsibility. The words, the thoughts behind what some of the Asian diplomats said were similar to the ideas of Prime Minister Nehru of India, especially his doctrine of peace and non-alignment in a cold-war world. The diplomats talked about Pancha Sila, the five principles of good will in international relations, and told us that it was quite as important to establish good feelings with other nations as it was to set forth closely-reasoned arguments. Western diplomats shrugged their shoulders or smiled with a tinge of impatience at

these notions. Well-reasoned arguments, clarity, what they called "facing the real world," were what they thought really counted, not all this talking about good will.

The conference was a useful introduction to a variety of Asian ways of talking and thinking. In the years to come this would become a major preoccupation of ours, which Howard would approach through intellectual analysis and I would learn about through individual friendships.

When we returned to Colombo, Howard found a European-style bungalow at the corner of Maitland Crescent and Horton Place in Cinnamon Gardens. Its bare whitewashed rooms contained a few chairs, couches resembling British veranda furniture, beds, and a Victorian lamp or two. We had to buy sheets, mattresses, silver, kitchenware, a refrigerator, wardrobes and bookcases. The cement floors with their brick red polish always made me think of a public building. I tried to make our house more attractive by filling it with bright watercolors on the walls and, later on, with the powerful block prints of Richard Gabriel, a Sri Lankan Catholic artist whom I admired.

To save money, we moved in while fifteen house painters were still busily at work. One day while I was taking a nap in the buff in our bedroom, three of them came in and began painting. I pretended to be asleep under a single white sheet until they finished their work, because I couldn't decide whether to let out a little squeak, or a big scream. (It was cowardly, I know, but that's what I did.)

A soaring jackfruit tree stood in front of our house. We planted elephant ears—giant foliage plants worthy of their name—in the front yard, and edgings of red and dark green coleus. Garden snails were legion, so I gave the children five cents for each one they caught. We bought several dozen poinsettia plants from the nursery of the Peradeniya Botanical Gardens; by the time we left, two of them had grown to be over six feet tall.

What a crowded bungalow it was! Wonderful, cheerful Julius, our houseboy, who always seemed to be running even when he wasn't, took care of everything. He slept by choice on a mat on top of a table on the side porch, which always shocked me. Our cook,

Sandy, with the toothy smile, made heavy birthday cakes but also sharp, eye-watering curries. A part-time gardener, who wore a charm on his chest to ward off the devil, came a few times a week. A nanny slept in one of the children's rooms. Add to this a busy typist and Howard's research assistant with his papers spread all over the dining room table, and children, bicycles, visiting American scholars. Irene De Silva, a Sri Lankan friend, often stopped by with mangos and pots of delicious buffalo curd. Even the garden overflowed with pet rabbits, the servants' children, and their friends who came to purchase rabbits. What a bunched-up existence! What delightful chaos!

Howard meanwhile worked long hours in his study, surrounded by tables piled high with books, pamphlets and documents. Stacks of newspapers lay on the floor. Several yellow jackfruit-wood bookcases, a file cabinet and a rush wastebasket spilling over with balls of crumpled paper filled that cramped space. This was the work-engine of the house, where my husband, on a grant from the Rockefeller Foundation, labored and perspired, the sweat dripping, his arms sticking to the foolscap pad in front of him. When Howard, sensibly, finally bought an air conditioner, he was able to work longer and the children could pull their mattresses out of hot, sultry bedrooms, shove them under his worktable, and sleep there at night.

The dining room was in a narrow wing off the living room. At breakfast the table began to fill up with long rows of bottles— syrups, pills, and vitamins—to ward off swollen glands, boils, and tummy troubles. (I can still hear Dr. Sproule saying, "What your children really need, Mrs. Wriggins, is a little bit of 'upcountry'"—or what we Americans might call "mountain air.") However, on nights when we had parties, this same dining room table was filled with dishes of chicken curry, cashew nut curry, dhal, rice piled high, eggplant and okra.

In the evening, the living room and the dining room often rang with political discussion and bursts of laughter. Once Howard had invited several less Westernized Sinhalese for dinner, hoping for an explanation of some of their cultural grievances. I remember wondering beforehand whether their wives spoke English and how I would manage if they didn't. After a hot curry dinner, the young men told us how they had organized a thriller movie which they called "The Perils of Pauline." They had pieced it together from fifty-two smaller films that had preceded the Saturday movie of the week. Rocking with laughter, the young men confessed that the heroine was always hanging on a cliff or tied up on a railroad track before an oncoming train. As a child in the twenties, Howard had seen the same melodramas with the heroine tied to the track in *The Perils of Pauline*. Oh, the folly of pride! Just when we thought we had reached beyond the elite of Cinnamon Gardens to Ceylonese who didn't know anything about America, we found ourselves back on our own cultural turf.

Other times we began to be aware of a whole stratum of life that we knew little about. Part of it had to do with astrology. After a good rice and curry meal among friends, a story would always come up about the birth of someone's niece. "Well, did you hear that they even tried to get the obstetrician to delay the birthing so that the timing would be more auspicious?" And then someone else would say, just as they might do in New York or London, "My gawd, the lengths some people will go to."

There were many such astrology stories. Some of them were harder to relate to than others, like the one about Ponna Wignaraja, who had come back from India with ancient records on ola leaves that depicted the history of his family members. They also foretold, in a general way, his own life, including the fact that he would go over "the black waters," a large ocean, for a significant period of his life. (He went to Yale.) There were also tales about Kataragama, a place in the south where Hindu and Buddhist firewalkers can walk over the glowing coals unharmed. The doctors examine their feet, "and, you know, there are no burns at all."

We went to the American Embassy Residence for Fourth of July parties; and once the Ambassador asked Howard to lunch with part of the defeated United National Party cabinet. But for the most part, we thought, in our youthful all-knowing way, that the Embassy was too isolated from the real Ceylon and that the further we stayed away, the better.

A wonderful upstairs balcony, equipped with solid bamboo chairs and lumpy cushions, looked down on variegated yellow and green vines that festooned the palm trees across the street. I took tea and digestive biscuits there at 10:30 every morning during that fall of 1956. I read, wrote letters, composed a few pages describing the monsoon. I tried to write about the firewalking at Kataragama, and also about fashions in childbirth, for I was going to have my third baby.

These were only fragments, for my mind seemed to grow smaller as my body grew larger; like the sap of a tree that retreats to its roots in winter, I slipped down to an instinctual self beyond the reach of words. If I obeyed the doctor and stayed upstairs for three months, would I be able this time to carry my baby full term and break a series of miscarriages that had followed the births of the other two children? Down below me, near the vine-encircled tree on the sidewalk, the banana man called, "Annamaluia, Annamaluia." The kerosene man banged on his iron drum with a stick. I listened to their cries and waited.

The 1950s

Colombo. Ceylon

Dinny, by now a gap-toothed six-year-old, and Chris, a quiet, curly-haired boy of four, came up to my balcony every afternoon for tea. I loved their paintings and their games, especially one called Douane or Customs, an idea they picked up in Switzerland on the way to Asia. First, Dinny dressed up in cowrie shell necklaces, bracelets, camera bags and straps, sunglasses and straw hat. She then loaded a suitcase with old clothes and toys. Chris pretended to be a stern customs official. "All right now, show me what's inside, lady," he said as he eagerly turned the suitcase upside down and dumped everything on the floor.

It was in our bedroom near the jackfruit tree, I remember, that Howard came down with an unknown fever on December 26, 1957. His limp body lay shivering under the sheets of our large bed. Never had he looked so small, so shriveled, so helpless.

I pressed the doctor for a diagnosis. "Is it malaria? His body shakes so much."

The doctor made the same "maybe-yes, maybe-no" movement of his head from side to side that the servants made whenever I pressed them for a definite answer.

"Is it cholera?"

He waggled his head from side to side again in this "figure-eight" head shake.

"But doesn't whatever fever he has have a name? If you say it is malaria or hepatitis," I said shakily, "then I can cope."

I wasn't sure whether I really could, but I kept pressing. "Do you at least have an hypothesis of what it might be?" I was helpless. The doctor waited for ten whole days to give the sickness a name—paratyphoid fever. Howard had drunk some contaminated water in the countryside and now in order to get well he would have to eat cream of wheat, little bowls of it, day after day, week after week.

I learned later that Howard had been talking to an Ayurvedic physician, trained in local herbal cures, three days before he became so ill. The doctor, looking at him, had asked the translator if Howard didn't have a fever. I found this uncanny.

At the time I didn't think of all the dreadful possibilities that might have occurred to me if I had been older. Something protected me. I was also very busy. It was a long time before Howard was strong enough to sit up in bed. Then his long, capable fingers began to work with pieces of balsa, rolls of fine paper and balls of string that came from Colombo stores well stocked with British-made construction kits. He transformed these into a splendid helicopter with a real jet engine, and an airplane with a network of struts between wings that spanned two and a half feet. Christopher was enchanted.

Meanwhile I was growing larger and larger with a baby expected to arrive in April, the height of the airless, steaming hot season. Early in my pregnancy, our nanny insisted we take down a demon mask which hung on the bedroom wall.

"Madam," she said looking at the protruding eyes and the cobra entwined around the beak of a bird-like creature, "that is a bad influence for the baby." A bad influence from a mere mask on the wall? What was she thinking about? Hers was a more threatening world than I had suspected, but I put the mask away just the same.

The nine months passed. Each time an auspicious day was approaching, we all found ourselves hoping that the baby would be born then. Sinhalese New Year, Tamil New Year, a full moon, Easter, even the doctor's birthday all went by. Nothing happened. One sultry night, my labor began. We drove to nearby Spittel's Nursing Home carrying several suitcases filled with rolls of cotton, disinfectant, a mysterious British concoction called Gripe Water, and various other medical supplies which mothers had to bring, along with clothes for the baby. We had settled down in a small room by about ten o'clock, and Howard began reading aloud to me from Nayantara Sahgal's *Prison and Chocolate Cake*, a book about the Nehru family. I am not sure how much I really heard, as I listened to the fans whirring overhead and watched the little pink lizards called geckos as they chased mosquitos on the walls and ceiling. I began the restful breathing of Natural Childbirth. A black cat walked in for a moment and then wandered down the hall. For some reason the cat didn't bother me; it just seemed funny.

As I waited for Dr. Chinnatamby, my obstetrician, I remember wondering what she would wear; not only was she well-qualified in her field, with two medical degrees from the British Isles, but she wore the loveliest saris in Colombo. With her Tamil eye for color, would she arrive in a dashing scarlet sari, or a violet georgette? I hoped she would be wearing a wine-dark one.

When Dr. Chinnatamby finally came, she had on a chartreuse green sari and a green oilcloth apron. She examined me, feeling my stomach here and there. "Your baby is doing nicely." She paused and pursed her lips. "But I don't think the baby will come until after midnight."

Gloria in Excelsis Deo, Jennifer came into the world the day after Easter at two in the morning, with the joyful cry, "I am!" Howard was with me, providing moral support just as he had done in Switzerland when he acted as interpreter during the birth of our first child, Dinny, and when he was with me in New Haven at Chris's birth. The encouragement shining from his deep brown eyes made it the best natural childbirth I had ever done. A special nanny, with a dark face as wrinkled and black as an old prune, held Jenny on her knees in a chair beside me as I half-dozed or slept at night.

My room at Spittel's Nursing Home was a garden of delight—bouquets of asters and zinnias, a golden shower of ethereal, tiny yellow orchids, an orchid of a subtle shade somewhere between violet and blue, and the spray of deep burgundy orchids from my new friend, Punitham Tiruchelvam.

An American friend active in the Ceylon Red Cross had introduced me to Punitham shortly after we arrived. "There's somebody you've got to meet," she said. "She's just a marvelous woman." She paused. "She'll probably try to enlist you in one of her causes, so don't say I didn't warn you."

Punitham was like many Tamils, intense and stimulating. Like many Tamils, too, she was dark-skinned with luminous black eyes. Her movements were quick, darting. She talked very fast. Punitham was small, wiry, and her ears were too big for her face. Outward beauty was not one of her strong points, but she had a kind of interior grace that expressed itself in an immense capacity for caring. Her many concerns might have been oppressive were it not for the flashes of merriment and humor that danced somewhere inside her.

I had no idea then that Punitham would color and enrich my life for twenty-five years. As I lay in bed at Spittel's, nursing Jenny, I used to save up stories for Punitham just to hear her laugh; like the one about the ants coming in on the stems of flowers and ending up in a bedside sterile solution, and how the nurses said that that made them "sterile ants." Oh, such a marvelous laugh Punitham had, setting all her pulsating energy free to vibrate in the air! Her eyebrows went up, she threw back her head, and her fine teeth showed white against her dark skin.

Ethel Grant, the lovely brown-eyed wife of the American AID Director, Jim Grant, came to see me, too. She arrived once on horseback, tethering her horse outside. The Grants had just come from India: Ethel wore a chignon held in place by hairpins with tiny Indian silver bells on them. She was a handsome woman. Our families saw a lot of one another and she had a knack for creating special occasions, such as Howard's first outing to the ocean after his illness. The Grants continued to be our close friends later, both in Washington, D.C. and in New York.

When Ethel died suddenly in 1988, I spoke at her memorial service at the Cathedral of St. John the Divine. There must have been a thousand people there who remembered her acts of kindness. As we were pouring out of the nave of the vast cathedral, a young woman in front of me said, "That's the kind of funeral I am going to have."

I was a little stunned, still aching from the loss of Ethel, and I thought to myself, "Well, dearie, you have to do something to earn it."

By the time of Ethel's death Jim was head of UNICEF (United Nations International Children's Emergency Fund) but I suspect it was Ethel's extraordinary humanity that brought such a crowd to pay their respects. Once, when a reporter asked her if there was a God, she replied by saying, "We were put on this world to show compassion for others." Isaak Dinesen captures the same spirit:

> There exists a true humanity, which will ever remain a gift, and which is to be accepted by one human being as it is given to him by a fellow human. The one who gives has himself been a receiver. In this way, link by link, a chain is made from land to land and from generation to generation. Rank, wealth and nationality in this matter count for nothing.[1]

On my last night in the nursing home, Sinhalese Buddhist priests chanted *pirith,* a monotonous intoning all night long for blessing a new house. Before I left, I stopped to visit the scion of a large Sinhalese family in the room next to mine. This boy baby with lots of black hair still didn't have a name a week after he was born, because his horoscope had to be drawn up, and certain sounds and letters had to be agreed upon in accordance with the particular second, minute and hour of his birth. Family and friends were all there, some of them playing cards with the nurses in one corner. The grandmother showed me a gold sovereign.

"We put it into the water in which his first bottle was boiled," she explained with a slow, shy smile. "We hope it will bring him prosperity."

When Jenny and I came home to Maitland Crescent, I struggled to keep up with her need for more and more milk, while Maggie, our smiling nanny, helped to take care of her. Upstairs, downstairs and into the children's rooms she went with the baby so that Jenny could be admired by everyone. I can still see her standing in the doorway of Dinny's room to catch the slightest evening breeze, rocking Jenny in her arms to the sounds of clacking palm fronds, an Asian madonna against a bright orange sky.

Three weeks after Jenny was born, Punitham dropped by to see us. Her deep black eyes were flashing with excitement. She talked very fast as usual. "Prime Minister Nehru of India is coming to Colombo. Let's go. We'll never have a chance like this. He's getting old. Have you ever read his books?"

"But I have to nurse Jenny every two hours," I protested. "I can't go." But of course we went, along with thousands of others, to listen to him at the Ramakrishna Mission. The Prime Minister wore a jaunty cap, jodhpurs, and his eponymous jacket with the high collar.

He spoke so softly that we had to strain to hear him. "The cold war is a war in which you avoid the use of weapons . . . but the atmosphere is full of hatred and violence. . . . You can't have peace coming out of a quagmire of hatred. . . ." I was thrilled to see Nehru, and Punitham whisked me through the crowds so I could get home as soon as possible to nurse Jenny.

But not long afterwards I came up against a strange and unexplained world. I was lying with Jenny in our bedroom when Maggie approached and put her fingers to her lips. "I will tell you something," she said. "When your baby cries at night, she is talking to the fairies. And the fairies tell her that her mummy is dead. She laughs because her tummy is full and she has just had a meal. Then the fairies tell her that her daddy is dead and she cries."

The nurse at Spittel's Nursing Home had told me the same tale, using angels instead of fairies. I never discovered what it meant. I did learn that the chants of the Buddhist priests that I had heard during Jennifer's 2:00am feeding were intonations to purify a house from the mischievous work of the Evil Eye.

The life of our old house was in our sufferings, our blessings, and our discoveries. Yes, and in the enrichment of friends. The sufferings? Weren't they contained in the image of huge, white bed sheets with Howard's limp form under them, and didn't they turn into something else? While Howard lay in bed so sick and so weak, the masses of material he had gathered for his book on Ceylon's dilemmas as a new nation grew in his mind. When he was finally able to get to his desk again, the book almost began to write itself. I had waited too, in this upstairs bedroom and on the balcony, for a child to grow in my body. And Jennifer was born into the world. What a blessing she has been!

The discoveries? The doctor's shaking his head in a figure eight to show he could not say, not know; the same head shake from the servants which opened up the world of neither yes nor no, of ambiguity, of trying to please, of saving face. The idea of the Evil Eye was everywhere in Ceylon, so that Buddhists and Hindus alike would often rent out their newly-built houses instead of moving in themselves. They felt this was protection against the danger that a jealous person may have cast an evil spell bringing harm to those who own the house. It showed a darker world of envy and mistrust than I had known. Astrology in Ceylon was surely very different from Western astrology. I didn't know quite why this might be so. Maybe I could find out.

Chapter 4

PUTTING GREEN, TRIDENT AND DRUM

The best way to escape the heat of Colombo was to go upcountry to the British hill station, Nuwara Eliya. It lies in the central southern part of the island where nearly inaccessible peaks rise to over 8,000 feet. In part of this mountainous area, British colonials had planted egg-yellow Scotch broom, stocked the mountain streams with trout, cleared the valley floor for a race track, and created a golf course with a putting green so smooth and thick, it was like the softest velvet.

Each morning of our stay at the hill station the soft rain and the mists intensified the green of the golf course and covered the green carpet with a thin coating of silver dew. Could anyone doubt that this was England or Scotland? Could anyone resist a flight of fancy?

"Why not?" I said to myself. At the edge of the putting green, I turned around and backed my way to the cup at the center so my footprints appeared to go out from the cup. Then I retraced my footsteps to the outer edge.

"What's thee doing now, dear?" Howard asked in an oh-so-patient voice.

"Playing a game," I explained. "Remember the Charles Addams cartoon in the *New Yorker* with the ski tracks going around both sides of a fir tree, one on each side? It is sort of like that. . . ." I paused and smiled to myself. "What will the first golfer of the day think? I wish I could be here to see."

At the time I didn't suspect that my playfulness could be put to any good use. But twenty years later it would express itself in my adaptation of the classic Chinese novel, my first book, which I called *White Monkey King*.

*****

When we returned to Colombo I realized that the putting green was a symbol of the Britishness in manners, food, drink, men's clothing, music, the English language, entertainment, and even ways of thinking that dominated the upper levels of Ceylonese society. Howard would surely add to that list political precedents and their parliamentary practices. The status-conscious society of Ceylon for generations had been in harmony with British social predilections.

Knowing someone's background shows how to deal with him: this was and is important in both societies. It doesn't fit quite so well for an American, especially a self-righteous American like me, who was sure it was wrong to ship race horses down from the mountains each week on a grueling train ride, to race for wealthy British and Ceylonese in the 98-percent humidity, 85-degree heat of Colombo. I knew with the certainly of someone thirty-four years old that it was unforgivable to use valuable foreign exchange for Lyons ice cream to be shipped biweekly from London. And I couldn't believe that the Joseph Fraser Nursing Home would exclude Ceylonese patients.

Howard, always more subtle, didn't have my self-righteous impatience. He merely pointed out that biographical sketches of prominent Ceylonese stressed rugby and cricket colors before academic achievements. Being a scholar, he knew how to fit these details into a larger picture. "After all, the elite attended Oxford and Cambridge and some know their Shakespeare better than we."

I don't know why Ceylonese society struck me as so Victorian. At first it was my discovery that a forty-five-year-old matron had never been alone in a taxi—one of her family servants was always with her—or the common sight of well-behaved Ceylonese children going off to school in their crisp, white uniforms with their drivers or their nannies. But when the Martha Graham Dance Company came to Ceylon, suddenly I felt very Ceylonese in my reaction. All those male and female bodies intertwining—well, it was too much. (Except for rather staid ballroom dancing among certain classes, men and women did not dance together.) Our Ceylonese friends didn't want to offend us, but it was clear that they thought the Graham dances were out of bounds, not in good taste. The sexual overtones seemed very foreign, from another world—as was the American avant-garde, indeed.

Our small children wore those crisp, white uniforms along with the Colombo elite when they attended Ladies College, a Church Missionary Society School with boys and girls in the youngest grades, and girls only in the high school. Each day began with Christian hymns and prayers. "What are we thankful for today, children?" intoned the headmistress. "For the lovely day, Miss Nellie," was the unfailing response. Elaborate prizegivings were surely modeled after British schools. The school play was about Christopher Robin.

I used to envy the parents of very small Ceylonese children at Ladies College when I would see the little ones sitting motionless during lengthy speeches and three-hour prizegivings. I asked Punitham about it once. She said, "Well, we have to put up with many more things in life than you do." I remember children's birthday parties where twenty or thirty aunts, uncles, and older cousins—in short, the extended family—came to celebrate; both the child and the birthday were almost incidental. Yet I also valued children's freedom to play and be creative, so I took comfort in the fact that, while Ceylonese children seemed to be content to sit quietly on the beach sifting sand through their fingers and looking at the ocean, ours were busy digging holes and shaping the sand into castles.

The 1956 election was upon us, only five months after we had arrived. This election was the beginning of the nationalist troubles that are still felt today. Because he was researching a book, Howard sought out the new groups that were being organized—the native language teachers, traditional physicians and Buddhist priests.

Howard and the Indonesian Chargé d'Affaires were the only ones who predicted exactly the outcome of the election. S.W.R.D. Bandaranaike became Prime Minister largely because he kept insisting that Sinhalese, the language of the majority, should be the official language instead of English. He also promised that the changeover would be made immediately. The Sinhalese victory and the "Sinhala Only" policy undermined British influence, brought the government closer to the people, and handicapped the Tamil minority who had done so well under British rule. Bandaranaike told Howard that he had never found anything to excite people so much as the language issue.

But was this Oxford-educated Prime Minister ignorant of the dangers of the forces he was unleashing? Surely he was aware of the vigor of Tamil minority culture, and also the association of that culture with the languages and traditions of India. In addition, many of the Western-educated elite, including one of Punitham's ancestors, were Tamils from the north who had been educated in American missionary schools.

There were riots after the 1956 election. Several hundred people were killed, and one hundred injured. The riots began in Colombo and spread to many parts of the country. Some Tamils fled to Hindu temples, others were sheltered by Sinhalese friends. Houses were burned, people beaten. How strange and ironic it all was! for 1956 also marked the celebration of the 2500th anniversary of the death of the Buddha.

That year also marked 2500 years since the legendary introduction of Buddhism to Ceylon and, as some said, the beginning of the Ceylonese race. For the first time since independence, the Ceylonese began to look to their cultural roots. They held many Buddha Jayanti celebrations, and put on plays such as "*Maname, or The Spirit of the Mahaveli,*" a huge panorama of Ceylonese history.[2] Dr. I. D. S. Weerawardene, a Sinhalese scholar, was busy translating the best English books that had never been translated into Sinhalese. He saw himself as a kind of Venerable Bede, the scholar monk, bringing Enlightenment.

India's Prime Minister Nehru made a state visit on May 17, 1957 to take part in the celebration of Ceylon's 2500 years of Buddhism, a religion that had been born in India but had long ago died out there. In making this visit, Nehru was acknowledging the cultural distinctiveness of the Ceylonese. They were quick to appreciate this, for they bristled when a foreigner assumed, as often happened, that Ceylon was part of India. Nehru attracted tremendous crowds. The Sinhalese constituted seventy percent of the population, Tamils another eleven per cent, and the Moors (descended from Arab traders) and the Burghers (Euro-Ceylonese) made up five per cent of the population. It looked as though people from every group had turned out to hear Nehru.

Ceylon didn't become Sri Lanka all at once; even its name was not changed until 1973. The country remained very British in many ways. The cricket match between Royal and St. Thomas, rival boys' schools modeled on Eton and Harrow, was virtually a national holiday. It was old boy this and old boy that. As in England, school loyalties still took precedence over ethnic backgrounds. At a children's handicraft exhibition in Colombo, a model labeled "Our House" was a *House and Garden* version of a British home, with paper cardboard figures in front, all of whom had white skin and curly blond hair. I wanted them to have dark skins and black hair like the families of Ceylon.

At that time Ceylon was primarily a rural society, identified with the land, the paddy farmer, the villages, the countryside. Ceylon had only three principal export crops—tea, rubber and coconuts. In the highlands I had seen Indian Tamil women picking tea, two leaves and a bud, from the dark green tea bushes. At lower altitudes there were the eerie rubber forests with rubber tappers milking the trees. Still farther down were the shining coconut palms, farmers and their bullocks, like those portrayed by the artist Richard Gabriel, and the chartreuse paddy fields that farmers carved so skillfully out of the hillsides.

I puzzled over the cultural juxtapositions. And then how startled I was to find, painted on rocks and trees at the edge of the golf course at Nuwara Eliya, a Kataragama trident, the symbol of the Hindu god.

I had heard about Kataragama from my Ceylonese friends, an obscure place five hours from Colombo at the edge of the southern Dry Zone, where pilgrims gathered to make vows and take part in religious rituals, including firewalking. Punitham had told me that believers with a pure heart really did walk on the coals and take no harm. But "once there was a Protestant minister who tried it," she said. "They had to take him to the hospital and he nearly died."

Some Ceylonese friends had urged us to go to Kataragama, and had offered to accompany us. At the last minute they opted out, so Howard and I went alone. Our first sight was of a small, muddy river where priests perform a secret rite, the Water-Cutting ceremony. People were bathing to purify themselves. Across the river was a bell tower, a stone pillar and a collection of small, somewhat drab temples inside a sixteen-foot temple wall. Several Bo trees, sacred to Buddhists, stood near the Hindu temples. Outside this temple enclosure was a burial ground, several more temples, shops, restaurants and a rest house. The site was not impressive. The people, in their religious intensity, were.

Everyone went to Kataragama, even politicians and students. They went to get advice, to make vows, to rid themselves of evil spirits. I saw pilgrims doing penance who were carrying on their shoulders heavy wooden yokes (rather like Puritan stocks) graced with peacock feathers. I saw men with needles through their cheeks without a sign of blood; men virtually naked rolling over and over in the dust; and men pulling carts by ropes fastened to hooks embedded in the flesh of their backs. It was repellent, but the atmosphere was undeniably one of holy resolve.

In the afternoon of our stay, I watched several men throwing coconuts into a huge trough, the shells splitting open on impact. This represented breaking the hard shell of human isolation and opening one's heart to understanding. Inside one of the Hindu temples I heard the eerie blast of conch shells, the ecstatic cries of pilgrims, and ear-splitting drumming. I saw priests performing mysterious rites in front of a curtain—pilgrims in a trance jumping up and down faster and faster, shouting, "Murugga, Murugga!"—one of the names for the Kataragama god.

We returned to the courtyard, where families squatted around small fires to cook their dinners. As the night wore on, the noises subsided. We lay down with pilgrim families sleeping on the hard dusty ground near the Bo trees. I looked up at the Southern Cross in the vast heavens. The ground was hard, but oh, so reassuring after a day of so much that seemed abnormal and strange. I was glad to hug the comforting earth as something solid and familiar. Once we got up to look at the roaring fire in the front courtyard. The pilgrims were shrieking as the fire beast leaped now this way, now that in the shifting winds. After another nap, we went back again to find a place as close as we could to the trench of coals. A bystander nearby asked me who we were. He told us that making plans to go to Kataragama was inviting bad luck.

"An American was in Colombo and he said that he was going to drive to Kataragama on a Tuesday afternoon, and you know what happened? His car broke down. The garage lent him another one and that broke down, too. It's always like that," he said.

So that was why our Ceylonese friends had refused at the last minute to accompany us, giving the flimsiest of excuses. Why hadn't they told us that the Kataragama god was jealous of his authority in his own precincts?

Suddenly the firewalkers were standing near the edge of the trench. A German Swami (whom we had met earlier) was raising his arms high in the air, his palms together as in prayer. He led the firewalkers across the orange and reddish coals, a still-burning trench ten feet wide and twenty feet long! The Swami in his ecstasy shouted the name of the god. A woman ran part-way across, faltered and went down on one knee. The crowd gasped. More pilgrims crossed and ran into the little Hindu temple on the other side. Loud cries came from the temple. Many walked or danced back over the coals once more. A man next to me whispered, "He is right beside Murugga, his god."

I don't know whether or not the shell of my understanding, like the coconut shells in the trough, broke; it certainly cracked.

Staying up all night at Kataragama turned out to be the beginning of many all-night ceremonies for us. We went to the south to a festival for Pattini, who cured smallpox and other childhood diseases. We went to exorcisms, designed to expel evil spirits of one sort or another. I began to see the Kataragama symbol, the three-pronged fork, almost everywhere I looked, even at the edge of the British putting-green. I couldn't avoid the supernatural here. I carried it with me always.

*****

If the putting green represented the pastimes of the British-educated elite, it also represented to me the well-ordered, groomed self, the veneer for all to see. If Kataragama expressed the needs of ordinary Ceylonese, with its symbol, the trident painted on the rocks, wasn't this the primitive in us all, even if it seemed so alien?

I found myself wondering what was pure Ceylonese. I wanted to know what was the symbol of the middle ground between the staid British veneer and the racing-of-the-blood Hindu religious passion. What typified the everyday self, the everyday society? What lay between the polished and the primitive in Ceylon?

Then it came to me, as I remembered a very special night when we stayed up to see a religious procession called a Perahera, near Kelaniya. There were girls playing their huge drums together. At the time of the full moon, the village people gathered by the roadside to wait. This largely Buddhist procession (there were some Hindu relics as well) would come by in two hours, four hours, or six hours. No one knew when. No one seemed to care. In the warm evening air little knots of families laughed and talked, or they spent the waiting time sleeping on the ground beside their children. I don't remember how long we slumbered on the grassy bund near Kelaniya, before we were awakened by the sound of the slapping hands of six young girls seated around a large rabana drum.

The sounds were peaceful, innocent, happy! In the middle distance I saw the light of a fire. (I later learned that this fire was built under the round bass drum to dry and tighten the hide that formed its head.) The fire was put out; a second group of girls began to sound their lively rhythms, one group of drummers answering the other, a kind of joyful rivalry in the night.

We moved closer to the players, whose white blouses and moving arms and hands I could barely distinguish from a distance. As we drew nearer I could see them smiling and laughing, tapping their fingers or striking the drum with the palms of their hands. One girl beat out a tune this time, another girl picked up a variation, a third played with that in turn, as though each was talking to the other. Then all of them made syncopated sounds together.

Rabana playing, that was it. The counterpoint of sound and rhythm of the young girls was a kind of conversation; it was an evening dance of drums. That was the median. That was the symbol of everyday life. That was where people lived, where rice was harvested, coconuts grew, rubber trees were tapped. Howard would say that it's where men sweated behind bullocks in the mud, where the backs of women were bent double weeding rice.

And in one of our endless dialogues about Ceylon, I would add, "And where after a day's work is done, young girls play rabana drums."

"Okay. It's true the villagers have stayed where they are in Ceylon. The peasants have not migrated to Colombo. The government has purchased their crops at subsidized prices and provided them with extensive health services. They have no reason to go. The cities have not become the crowded metropolises of Bombay, Calcutta, Bangkok, or Djakarta."

"And maybe they will stay there as long as they have a source of livelihood, as long as they can listen to the magic of girls drumming in the night."

PART THREE

AMERICA, ENGLAND
AND AFGHANISTAN

Chapter 5

FINDING MY VOCATION AT 55

Whughen the time came to leave Ceylon and return to America, we took an Italian ocean liner from Colombo through the Malacca Straits and the South China Sea, to Hong Kong. We were six—Howard, Chris, Dinny, three-month-old Jenny, and Charlotte Bunker, the young student who was to help with the new baby. I was thirty-five years old.

After a few days in Hong Kong, we made a side trip to as close as you could get to China in 1957, to the New Territories (leased by Britain from China for ninety-nine years). We saw duck farms and the transplanting of rice in neat rows by straw-hatted, bent-over Chinese. The rest of our trip was a memorable pre-jet engine, thirty-six-hour flight. Jenny was a large baby and I couldn't meet her needs with nursing alone. Charlotte held her, and the stewardesses were busy heating her bottles during the night. We stopped at Guam, Taiwan, and Japan, and, on a desolate air strip in the Aleutian Islands, we saw two sunsets and active volcanos, and felt the first wash of cold air against our faces and the smell of distant snow. At an airplane hangar in Seattle the customs clerk, looking at

Howard's passport, asked him with a raised eyebrow what his occupation was.

"I teach at Vassar College in New York."

"Excuse me, may I ask you a personal question? Do you get paid for it?"

"Not very much. But yes, I do get paid."

Then the clerk yelled to his colleague at the other end of the building. "Hey Joe, listen to this. Here's a guy who says he teaches all those pretty dames at Vassar College. And you know what, he says he gets paid for it. What do you think of that!"

We stopped first for a reunion of my family in Seattle, the first since 1939, before the war. My eldest brother Jim had been in the Navy and served on a destroyer in the Pacific. My brother Win, badly wounded by a land mine in Sicily, had been recovering in a hospital for over a year. It was a poignant reunion, for my father was dying of cancer.

After a generous two-year leave we returned to our old house on Overocker Road, at the edge of the Vassar campus in Poughkeepsie, only to find that our well had run dry. Each day we filled a forty-gallon milk can in the campus pumping station and then used the water over and over again—all with a baby in diapers. When we wrote to our Ceylon friends that our well had run dry, they didn't believe us. "People in America don't have wells!" they said.

There were other problems beyond their ken. That winter the furnace failed when an old boiler cracked. The plumber had to stuff the crack with lead shavings so the furnace would produce some heat. It took most of the night for the shavings to melt. "Reminds me of the years when I was a locomotive engineer on the railroad," the plumber said nostalgically, with a far-away look in his eyes. "We used to press the limits of the boiler so the engine would go faster. Why, one time . . ." The gauge rose ever-so-slowly as the shavings melted.

Howard had a heavy teaching load but he loved teaching all those articulate and beautiful-on-weekends Vassar girls. Our children, now six and eight, went off to the local public schools and a nanny took care of Jenny. I cut Howard's 1,300-page manuscript in half—a recipe for disaster which I will never repeat. I had edited many a document when I worked at UNRRA, but witnessing the intense experience of the writing of a manuscript, how it involved Howard's whole being—all this was new to me. The cutting of my husband's first book was ill-advised; it had the potential of destroying our marriage.

It was an ingrown year in many ways, except for our reaching out to Patsy and Henry Wheeler, Quaker friends who were starting a new Friends Meeting on Bulls Head Road, right across from their dairy farm in Dutchess County. We saved Sundays for Quaker Meeting. Afterwards, there was always a picnic lunch and good talk with the Wheelers, who were less driven than some of our academic friends.

We were just putting down roots in Poughkeepsie—the new pump in the freshly drilled well and the furnace working perfectly—when Howard was offered a job in Washington, D.C. The Library of Congress has a Legislative Reference Service which provides Congressmen, regardless of party, with background research data, specific information, and speech drafts. Howard's new position was head of the Foreign Affairs Division, which worked with Congressional staffs. He had a fast course on how the American Congressional system functions.

Howard found a large house in the village of Chevy Chase, just outside Washington. We settled in at 9 East Lenox Street and the children had a wonderful time exploring what they called "the mica mine" in the basement, and playing in the attic in a sizeable cage for storing trunks. Howard had a roomy study. I marveled at the five fireplaces, two of them in upstairs bedrooms. The attic also had a quiet room where Vernon Aluwihare, an old friend from Ceylon, lived with us for a year. Later on Louise Burroughs, John Oliver and Judy Brown each stayed there for long periods as well.

We missed the countryside of Dutchess County outside Poughkeepsie. Our new house was just off Connecticut Avenue, a major artery in northwest Washington that led into Chevy Chase Circle and beyond. Still this house turned out to be a good choice, for in a few years the children went to Washington to school. Dinny, at twelve, started at National Cathedral School for Girls, and ten-year-old Chris went to Sidwell Friends. Because we lived close to the Washington buses that came along Connecticut Avenue, they could come home on their own after school. These were the carpool years, and what Anne Lindbergh calls the Oyster Stage of Life: the constant growth and expansion of living, the proliferation of bicycles, musical instruments, games, dogs, cats, the impossibity of getting into the garage any more . . . "the wild creativity of it all," as she described it.

Mother came to see us once in our house on Lenox Avenue. Daddy died in 1959. Mother died only a few months later and Win scattered her ashes off Anderson's Point. I felt very alone in the world. Mother was always a strong source of support even though she had been thousands of miles away ever since I had come East to graduate school. When I think of Mother, I picture her the summer she and Daddy came to see us on Little Cranberry Island. In my vision, she's on the beach, reading *Dr. Doolittle* to Dinny and knitting a sweater at the same time. I think back to our time on Anderson's Point when I read to my mother Eva Curie's biography of her scientist mother. I see Daddy in his brown khaki t-shirt and pants in the Cascade Mountains, fording a rushing river with his boots on. We pay tribute; Howard admired them too for their courage, their enthusiasm, their close kinship with the world of nature.

I still remember Ethel Grant trying to comfort me after Mother died. When our children were small, Ethel and I used to go to the National Gallery of Art once a week. We listened as James Cahill lectured on Chinese landscape painting for the "Treasures of the Palace Museum in Taiwan" exhibition that came to America in 1961–62. Ethel always surrounded herself with beautiful things: museum quality Chinese chests, wardrobes and low tables made of rosewood (which had come from Jim's family, for he had grown up in China). Ethel was supremely competent: as a hostess, driving a car, in relating to the physical world—all activities that were effortful for me. Our friendship must have been an attraction of opposites, for I always had the feeling that she appreciated the life of the mind and the spirit and was longing for something I represented to her.

Our spiritual home was the Sandy Spring Quaker Meeting, twenty miles outside Washington, an unusual community whose Meetinghouse was built in 1817. It was a handsome old red brick building. Dean Acheson's farm lay just beyond the Meetinghouse. Once he told our British friend Geoffrey Wilson, who also knew this famous place of Quaker worship, that when he drove past our Meetinghouse to his farm after an agonizing day during the McCarthy period, he felt as if he were passing through a sort of "spiritual delousing station." We loved the Meeting and Sandy Spring and introduced our friends the Boozes to it, which turned out to have far-reaching consequences in years to come.

Very soon after we came to Washington, we began to work on an exciting project for a new Friends School—high school grades to begin with—in Sandy Spring, Maryland. Land had been given by Esther Scott, a retired school teacher—fifty-six acres as a start. Building plans had been made, and Sam Legg, Vice Principal of Oakwood School near Poughkeepsie, had agreed to be principal. But the guiding spirit of the project was Brooke Moore, a cabinet maker with solid roots in Sandy Spring. It was his vision that had built the school.

"It won't just be for a few bright people. It won't be only to train students' minds. It will be to develop the spirit, the mind, the skilled hand. I can't describe it exactly. But you're a teacher, Sam."

"I know what you mean," Sam responded. "Intellectual segregation like there is in a lot of schools. I don't believe in it any more than I believe in racial, religious, or any other kind of segregation."

A few Quakers formed a school committee. They were Friends of all trades and occupations: an orchardist, a cabinet maker, a building engineer, a construction supervisor, teachers, housewives, a doctor, a research director, a public relations specialist, and an insurance man. I wrote articles for *Friends Journal* about Brooke Moore and starting the School.

The school didn't have any real money and we couldn't see where any would be coming from. So one bleak evening when we had gathered together, Brooke suggested that if he took his tractor and made a road in to the property to where Sam Legg's house was supposed to be, people might think that we were flush. "Priming the pump," he called it, and so it was. Not long afterward, Hadassah Moore Leeds Holcombe gave us $20,000. And a local bank, knowing the solid reputation of Brooke Moore, made a substantial loan. There was a time when it was clear that the project had grown to such an extent that it had become necessary to hive off subcommittees and form a corporation. These were uncomfortable times for Friends, who prefer individual relationships. We laid the cornerstone for the new Sandy Spring Friends School July 10, 1960. The school opened in 1961 with grades ten and eleven. Both Ben Booz and her eldest son ended up teaching there. In 2005, it is a thriving 550-student Quaker day and boarding school for children from kindergarten through high school.

Just as we had done in Dutchess County with Patsy and Henry Wheeler, we continued to spend all day Sunday with our new Quaker friends, Mary and Roger Farquhar, out in the country, swimming in their pond in the summer, the children building dams in their river, some of us ice skating on it in the winter. Although Roger was a dynamic editor of the *Montgomery County Sentinel* newspaper (he has the distinction of having trained Bob Woodward before he became a famous Deep Throat reporter), the Farquhars were very different from the ambitious politicians and driven public servants we knew in Washington. They were warm, more down-home.

The 1960s were exciting years for us. These were the years that David Halberstam wrote about in *The Best and the Brightest.* There was the sense that change was needed and that the new arrivals in government would be able to make those changes. Along with many other scholars, Howard was pleased to participate in the Kennedy administration, taking a job in the State Department's think tank, the Policy Planning Council. They were troubled times as well; the civil rights law was before Congress and racial unrest was everywhere. On the international front, things were just as bad. Howard began his new job April 21, 1961, the day of the Bay of Pigs invasion, where American-supported forces invaded Cuba in a failed attempt that might have resulted in a nuclear war. Our military presence in Vietnam was also controversial. Then President Kennedy was assassinated, ending a dramatic era of a thousand days.

Howard's job on the Policy Planning Council took him back to his interest in South Asian affairs. His *Ceylon: Dilemmas of a New Nation* had been published in April 1960, and people were talking about political development. We had many old friends around Washingon who knew Asia well: Jim and Ethel Grant, Paul and Ben Booz, and Mildred and Phil Talbot. When Dean Rusk became Secretary of State, Phil was President Kennedy's choice for Assistant Secretary of State for Near East and South Asian Affairs. His wife Mildred was just starting up a new organization to build a dialogue between Asian and American women, something more substantive than cocktail parties and dinners. At the time there were very few women in the upper echelons of government (Ambassador Carol Laise was a noteworthy exception). The new organization needed a chairman, someone to get things started, to form an international board, and I volunteered.

This organization, which for several years kept me on the telephone and the children surviving on french fries and fish sticks, was affiliated with PPSEAWA, Pan-Pacific and South-East Asia Women's Association. During the second year, we became independent and changed our name to the Asian American Forum—for that is what we were.

We didn't know, when we started, whether we could find a level of discourse between women from twenty-four Asian and Commonwealth countries—among them India, Pakistan, Ceylon, Burma, South Korea, Japan, Indonesia, Thailand, Australia and New Zealand—and American women. We found that level by discussing the role of women in a rapidly changing world. We focused on definitions of progress as it relates to women and education, women and work, the nuclear family and the joint family, the role of the artist in society. Our dialogue—the word was new then—was exciting. It gave the Asian women insights into American life, and we learned a great deal about Asia and Asian women. We had two Asians and two Americans in each of our seminars, brilliantly led by Sally Smith, an international educator. These seminars were so stimulating that we followed them up with small discussion groups where Asian women were often more ready to speak and share their ideas than they would be in a large public gathering. Lady Jackson, better known by her professional name Barbara Ward, the well-known economist, spoke at our first annual meeting at the Indian Embassy. We produced a record of our seminars, *The Roots of Progress,* whose artistic cover was designed by Ben Booz. It was eventually distributed in Asia by the U.S. Information Agency. In 1964 PPSEAWA held an International Conference in Samoa, on the topic of women preserving cultural values in a rapidly changing world.

About this time I was asked if I would consider a paid job working with Leo Szilard, the atomic scientist. I was tempted, but with a busy diplomatic life in Washington, three children and a big house, I knew it would be too much for me. I simply didn't have the energy. Perhaps in another era, I might have found full-time help and given the job a try.

As it was, our children were coping in their own way with the turbulent sixties. Dinny was bell-ringing at National Cathedral; Chris was absorbed in drumming with a band, as well as the desirable length of hair, certain clothes, intensity of sound; and our youngest, Jenny, was playing the recorder. The name of Chris's band was "The Primitive Sect," which is what Quakers were called in the seventeenth century.

In 1965 I joined the Board of Sidwell Friends School, a large Quaker day school in Washington where Chris was a student. I was on the search committee looking for a new headmaster. Howard interviewed Bob Smith, who was in the Admissions Office at Columbia, and I recommended him as a topnotch candidate for the post of Headmaster. Everyone was impressed with his gentle demeanor and unusual capacity for listening—faculty and administration alike said to us, "You know, Bob listens, he really listens." Bob became Headmaster, and reinvigorated Sidwell's Quaker ambience.

1967 was the year of the unexpected. Howard was asked to go to Columbia University in New York City to direct a new graduate Institute of South and Southeast Asian Studies. Then, having decided to return to academic life and having bought a new house in Riverdale in the Bronx, just up the Hudson River from Columbia, we stayed in Washington for another year. Columbia University granted Howard a year's leave of absence to work with Walt Rostow in the White House as a member of the National Security Council staff. His bailiwick was South Asia, the Middle East and parts of Northern Africa. During that last year in Washington, I went back to school again after twenty years, taking painting courses at American University under Ben Summerford. After the Asian American Forum years, it was a welcome change to be free of responsibility.

Howard had a fascinating time working in the White House for the National Security Council. There were troubles between India and Pakistan in Kashmir, so he worked with President Johnson and Secretary of Agriculture Orville Freeman on India's food problems. The two of us attended White House dinners in honor of the King of Saudi Arabia and the Prime Minister of Aghanistan.

Howard may have thought Columbia would be an anticlimax, but such was not the case. It was 1968, the year of revolt in American universities, Columbia among them. That first year his office was trashed by the Students for a Democratic Society, a radical group that led a campus-wide student strike.

When Howard knew that some of the ardent rebels were coming to see him in his office, he asked Chris, who was then a student at George School, what he should do. "Well, why don't you get a hookah, sit like a yogi crosslegged and smoke it? That would surprise them." Howard found a hookah, put it in a conspicuous place, and faced his stony SDS interrogators, secretly glad to be reassured that his son had been on his side.

Even though Howard's work in Washington was on quite different problems than Vietnam, it wasn't easy for him being on the inside of the White House while our Quaker friends were on the outside picketing against the Vietnam War. And Dinny, a student at Brown University, had been part of the March on the Pentagon. Even though the *New York Times* denied it, Dinny reported that tear gas had been used to quell the rioters.

In that year of national discontent, conversations in Washington were about what decisions were being made and who was making them. Even though in New York the Vietnam War was still on everyone's mind, it was not the only subject of discussion; people were also talking about THE CITY, the theater, music, the worlds of publishing and finance, the arts, and the United Nations.

I went into Manhattan two days a week to study drawing at the Art Students League. Their classes with leading artists were very flexible. I could sign up for a month or several years. And we did a very New York thing: we allowed an advertising company to use our home for a commercial on automobile shock absorbers. We gave the money we earned to Eugene McCarthy's campaign and we bought a Kousa dogwood for our garden.

But life with Howard was filled with the unexpected. We were just settling in when Howard asked Columbia for a sabbatical for the fall of 1969 so that he could visit the Centers of South Asian Studies in Western Europe and the Soviet Union, as well as major academic institutions in South Asia. Dinny stayed on at Brown University. Chris was given permission by his school to travel in the fall semester, and so was Jenny.

As Kipling would have it:

> Still the world is wondrous large,—seven seas
> from marge to marge—
> And it holds a vast of various kinds of man;
> And the wildest dreams of Kew are the facts of
> Khathmandu...[3]

Off we went. When the first suitcase was left at home by mistake on the 12th of June, we all agreed that we wouldn't keep track of luggage mislaid in our almost eight-month trip around the world. Jenny, however, did keep a few statistics on our globe-circling: sixteen countries, forty-one flights, ninety-six different beds slept in and about 105 temples visited. She also kept track of conveyances—all manner of trains, buses, rickshaws, subways, airplanes, horse-drawn carriages called tongas, Victorias, cycle-rickshaws, bicycles, taxis with black tiger stripes in Kathmandu, funiculars, motor scooters, gondolas, Land Rovers, a nineteenth-century paddle-wheel riverboat, a sampan, and two punts.

In England, Switzerland, and France, we visited a number of close friends Howard had known in his refugee work with the American Friends Service Committee. Howard conferred with scholars and we attended an AFSC Diplomats Conference in Montreux (like the one we had attended before in Colombo). After a stopover in Moscow, we flew to South Asia.

In India, we traveled for six weeks among its people, from Mahabalipuram and Madras in the South to as close as we could get to Tibet. In Nepal, Chris saw a caravan of laughing, jolly Tibetans with their jostling ponies, bells on their necks, and he was smitten. I was not sure what the high point was for Jenny, but perhaps it was our five days in Cambodia exploring the vast temple area of Angkor Wat with its huge Buddhist heads and temples, some of which were being devoured by jungle vines. For me it was the OVERVIEW of Asian art: the cave paintings at Ajanta, the astonishing Silk Road museum in Kabul with its Gandharan Buddhas, and the Kannon Buddha in Japan. I would draw on these visual images for years to come.

In Colombo we showed Jenny where she had been born, and were amused that our old house bore a sign saying "Ceylon State Bank Redemption Department." Howard talked with everyone until in the end he lost his voice. I saw Punitham, who was hungry for information on the outside world. Under the Bandaranaike government, there had been foreign exchange restrictions (largely for economic reasons) on imported books, so that very few foreign books and magazines were available. Before we left Colombo we visited Arthur Clarke, space writer and scientist, just as he was finishing off a final report on the Apollo 11 space mission.

We were glad to spend Christmas of 1969 in Indonesia with the Booz family, with whom our children had become good friends at Sandy Spring Meeting and then at Little Cranberry Island. Chris then returned, along with Paddy Booz, to George School with a movie he had made on our trip, but Jenny went on with Howard and me to Hong Kong and Japan.

It was hard getting back to a more normal life in Riverdale again. Jenny was twelve going on nineteen, and eventually we concluded that Riverdale Country School was more confining than she remembered. Eventually she attended Friends Seminary on the Lower East Side of New York. She traveled about twenty miles each way instead of walking five or six blocks; first the train to Grand Central and then one stop on an express subway. I too went back to school, becoming a member of the Bank Street Writers Workshop (1971) in order to learn more about the art of writing children's books. I liked the anonymity of writing; what mattered was not who the author was, or whom she or he knew, or where the author came from, but THE STORY itself.

One of the first people we met was Jane Smythe Brown, who came to Riverdale about the same time we did. Jane had recently married Wentworth Brown and had been instrumental in getting the de Young Museum started in San Francisco. She was very knowledgeable about Asian art; in fact, she was knowledgeable about almost everything and she was not reluctant to divulge what she knew. "It's like this, see," and she would begin. She had been brought up in Panama, married young and lost her husband in a motorcycle accident early in the marriage. Jane then went on to marry Bob Smythe, who had been Consul General in Chungking in the very early days—which is why she was able to organize a Riverdale/San Francisco art trip to China in 1977, well before the United States had established diplomatic relations with China. She had no children of her own but she had many friends of all ages. Jane was artful in her cooking, in hostessing, managing people, and painting. I don't know of anything she didn't do.

Riverdale proper started out in the 1850s as a group of villas and a railroad station.[4] Some of the ancient copper beech trees are still standing, one with a girth of sixteen and three-quarters feet. Our house had been the gardener's cottage to the Wave Hill mansion. It was not only a beautiful place overlooking the Hudson River, but our home—much smaller than the one in Washington— was only one block away from the eighteen acres of Wave Hill Botanical Gardens and Environmental Center. It was at a Wave Hill reception that I first met Sally Kerlin, whose husband Gil had saved Wave Hill from the developers who were flocking to Riverdale in the fifties. I was attracted to Sally from the beginning. She was about ten years older than I, about my height, very feminine, with blue eyes, fair skin and an enchanting laugh that still rings in my ears.

"I am Sally Wriggins," I said.

She smiled and said, "Yes, I know who you are."

I remember being surprised, and we became fast friends. Many of her interests—Wave Hill, Bank Street College of Education, geography—coincided with mine. We both went to the Society of Women Geographers meetings at the Explorers Club and to social events at the Cosmopolitan Club. It was Sally who introduced me to the "Lady Philosophers," an extraordinary group of women, many of them much older than I, who had been meeting together in New York for over twenty years before I joined them. Howard and I attended Scarsdale Quaker Meeting for several years, but in time we began to meet with a group of congenial friends and Quakers in one another's houses. Sally Kerlin was part of that worship group too.

The 1970s

magic circle of lady philosophers

Riverdale N.Y.

and back to SRI LANKA

Those of us who lived near Wave Hill, on the slope leading down to the Hudson River, saw the sun set behind the craggy Palisades in New Jersey. Because the station was right on the river, we felt the whipping winds roar up and down the Hudson as we waited for a train to Grand Central Station. To get to Manhattan, we could drive on the Henry Hudson Parkway to the West Side Highway; we could take the Broadway Local subway at 242nd Street at Van Cortlandt Park to go to Columbia University; or we could take the bus to Manhattan. Riverdale in the Bronx was a very cohesive, well defined community; we saw our neighbors commuting, at parties and at community events. So it was odd that we didn't get to know the Goodriches until several years after we moved there. Perhaps it was because they were so much older than we were. By then, Carrington was an Emeritus Professor at Columbia.

I remember the first time I met Anne Goodrich. As I entered her dim living room, my eyes fastened on a scroll of two swirling fish, with a lengthy inscription running down one side in squiggly Chinese characters. I strained to see it in the near darkness.

"The Silent Traveler gave it to me," Anne explained, turning on a nearby lamp so I could see better.

"Oh, the travel writer who illustrated all those books? *The Silent Traveler in London, The Silent Traveler in Tokyo*? My mother used to read them," I said, happy to have found a connection, for I knew very little about Chinese writers.

"He was a good friend of the family and used to teach at Columbia too."

The weather was excessively dreary that afternoon. The Goodriches' home was the only private house left among a maze of tall apartment buildings. "When the children were growing up there was nothing but an old farm between the house and the river," Anne told me once. Carrington and Anne had come to Riverdale in 1932 when Carrington began to teach at Columbia. These were the days before the height of the real estate boom in the fifties, when all the apartment buildings began to tower over their house and blocked out the light.

I remember the afternoon as a study in stark black and white: the dark, dark living room with its Chinese bronzes and strange gods and goddesses standing in the corner, Anne as a figure of light with the nimbus of her white hair and her eyes of pure cerulean blue.

She told me that she was writing a book on Chinese hells—a word she pronounced with great gusto—"all eighteen of them. Did you know there were so many? I didn't."

With someone as direct as Anne, it wasn't hard to confess that I had been trying to write children's books. Writing was my way of trying to capture some of our family's adventures. After our 1967 trip out West to show Chris and Jenny where I had grown up, I had begun a book about white-water rafting on the Middle Fork of the Salmon River in Idaho. I wrote about a colorful hermit who lived there. I started to tell Anne that I was working on a story for younger readers about an exchange of ghosts between Nepal and America—a story inspired by our round-the-world trip in 1969.

Anne interrupted. "So you are interested in introducing American children to Asia?"

"Sure."

"Well, if you are so interested in writing for children, why don't you look at Chinese folk tales?"

69

Here is Sally, deep in conversation with Anne Goodrich, in her dark, inscrutable living room.

"Like what?" I asked her.

"Monkey," she said instantly. "It is a wonderful story that every Chinese knows. Children love it and American children would love it too." She continued, "It is about a very naughty Monkey who steals the peaches of heaven and gets into a lot of trouble." She lent me a copy of Arthur Waley's translation of *Monkey*.[5] I had never heard of it. Waley has been called "The Explorer who Never Left Home" because he never went to Asia; his translations of Japanese and Chinese classics are nonetheless without peer. Arthur Waley had translated about a third of the original Monkey story during World War II. Since then, Waley has been superseded by Dr. Anthony Yu, who had gone on to translate the entire *Journey to the West* or *Monkey*. The first volume came out in 1977.

I remember putting off reading *Monkey* for quite a while, but from the moment I began, I was entranced. Howard always says with mock anguish, "AND THAT'S WHEN IT ALL BEGAN."

As I came to know Anne better I learned that she had gone to China as a missionary after studying at Vassar. Anne was diving champion of Beijing in those days. She also told me that, thanks to an engineering friend, she had had a Beijing sewer named after her. She met Carrington in Beijing. She used to tell me how handsome he was and how all the girls were after him. He was quite a catch. When I first met Carrington, I was impressed with his courtly manner. He seemed quiet and gentle, slow of step, but still vigorous. In temperament the Goodriches were not unlike Howard and me, Carrington reserved and careful, while Anne was outgoing and optimistic.

Although Anne was a devout Christian, she became fascinated with Chinese folk religions. After she wrote *Temple of the Eastern Peak*,[6] about a famous temple in Beijing, she went on to write *Chinese Hells*,[7] about two temples filled with fearsome images of gods and ghosts. Anne also loved Chinese paper gods. The closets in their Riverdale house were filled with boxes and boxes of notes and slips of paper printed with images of the gods. Her paper gods were charms or objects of household devotion used to ward off evil spirits. I heard her say once that to get to the heart of a culture, "it is well to study its gods, the objects of worship of that culture. Every ritual, every altar, every image reflects some hope or fear that dwells in people's hearts." *Peking Paper Gods*[8] was finally published when Anne was 94 years old. But she didn't stop. When she was 103, she wrote an article about a pilgrimage she had made to a famous temple, Miao-Feng-Shu (Mountain of the Beautiful Peak), which was published in *Asian Folklore Studies* in 1996.[9]

We spent the year of 1973–74 in England, for Howard had been awarded a Rhodes Fellowship, at St. Antony's College at Oxford, to write about the relation of rich and poor nations. Inspired by Anne Goodrich, I had worked hard on my Monkey manuscript for several years and had a finished draft to take with me. On the recommendation of Henry Allen Moe, former head of the Guggenheim Foundation, we were able to rent a substantial house with a garden on Northmore Road in Oxford, from his good friend Sir Peter Gretton. I felt very much at home, for the flowers and trees in our garden there were just like the ones I had known as a child in Seattle. I didn't mind the light rains and I loved the long and beautiful springs in England. We were only a ten-minute bicycle ride from St. Antony's, and enjoyed living without a car. Jenny attended Great Ayton Friends School, not far from the Yorkshire moors.

What E. M. Forster once wrote of Cambridge, we found to be true also of Oxford: "Body and Spirit, reason and emotion, work and play, architecture and scenery, laughter and seriousness, life and art, these pairs which are elsewhere contrasted were there fused into one."[10]

Once in Oxford, my retelling of the Monkey story almost came to a full stop when Arthur Waley's widow refused me permission to use his translation of the story. Wayne Wilcox, one of Howard's colleagues at Columbia who was now Cultural Attaché in the American Embassy in London, had found me a literary agent with the poetic name of Diana, Lady Avebury. She arranged a memorable meeting with Waley's widow, Alison, who was the executor of his estate, a New Zealand woman who had married Waley shortly before he died. Mrs. Waley alternated between ignoring me and treating me as if I were just a gauche, boorish, American woman. She flirted with Howard, but even he got nowhere in negotiating permission for me to use the translation.

I didn't know what to do until I met Dr. Glen Dudbridge at the Oriental Institute at Oxford. Such a unassuming and brilliant scholar he was. He assured me that Arthur Waley didn't own the Monkey story any more than King James owned the Bible. He suggested that his wife Sylvia Lo, who was Chinese, could translate the original Chinese of the first fourteen chapters, the part I had chosen to retell. No matter that I had retold the Monkey story already using the Waley translation. So that is what I did.

During that remarkable year at Oxford, my interests expanded. They began to shift from the Monkey story itself to the seventh-century Chinese pilgrim, Xuanzang, whose journey had inspired the Monkey epic. This Buddhist monk had traveled to India to obtain copies of the original, pure texts of Buddhism from the land of its birth. His journey ended up taking sixteen years. Indeed, it was at the home of Dr. Dudbridge that I first saw pictures of the Wild Goose Pagoda in Xian, which the Chinese Emperor had built to house the Buddhist scriptures Xuanzang brought back from India to China.

I remember how excited I was when I found cheap Indian editions of two translations, by Samuel Beal and Thomas Watters, of Xuanzang's report to the Emperor,[11] as well as Beal's *The Life of Hieun-Tsian*[12] (Xuanzang), at Blackwell's Bookstore. Inside Watters's translation was a small packet containing a stunning 8"x 21" map that showed Xuanzang's journey from China to India and back to China. It was a very detailed topographical map whose heavy cross-hatching marking the mountain ranges made it very difficult to read the names of places. I also found a remarkable second map by Vincent Smith, in the Beal. This one included the whole of Asia in about 650 C.E., with the itineraries of two Chinese travelers, one of whom was Xuanzang.

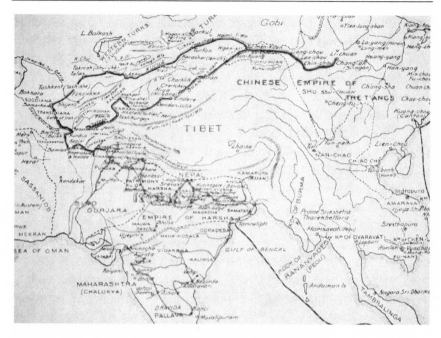

Map of Eurasia, about 650 A.D.,
showing the itinerary of Xuanzang.

In that same auspicious year of 1973–74, we visited Iran and Afghanistan during the damp and dreary month of January. We wanted to go to Bamiyan in Afghanistan to see the famous Buddhas, but a snowstorm in the mountains made it impossible. Alas, I also arrived in Kabul with a high temperature, so my clearest memories of our stay are of fighting what looked like it might become pneumonia. However, when I felt better, Ambassador Ted Eliot and his wife Pat arranged for me to talk about Xuanzang with Haruko T. Motamedi, an independent scholar whose husband was the head of the Kabul Museum.

In the Embassy library she spread out a large map of Afghanistan and patted the creases flat, and we pored over the map together. It was a revelation. She showed me exactly where Xuanzang had gone in Afghanistan on his 10,000-mile way to the Buddhist Holy Land in India, and his trip back to China. To me such a detailed knowledge of the places Xuanzang visited was unbelievable, and Dr. Motamedi talked in her low voice as if he had been by last week or maybe last month. Did they really know where he had stopped in 632 C.E? Wasn't his pilgrimage only a century after King Arthur was supposed to have lived in Britain? What impressed me as well was that she talked about Xuanzang in the same way that modern detectives talk about a live witness.

In 1975, soon after we came back to Riverdale from Oxford, Gran Wriggins died at the age of ninety-three. It was almost as if she had been waiting for our return. In her later years she had become an expert weaver. She taught us all about patience, keeping secrets, and how to be gracious.

A whole new world had opened up at the same time that our three children left home. Chris had graduated from Bennington and was off to Ladakh. After Dinny graduated from Brown, she did graduate work in nursing and was planning to marry Ed Cundy whom she had met at Brown. Jenny was about to go to Yale. People told me that it was a time when mothers often felt empty, without purpose. Quite the contrary. I remember going around saying, "post-menopausal zest, post-menopausal zest!" I was free to pursue a career, and I did so.

White Monkey King was published in 1977 by Pantheon Books. I was pleased that the New York Public Library had chosen it as one of its 100 Best Books of the Year. The illustrator Ronnie Solbert persuaded the publishers to design the book in a way that emphasized the great antiquity of this classic. The paintings in the Dunhuang Caves had inspired Solbert's fine sepia illustrations, printed on light brown paper in brown ink. It was a handsome book, and was well-received. Nancy Wilson Ross was quoted on my book jacket, saying that Monkey added to our knowledge of world mythology. I dedicated the book to Anne Goodrich and Ben Booz, who had been my mentors.

Few Americans were familiar with this classic that for centuries had captivated Chinese children and adults. They had no idea of its rich historical background, that began with a seventh-century Chinese pilgrim. I organized an exhibition for the New York Public Library called "The Ancient Background and Nine Lives of Monkey." Random House had the book sent to libraries in

Brooklyn, Philadelphia, Boston and San Francisco. I was looking forward to introducing this wonderful story to American children, schools and libraries. I was ready to share my newfound field of concentration. I was fifty-five.

PART FOUR

SRI LANKA
(1977-1980)
Diplomatic Life in
Colombo and Asia

Chapter 6

DIPLOMATS ARE LIKE SWANS

I could hear the excitement in his voice when Howard telephoned in late March 1977 to say that he had been asked to be the American Ambassador to Sri Lanka. I felt my fingers tighten and my face grimace. I was proud of him, of course, but the timing couldn't have been worse. My first book had just been published and I was planning to promote it to schools and libraries. I was poised, ready to share my new-found field of concentration.

When Howard hung up, I rushed to the kitchen and scraped carrots furiously—scrape, scrape, scrape—as if this would be the last time I would be allowed to do so. I knew, from having lived in Sri Lanka before, that the servants were always in the kitchen. As an Ambassador's wife I would not be free to scrape carrots as an outlet for pent-up emotions—and I knew that one of the hardest parts of living in the tropics was finding an outlet for pent-up emotions. I remembered Howard's quote, "Diplomats are like swans, elegantly floating on the surface of things, but paddling like hell underneath." Within three months I came to know exactly what he meant, as we learned how to float elegantly on the surface while working very hard behind the scenes as brand-new diplomats. Howard did agree that, however great the demands of the new assignment, nothing would interfere with my long-planned-for trip in November to China.

It was pleasant to conjure up a chauffeured limousine, a sumptuous residence with servants in abundance, a whirlwind of travel, and luncheons for famous people. I remembered, from the time Howard had worked in the White House, that we had attended exotic embassy dinners with mounds of caviar flown from the Caspian sea, and flaming desserts. We did a great deal of entertaining ourselves at the time. Life would now have a glamorous aura, but was this what I really wanted? Part of me liked the idea that we could work and learn together and try to represent America with the right mixture of understanding, restraint and style. We had worked and helped each other in the past and would do so again.

HERE IS DEAR HOWARD AT TWICE-TIMES THIRTY
WITH A SPARKLE IN HIS EYE
        THAT IS FINE AND FLIRTY.

HIS SMILE IT IS MERRY
            (WITH NARRY A WRINKLE)

AND HE'LL DANCE THE HERRI-GERRI
            ON TOES THAT TWINKLE!

HERE'S THE AMBASSADOR AT HALF A HUNDRED TWEN
WEIGHTED DOWN WITH KNOWLEDGE
    AND HONORS A-PLENTY!
BUT NEVER MIND THE GLORY,
    NEVER MIND THE FAME,
HOWARD KNOWS
    THAT GOOD FUN
IS THE NAME OF THE GAME!

One of an Ambassador's most important decisions is the selection of his Deputy Chief of Mission, his alter ego who must run the Embassy in his absence. My husband's choice was a brilliant foreign service officer whom he had scarcely met, Herbert Levin. At our first dinner with this new colleague and his thoughtful wife, Cornelia, there was a certain amount of sparring, the oh-so-casual dropping of achievements and distinctions on his part and on ours. I noted that Howard was less modest than usual.

Our association continued that night in my dream, in which the four of us were standing on a Persian carpet under an imposing chandelier. Everyone in the circle was singing, their voices tripping up the scales higher and higher. All in this operatic quartet had reached high C, except me. I was valiantly trying to do so when I woke up.

The truth was that I didn't really want to reach high C. I didn't want to be on a diplomatic stage. As one of the founders of what is now called the Asian American Forum, I had been interested in broad cultural issues that had diplomatic implications. But from this experience of coming to know such able women, and hearing them talk about their areas of expertise, I had concluded that I wanted to find my own specialty. After three or four years of floundering, I had found it, thanks to Anne Goodrich, in an area in Chinese literature and history. For the first time in our marriage I was exploring an interest that was wholly my own.

So while the Ambassadorship was a culmination of Howard's career, first as a scholar, then as a government advisor, a policy planner, a professor, and now as a diplomat, this time we were no longer in sync. I was not an old-fashioned wife without a career, nor was I a totally modern woman who could opt to stay home in America.

Preparing for three or four years of embassy life in the tropics required two major outlays: a new wardrobe and a small grocery store's worth of canned goods and drug store supplies. What summer clothes I possessed were chiefly sweaters and non-designer jeans for summers on Little Cranberry Island. I soon became an expert on comfortable reception-line shoes and one-hundred-percent-cotton clothes. Expecting local food supplies in

Colombo to be unreliable, we spent a hectic Washington morning in a wholesale warehouse with a helpful man whose name was Luscious. I pointed to the food we needed and Luscious loaded up cases and cases of consommé, tomato soup, applesauce, pears, V-8 juice, American condiments, coffee, and so on. These would be shipped for us, along with our household effects, to Sri Lanka.

The State Department provided an excellent course for ambassadors and their wives, as well as a family workshop for government personnel going overseas. There were language courses; role-playing workshops on cultures strange to us; and lectures on long-range planning for women, State Department organization, representation and protocol—all of the highest quality. Howard conferred with Adolph Dubs, then Deputy Assistant Secretary of State for Near East and South Asian Affairs. Dubs, whom everyone called Spike, recognized that Howard had several strings to his bow—a definitive book on Sri Lanka as well as policy experience with South Asia politics. Spike also knew Howard's writings on political leadership in developing countries. With this in mind, he urged Howard to travel widely in the area and not to limit himself to Sri Lanka. This was great news for me.

The last few weeks in July I spent trying to obtain attractive pictures for the walls of the Residence, among them a blown-up NASA photograph of Sri Lanka as seen from twenty miles out in space. While enjoying a round of farewell parties, we were swamped by financial arrangements: closing out bank accounts; changing our insurance policies; finding owners for our dog, our car; packing for air freight, packing for sea freight; tidying up the house; making inventories; getting medical and security clearances; sending out change-of-address labels; renting our house; filling out conflict-of-interest forms; redoing our wills. Finally we boarded our plane in New York, flew across America, and were still catching our breath on our flight from San Francisco to Hawaii, when the pilot announced: "We are about to cross the Atlantic, oops, excuse me, I mean the Pacific Ocean." I knew just how he felt.

We rested for a few days in Singapore, where we lunched with the American Ambassador, John Holdridge, and his wife Martha.

Just before we sat down—he was late —I noticed that he handed his wife a manila folder. After we adjourned to the veranda for coffee, I asked why.

"Oh," she said, "that's the way it's done. All invitations, suggested guest lists, diplomatic calls we must make, and my husband's schedule are in that folder. Any questions I may have about procedures, accounting or correspondence go in there, too, for the return trip when he goes back to the office."

My chin dropped "That's how you keep up with what's going on all around you?"

She nodded. "Yes, we exchange them twice a day, when my husband comes home for lunch, and again at night." Perhaps she smiled inwardly too, thinking how much this new girl had to learn.

Learn I did, in the elegant American Residence in Colombo, filled with bouquets of blue, wine, red, violet and yellow orchids the night we arrived in August, 1977. But that first night we wanted to go for a walk after our long flight—only to find that all the windows were barred, the servants had locked all the doors and gone to bed, and we didn't know where the keys were.

"Oh darling," I groaned, "we're prisoners in our gilded cage." I went to Howard's arms, seeking support in his tall frame and broad shoulders. "We've come half-way around the world for this? We were free before."

The State Department Post Report described the Residence as follows:

> The air-conditioned residence is set in one and one-half acres of land, is a two-story house with reception hall, dining room (seats 24), two reception rooms, guest lavatory, two verandas, kitchen, pantry, storeroom, servant's quarters, double garage in one story located to the rear of building, four bedrooms, three baths, large sitting room upstairs. Residence is equipped with one gas, one electric stove, three refrigerators, two deep freezes, a washing machine, two dryers. Local market is unpredictable.[13]

The brochure didn't say that one of the previous Sri Lankan owners had seen a ghost in the bathroom mirror; or that the jewelry of a previous Ambassador's wife had been stolen when they first arrived, following which they acquired a gaggle of geese to keep out all intruders. The geese, alas, were gone. The sad state of the well-landscaped garden was not the result of their depredations, just of neglect. Maybe I could restore it.

The Residence was spacious and offered attractive possibilities—beautifully furnished reception rooms; a small downstairs room which became our music room; a large sitting room upstairs where I could write; a covered veranda for breakfast, close to trees filled with giant climbing philodendrons. Here we could hear the early morning birds. The veranda could be used for large dinner parties as well, with soft modern floor spotlights to highlight the exotic plants hanging from the ceiling. There was also a large outdoor veranda overlooking the back garden where I could serve tea.

Our first grand dinner was an exercise in suspense. Even by the morning of the party we didn't know whether there would be a curfew because of racial discord on the island, and if there was, who would have police permission to be out after 8:00 p.m. Would there be four for dinner, or eighteen?

On one of our early morning walks we passed by our old house, which seemed empty, desolate-looking. "Zircon Typewriter Company," said the sign out front. Too much was happening for me to think much about what Ceylon had been like in the fifties, what I had been like as a young mother whose primary concerns were the health and well-being of her family. Dinny, I remembered, had learned to ride a bike on this very street when Howard was away for six weeks in India and Burma. The children and I had gone to Kodaikanal, a hill station in south India, during the hot season. We throve. Color came back to their cheeks and I shed a minor infection that I didn't mind losing. I'll never forget the pallor, an off-color green, of Howard's face when he finally joined us there.

The smell of wood fires hung on the early morning air near our old house back in Colombo, as men and women made breakfast tea by the side of the road or in vacant lots. It was the time of year when sarong-clad men in the streets walked along dodging puddles, holding up above their knees the corners of these comfortable skirts so they wouldn't get wet. The men swung their sarongs back and forth in a kind of rhythm that was lovely to watch.

People always seemed to be in groups—whether on the passing buses and trains, three or four to a seat; or in cars, a sea of faces at the windows; or as they washed themselves by a village stream. Though Sri Lankans are a many-sided and complex people, on the surface they showed laughing smiles and happy faces. They have a veneer of gentleness and great charm, but I felt there was a dark side and I wondered when it would appear. I fancied they must see us as loud, impatient creatures with few manners and lacking in the social graces which they wore so lightly and with such ease.

Warm personal occasions helped to alleviate my depression brought on by the recent racial turmoil between Sinhalese and Tamils. I saw my old friend Punitham—but not as often as I would have liked. We had several nice occasions with old friends, Dr. Chinnatamby, who had delivered Jenny, and Vernon Aluwihare, who had lived with us in Chevy Chase—people we had known for twenty years. Vernon was almost a member of the family. He had a wide, open smile, a large mouth and a comforting laugh, and was the soul of gentleness and human wisdom. He was married to a Tamil, though he himself was from a distinguished Sinhalese family from Kandy. He represented the very best of the Sinhalese with his relaxed, low-key warmth and charm. If he looked occasionally perplexed with that dent between his eyebrows, the happy expression so characteristic of Sri Lankans quickly pushed this aside.

One of the ways in which I tried to make the Embassy Residence a drawing card was with good food. Accordingly, my relationship with a lovely elf of a man, our number one cook Crooz, was crucial. I had heard that his reputation was a mixed one, but I enjoyed this aging little man who walked with swift steps, who had a few missing teeth, a winning smile, and sometimes a nervous giggle like a child when I caught him out on something. He wrote "spanage" for spinach, and "parsalay" for parsley, but since I can't spell either, this was yet another bond between us. He was so *sympathique,* and I felt bad when his heart or his innards were out of whack, and even when he went out on a drunken spree.

His meals were sheer artistry. The memory of his Shrimp Viennoise, a concoction of shrimp, heavy cream, mushrooms and noodles, makes me sigh deeply to this day. Crooz made velvety vichyssoise and the most sumptuous avocado, cream of carrot, and cream of cucumber soups. I don't know how he did it. Not to mention those jelly omelettes, and his greatest triumphs, chocolate and Grand Marnier soufflés. I could go on and on.

Crooz also made a very good whole wheat bread. This surprised me. We spent a lot of time, he and I, either planning menus or in our locked-up grocery storeroom plucking ordinary cans of sweet potatoes or pears which he then transformed into haute cuisine dishes of distinction. Big hunks of lamb, ordered three months in advance from Singapore, became fragrant cuts swimming in gravy and cooked to perfection. I cannot vouch for all those hot curries or his Sinhalese dishes, but I assume they were of equal quality.

He shopped for vegetables, chicken and fruits in the local markets and gave us succulent mangos, papayas, and pineapple for breakfast. I can still make Howard drool by mentioning the endless variety of plantains and bananas we used to have. I shopped at Elephant House for ice cream, sodas and cheese. I ordered wines, liquor, American cereals from the small embassy supply store.

Once I learned how to do the inescapable paperwork, running the Residence and entertaining were much easier than I thought they would be. "Yes," you may say, "with a cook, three houseboys, three gardeners, one laundry man, one sweeper, four guards in rotation, two drivers and a special man to help with customs at the airport, how could it anything but be easy?"

Well, there was usually a blackout whenever the Minister of Irrigation and Power came to dinner. There was the time when one of the kitchen servants was discovered to have worms, so everyone in the Residence had to have stool tests. I explained this delicate matter to all the male staff, and then my husband put it in plainer English. Still they all went to the hospital thinking that their chests would be x-rayed. Why? There were many such misunderstandings, some more serious. I once estimated that we grasped forty percent of their English and they forty percent of ours. The discouraging part was that none of us improved. Later I learned that the Sinhalese colloquial word for English was "sword."

Much to my surprise, I enjoyed the round of diplomatic calls. My heart went out to some of the wives who had come so ill-prepared for their tasks or whose futures were so uncertain. Where are they now, these diplomatic couples from Korea with its change of government? What became of the Libyan Attaché, the Czech Ambassador? I loved watching the expressions of the East European wives when I casually mentioned that I had worked one summer in the shipyards during World War II as an electrician. This soft, bourgeois wife of the U.S. Ambassador a member of the electrician's union?

There were many simple tasks to keep me busy. When one of the Marine guards was sick in the hospital I brought him a big bouquet of flowers from the garden. "I haven't seen so many flowers except at a funeral," he told me solemnly. To his pals he said, "I guess Mrs. Wriggins was trying to decorate me." One time I had a staff person to lunch whose mother had just died. Cely Arndt, the wife of the director of the Agency for International Development, came to lunch too, and commented on the way out, "You're sort of like a den mother, aren't you?" That's not the way I would put it, but it was true that many of the Embassy team were single or divorced, or their spouses were in another country. They were lonely. I would be too. I worked with the American Women's group on a comprehensive guide to Colombo and they, in turn, helped me with a project of setting up a canteen for the National Museum, which was sorely in need of one.

My writing life finally surfaced when the United States government formally recognized China in January, 1979. We were invited for dinner at the Chinese Embassy. I thought it might be useful to bring along a copy of *White Monkey King*. At dinner I presented it to the Consul General with a toast, saying how much I loved the story. Again to my delight and astonishment, it turned out that the evening's entertainment was a television version of the Monkey story, the very same episodes that were in my book. I couldn't believe it!

In December of 1977 a regional Ambassadors' conference was held in Katmandu, Nepal. All the American Ambassadors stationed in Pakistan, India, Nepal, Afghanistan, Bangladesh, Sri Lanka, and Iran, were there, as well as their man in Washington, Assistant Secretary for the Near East and South Asia, "Spike" Dubs. Each Ambassador discussed his country's problems. What would the Pakistan government do with deposed Prime Minister Bhutto while he was awaiting a decision following his trial for murder? In India, what was going to happen to the Janata government which had replaced Mrs. Gandhi? In Afghanistan, would the Daoud regime tighten up on its leftist civilian politicians? What would they do to counter Soviet influence in the army? In Sri Lanka, what would come of the dramatic changes in economic policy toward the free market? What about the growing restlessness of Tamil youth in Jaffna? Would the student unrest in Iran, which very nearly kept Bill Sullivan, Iran's U.S. Ambassador, from attending the conference, grow worse?

The tranquil garden setting of the Katmandu Residence seemed far removed from these potentially explosive issues. The Ambassadors sat around a long table under an open-sided tent with a fine view of the snow peaks of the Himalayas. Soldiers stood at out-of-hearing range on the grass. We wives sat at a respectful distance in lawn chairs drawn up in a circle, giant twelve-foot-tall poinsettia bushes all around us. I had been in Colombo only a few months at the time, so I listened intently as other Ambassadors' wives expressed their feeling that we were worth more than the State Department acknowledged. We needed more financial support for travel to similar conferences, or to orientation courses in Washington, so that we could learn more about our jobs. Some wanted access to more classified information. "After all, we are the ones at dinner who sit on the right of the Foreign Minister." Pat Eliot, our old friend and wife of the Ambassador to Afghanistan, had circulated a paper entitled "The Possible Roles within the Non-

Role of the Ambassador's Wife." In it she listed Ombudsman, Ear to the Ground, Confidante, Catalyst for the American Community, Second Best Role (as Consort to the Ambassador) and Resident Greybeard. She cited the long overdue opening up of the male-oriented Foreign Service, now slowly being brought up to date by less paternalistic management practices. The Family Liaison Office in the State Department and the Family Liaison officers in the field help women in the State Department find jobs, evaluate their skills, cope with special education and health problems, and acquire language training.

The customary group photograph of the diplomats, their wives, and Spike Dubs was taken later that day. Among them, of course, was Howard, whose clearly patrician looks—high sloping forehead and bushy eyebrows—reminded me of the movie star Franchot Tone.

I think now what a poignant photograph it is. Yes, they are mostly smiling, looking squarely at the camera. They are good at relaxing; they have to be. How could anyone have guessed that Ambassador Sullivan, American Ambassador to Iran, would lose his Embassy when it was invaded and his staff taken hostage almost two years later? Or that Spike Dubs, who became American Ambassador to Afghanistan, would be tragically assassinated on February 14, 1979 in Kabul? Or that Ambassador Hummel, American Ambassador in Pakistan at the time, would be having lunch at the Residence when his Embassy was burned down by a mob? What a testament to how much the Asian world changed in the three years we were in Sri Lanka.

Only once did I fear for my husband's life. The burning of the American Embassy in Pakistan, when the staff barely escaped with their lives, occurred in November, 1979, after Radio Tehran had blamed the Americans for the seizure by a gang of Moslem radicals of the Grand Mosque in Mecca. Newspapers reported that Moslems were inflamed all over the Middle East, spreading down into South Asia. Howard was recovering from the flu and I was recovering from a pulmonary embolism. Our assignment was coming to a close and we were preparing to go home via western China, packing and saying farewell. The air freight people were coming and we were expecting the New Zealand High Commissioner and his wife for a visit.

As Howard marched out the door in his academic gown, ready to give a graduation address at the university, I asked him if he really had to do it, for there could be some bitterly anti-American students present. With a twinkle in his eyes, he said he wanted "some spice."

"Spice?" I could have screamed.

Nothing happened to him, but I was glad that precautionary measures had been taken to protect him. Julie Hennsley, the wife of the New Zealand diplomat who stayed with us, laughed when I told her my husband's parting words. "Don't you know that men are always boys?"

Perhaps it has always been a politically volatile world, but until the late seventies the tradition of diplomatic immunity had been widely accepted. An Ambassador's Residence and Embassy were considered as the territory of the country he or she represented. An Ambassador was also immune from local jurisdiction and police interference, although the host country was obligated to offer protection. We discovered that now diplomats could no longer float quite as gracefully on the surface as they had in the past. Now they had to duck the bullets of those hunting them, and the terrorists who bombed their Embassies. Just as the hijacking of airplanes had become common, many a modern diplomat had begun to feel that he had more in common with a sitting duck than a swan.

Chapter 7

IN THE EMBASSY GARDEN

Never for a moment did I forget that we were living in the tropics. But I could close my eyes when I walked around the Embassy garden and remember that Mother taught me to say *"Caprifoliacea symphoricarpus albus,"* the botanical name for snowberry, as a parlor trick when I was three years old. She was taking a course in botany at the University of Washington at the time, and she must have liked the sound of it. She also taught me about kinikinick—the Indian name, which means "burning leaves," for the small shiny leaves of a creeping groundcover that the Indians liked to smoke. Mother taught me many such names. This one had lain dormant in my mind for many, many years until the 1980s, when we were traveling around Banff and Lake Louise in Western Canada. I looked down at the tiny green leaves and knew immediately what it was, even though it had been sixty years since I had seen kinikinick or thought about its tiny leaves! Mother told me the names of birds, too; especially she loved the song of the hermit thrush, whose voice trills higher and higher till it seems it will never stop. We always carried a copy of *The Birds of Western*

Canada; its binding had broken a long time ago and had been mended with strips of adhesive tape.

In Seattle I had a tiny garden of my own, filled with small ferns gathered on one of our camping trips in the Cascade mountains. There was even a little pool fringed with ladyslippers. But what was truly original and altogether inspired were my mother's miniature fern gardens. She found tiny ferns on the tops of tree stumps in the forest and brought them home to put them in small cradles made of bark. These she placed in the windowsills of our dining room. I have loved ferns ever since. Eventually I found a small tree fern for the Embassy garden. Would that Mother had been still alive so that she could see it!

It would have been such fun to take her around the acre and a half of land in Cinnamon Gardens, the part of Colombo where we lived. At one time Cinnamon Gardens had been a Dutch plantation, but its spice bushes—hence the name—had long disappeared to make room for the city's most fashionable suburb. The Ambassador's Residence was surrounded with wondrous—and new to me—exotic plants, variegated vines, palm trees, a spice grove, a huge scarlet Flame-of-the-Forest tree, colorful ginger bushes and a whole hedge of gardenias.

In Cinnamon Gardens, the best part of the day for me was the cool of the morning before the heat bore down. What did the eternal summer do to someone who was attuned to the four seasons? Well, deprived of winter and of springtime, I telescoped these seasonal rhythms into a single day. I experienced as seasons the coolness of the early morning, the still heat of the midday, the freshening late afternoon, and the sudden darkness. Often I dressed differently for each one. I moved through them in different ways. I lived by small rhythms.

MORNING

While it was still dark a brain-fever bird screeched from a mango tree, and, at the moment that the dawn-light struck the highest pinnacle of the Embassy Residence, a robin magpie answered. A swish of green parakeets streaked across the lawn, and in the bamboo grove near the street two parakeets touched each other as the male fed a morsel to his consort, the prelude to mating. Very early in the morning, the Embassy garden was a haven for birds and for us inside the Residence, who treasured this time of day.

Scratch, scratch, scratch. Sounds of a bamboo rake on an asphalt driveway. Karpish, the head gardener, made sure that I heard the noise of his sweeping as I discussed the December 30th ministers' dinner with Howard during breakfast on the side veranda.

Later I went for a garden tour with Karpish, an intense, black-eyed young man who always wore a brown khaki shirt and shorts. His bare feet touched the still-cool asphalt as we walked together on the long driveway leading to the palm-screened porte-cochere of our Victorian bungalow. The driveway marked off the rest of the lawn from the spice grove and kitchen plot on one side, and the more traditional garden on the other side. The rest of the Residence grounds changed in mood and feeling, from wild jungle places tangled with vines and heavy undergrowth, to the intimacy and refreshment of a fountain and a pool with swimming carp, to the more formal back garden on two levels. Splashes of bougainvillea, pink and heliotrope in pots, sat on a graceful balustrade. Plants and trees flourished. We were only eight degrees north of the equator, after all, with two monsoons a year. All life grew rampant here, and we needed two able-bodied men and an aging third to water and tend one and a half acres of garden.

"Doesn't Madame think the dracaena bush should be moved away from the bungalow?" Karpish asked me.

My lack of enthusiasm caused him to look worried as he sometimes did.

"But, Madame, the bad snakes like this bush. Better to put it outside the garden wall. That is what other people are doing."

"How is our traveler's palm? It has been in the ground quite a while now."

He nodded his head in a figure-eight gesture. "Fine, Madame."

We stopped to admire a giant green fan of the palm, more than twenty feet tall. The sheath was full of water for travelers, hence the name. In another nine months it would be as tall as Somerset Maugham's travelers' palms in the Raffles Hotel garden in Singapore.

"And the cannonball tree?" I asked, starting to cross the lawn. I was thinking of how it would one day have peach-colored blossoms and fruit shaped like wooden apples, pushing out of its leafless trunk.

We walked on.

"Excuse me, Madame, that bush you like. It is blooming. The purple blossoms came out yesterday. Today the white. Tomorrow the blue." And I remembered that this bush is called "yesterday, today, and tomorrow" for this reason. We admired it and we continued our inspection until he sensed that I was about to go inside.

"Excuse me, Madame," he said earnestly. A crease furrowed his young brow. "That boy I recommended for the Embassy lady on Maitland Crescent. He is not good. She should get rid of him."

"Oh?"

"Yes, he is very bad." Such an unexpected disclosure would require time to investigate, so I said nothing.

After many such early morning rounds, I discovered that what initially appeared to be a scattering of nondescript trees on the left side of our garden as one entered was actually both a tropical showcase and a spice grove. What the sixteenth- and seventeenth-century Portuguese and Dutch were searching for across the seven seas—clove and cinnamon and nutmeg—were all there. Tightly-closed flower buds on a small conical tree were picked green and spread on the ground to dry for several days in the sun, whereupon they turned brown to become the cloves we keep in our spice bottles. Two cinnamon trees whose bark gives us our spice stood at least forty feet tall. On occasion, the gardener would pick a cinnamon leaf, crush it in his fingers and hand it to me to sniff its sharp, pungent aroma. A tall nutmeg tree stood nearby which produced a hard, brown shell with the nutmeg kernel inside. Around the nutmeg was a scarlet aril or wrapper, and this was called mace. Three hundred years earlier, like many a distant government body, the Dutch authorities dispatched an order for the colonial government of Ceylon to reduce the number of nutmeg trees and increase the number of mace trees!

Years before, Mrs. Bernard Guffler, wife of the then Ambassador, had planted the spice garden along with tea bushes to show visitors from cruise ships—who had no time to go up-country—how spices and tea grew. Cocoa beans hung in large pods from the bark of a chocolate tree. Bright red coffee berries in season adorned a fifteen- to twenty-foot coffee tree. Not far away were guava, rubber, avocado, mango, banana and papaya trees.

Nearer to the bungalow stood the smooth grey trunk of a Bo tree, whose lofty branches grew taller than the Residence. In Buddhist temple courtyards the Bo tree's boughs, reaching out in a sheltering way, are decked with colored flags on holy days. The Lord Buddha, in the grace of the Bo tree's shade, received Enlightenment in the sixth century B.C.E. Three centuries later, a branch from this same tree was supposed to have been carried from India to Anuradhapura in Sri Lanka. There it was planted and still grows, five thousand years later, the oldest tree known to mankind.

Legends abounded about the life of the Buddha. One of these, from China, concerned the origin of tea. In the fifth reincarnation, the Buddha meditated for many years. Unblinking. Unsleeping. Then one day his chin dropped and he did fall asleep. When he awoke he was so furious that he sliced off both his eyelids with a knife and threw them on the ground. Immediately upon hitting the earth, the saintly eyelids sprouted roots and grew into what became known as the tea bush, symbol of wakefulness.

NOON

It was pleasant in January at midday. Three or four months later in the hot season it would be too humid to go out in the oven-heat. In the April-garden here, the spreading Flame-of-the-Forest tree would become a huge scarlet umbrella shading the driveway. Its splendor, and the succulent taste of mangos, which ripened at this time, almost compensated for the relentless heat.

In January we lunched with a view of the pond and its fountain, which a servant turned on in the sunshine and in the rain. What better symbol for the spirited forces of nature than the joyful play of water in the air? The birds came to watch the rising and falling of jets of water and to bathe in its coolness: a flashy, iridescent blue kingfisher; the pond heron, his long neck deceptively hidden. On some days a shrike, with his pivoting head like a tomahawk, perched on the rim and waited. I loved to watch his fierce yellow eyes as he scanned the garden for a meal or enemies.

AFTERNOON

"Why don't you pick off the dead gardenia blossoms?" I asked Karpish in the afternoon. The gardenia hedge stood next to the bungalow beyond the Flame-of-the-Forest tree. Just opposite was the jungle part of the garden, where black boughs of trees were festooned with vines and covered with sodden moss and small-leaved ferns. Giant climbing philodendron leaves stenciled with holes and deep indentations, the grand perforated leaves of *Monstera deliciosi*, hid the black trunk. All philodendrons, as the origin of the name indicated, were tree lovers. All were climbers, though they might not seem so, and this was one of the most exotic.

Above its slashed leaves were parasites and air-plants whose rare beauty excused their indolence. Bunches of mistletoe hung down from a mango trunk. I discovered that here once a year, under the cover of darkness, occurred a miracle.

Myriads of rose-colored buds unfurled from the leathery pink and green straps that hung from the mango trees, revealing one narrow pointed white petal and another narrow white petal, so that you could almost see the unfolding. A photograph of night-blooming cereus taken at one moment was different from one taken two hours later, the white petals fully opened, and the delicate yellow stamens inside were revealed. Why at night? Why a brief existence of only a few hours before it died? Perhaps that is why I found the night-blooming cereus so poignant. On one occasion their blooming coincided with a dinner party. Our friend Mildred Talbot, founder of the Asian American Forum, was visiting Colombo, and I was able to time the presentation of an ethereal bloom after dinner with a champagne toast.

"Excuse me, Madame," Karpish accosted me on another afternoon. "While you were away in America, the houseboys took all the king coconuts and sold them."

I pretended to be concentrating on a tall spear of ginger and did not comment. Later I would ask him if he got a good price for the flower pots he had stolen. Everyone tattled on everyone else, so of course the houseboys had told me about this earlier.

Usually when Karpish made such an immoderate demand I would ask him about one of his failures, such as why so few of our orchids had bloomed. We chose our moments. Usually Karpish and I avoided confrontations. We planned and dreamed of new varieties of flowers, new trees, and plants we wished to buy. Or we worked on balancing shapes, forms and colors and continued with our aim of adding more cut flowers for the Residence. Carrying out our ideas was another matter, for although the gardeners could save the seeds from our zinnias and marigolds for later planting, the few nurseries in Colombo would sell a branch or a small bush but seldom a full-grown tree.

Even more than perusing good nursery catalogues, I missed working in the soil myself. I loved the feel of the earth, of loam, of friable ground, of getting down on my hands and knees. I even enjoyed weeding and making room for the plants I wanted to encourage. On Little Cranberry Island in Maine, I liked to dig peat from the forest floor to use when I planted young balsam and spruce trees each year. And I liked the garden as a place of analogies: of seeds sprouting, plants growing and flowering, slowly dying and becoming part of the earth again.

I can't remember when it was, that we were going down the steps past the pink bougainvilleas to the lower garden, when Karpish stopped suddenly. "Did you speak to Madame about getting rid of that boy at Maitland Place?" he asked.

"Yes, I told her that he was a bad lot," I replied.

"But is she going to fire him?" The worried look, the tightness in Karpish's voice came back. Again I was puzzled by his strong emotion. "He was in jail two years ago. I can prove it." Again I did not reply. I needed time to check out this latest piece of information.

EVENING

The croton bush had a fine Latin name: *Gloriosum superbum.*
A single leather leaf might be partly green, partly red-black with
yellow veins and have a margin of crimson. Such reds, yellows and
oranges took me back to painting autumn leaves at school as a
child and letting the crimson and lemony colors run together just to
see how they would look.

In the hour before sunset my old friend Punitham came for tea
on the veranda, next to the riotous crotons. Before she arrived, I
had already sat down in a garden chair and was thinking about how
she talked so fast, how wonderful it was to be with her again. She
arrived wearing a wine-red sari with a simple border. Whatever she
wore, she had an incandescent quality that showed itself in an
extraordinary combination of intelligence, wit, and the charity of a
Mother Teresa who was desolate without those she could help.

There was a slight breeze in the air so that it was almost, not
quite, nippy. As we drank our tea we waited for the large fox bats;
they flew from the center of Colombo to change places with the
outlying crows from our neighborhood in Cinnamon Gardens. The
crows, having raided the fruit trees and refuse from our garbage
cans, could now return to their nests in what used to be called
Victoria Park. The bats, having slept upside down in their bat-trees
all day, came here for a night's good hunting.

"Doesn't everyone watch for fox bats in the sky at sunset?" she
asked. We looked at one another and laughed.

We sipped tea and, in talking of the past together, I felt very
close to this woman I had known in the fifties and had seen only
once since then. Punitham and I stayed out-of-doors in the cool
evening. Night came suddenly, for there was no lingering twilight
in the tropics. Two bandicoots, rather like our woodchucks, were
playing hide-and-seek in the dark in front of the spotlights at the
edge of the lawn, as if they were enjoying seeing their own
shadows.

"I found out why Karpish is so worried about the man he
recommended for the lady at Maitland Crescent," Punitham
remarked casually, breaking our silent watch. "He isn't a thief at

98

all in the usual sense, though he may have done something wrong at one time. It seems that the man ran off with Karpish's sister. A family disgrace, in other words."

"Oh, so he is trying to take revenge. I wonder if I should tell Karpish tomorrow that I know what he is doing. I don't think so," I said, thinking out loud. Punitham got up to leave. "I think we'll just continue our garden talk about thriving dieffenbachias, the fraying silver-veined anthuriums and how pleased I am with the red alocacias."

Chapter 8

PUNITHAM, HINDU FRIEND

Punitham is wearing a wine-dark sari and I am wearing a pale flowered cotton, in a small picture on my desk in America. Characteristically, she has her hands on the shoulders of a grinning little boy in front of her who had just wormed his way into the picture of the two of us in front of a stupa. We are in a Buddhist courtyard in Colombo, similar to the one where I would go to for a Buddhist tutorial.

Similar, except that this one has a building containing the paintings of George Keyt, one of Sri Lanka's best-known contemporary artists. I hadn't known of these paintings at the Gotami temple in Borella until Punitham took me there. They offer a good way for strangers to begin to understand Buddhist traditions. Here is the Lord Buddha's first sight of an Old Man, a Sick Man, and a Dead Man, who were to influence his life so profoundly; the Tempting of Mara and the devils—so similar to the Three Temptations of Christ—indeed, the major events of his life. Religious art in Sri Lanka is usually in traditional style, so these murals are additionally fascinating because they show clearly the influence of Picasso. I took many an art lover and international visitor to see them.

When I first knew her in the fifties, Punitham was Director of the Red Cross in Sri Lanka and had already started Talking Books for the Blind there. She was clever enough to enlist our seven-year-old Dinny in some of her Red Cross work. I was drawn into it too, to help with some of the publicity. When Punitham's eyebrows were pinched together, I always knew she had a new proposal. Sometimes it was "those poor children on the tea estates who have no schools, no books, no paper, no pencils," or she wanted me to go to a fancy Hindu wedding which she had to attend because the groom was marrying her fourth cousin. I learned a lot by helping her and attending family ceremonials.

Even in the fifties I sensed that Punitham transcended the usual East-West stereotypes. She could be a driving Red Cross executive employing the logical, analytical and directed thinking of the Western world. At the same time, she was a devout Hindu who embodied the intuitive, diffused, synthesizing, more tolerant-of-paradox world of the East. And she didn't accommodate, didn't subordinate rational thought to intuitive feeling or the other way around. She kept an extraordinary balance.

Punitham was the first one to tell me about the religious site of Kataragama where the firewalkers could walk over the coals unharmed. No one seemed to know whether this ability was a question of possessing "the right faith," or preparation ahead of time. Many devotees do prepare by fasting for weeks, walking to Kataragama and then going through purification rites. I don't recall how Punitham explained it. I think she left it as a kind of mystery, something for me to think about. But she wasn't condescending and she didn't try to hide behind "the mysterious face of the East."

Punitham's husband had been Minister of Local Government. Tiru had grown up in Malaysia at a time when Ceylon didn't exist as a nation-state, and an astrologer had forecast that he would be a Cabinet Minister when he was fifty-seven. When she told me this, I asked her whether she believed in astrology. I still remember her answer. "How can I not believe it, Sally?" Tiru had resigned his post when the Prime Minister backed away from his proposal for setting up District Councils—the condition under which Tiru had

Here are Sally and Punitham at a Stupa.
the little boy who invited himself into the picture.

accepted the cabinet position. This failure to institute District Councils (which would have given more autonomy to Tamils in the North) was a serious disillusionment for Ceylon Tamil political elites, and Tamil youth gradually moved toward violent forms of agitation.

Already in 1978 when we returned to Sri Lanka, groups of young Tamils called "the boys" were robbing banks, attacking police stations and seizing whatever arms they could. Government offices in the North were trashed; even the mayor of Jaffna, the cultural and political capital of the Tamils, had been assassinated by a young activist, Vellupilai Prabhakaran, who by that time had founded the Tamil Tigers. In addition, the ill-conceived shift to a Sinhala Only policy in government meant that there were now few Tamil-speaking officers in the police and the army. What earlier had been a truly national army was now seen in Jaffna in the north as an army of occupation.

Punitham still lived only a few blocks away in Cinnamon Gardens. When I visited, I went upstairs to see if she still had the haunting picture of the face of Christ. It was just as I remembered it, the face whose eyes were closed until I had looked at it for a very long time—and then they seemed to open. Some things were the same, but her husband, a lawyer, had died. Ironically, he left her without a will. Her children seemed to be doing well. Neelan was a distinguished lawyer whose home was nearby. Another son was studying medicine in Great Britain. Janaki, her daughter, lived with her. Punitham continued to have Sinhalese servants.

Punitham's face in the late seventies was fuller than it had been, the result of taking medicine for both asthma and diabetes. She always carried a small inhaler to help her to breathe. Her movements were still quick, darting; her dark eyes shone with the light of humor and a glowing intensity that I loved. This time she talked more about her grandchildren and less about her causes, but she still had the usual entourage of needy friends. I remember her laughing about it. "My children call them 'my nutties' and tease me about them."

Sure enough, her old entrepreneurial spirit was functioning well. I can still hear her saying, "Howard, there's this wonderful sculptor who is head of a school. They don't pay him anything and he's so poor. What if he did your head, Mr. Ambassador?" She spoke in her usual teasing way. "You couldn't afford to do a proper one in America and you'll really be doing him a favor."

She was able to help those in need through a mixture of very practical ideas and sometimes shameless flattery. The poor sculptor/headmaster would have an Embassy commission that would help him sculpt the children he loved; and Howard would have an inexpensive bust. It was a perfect combination. She was right, for after he sculpted Howard's head, he received a number of commissions from other Embassy families.

"Why don't you have your Ceylon library, all those paperbacks I see, bound in fine leather? I know a bookbinder who doesn't speak much English and I could help him with the titles. He's dirt cheap and he could emboss the titles in gold . . ."

She was tirelesss. One time she took Howard to an "astropalmist" who made a print of Howard's hand. The astro-palmist read all kinds of things in it, such as the fact that I had had "five conceptions" [two miscarriages], which he hit correctly, and "some years," he said, "had been more important than others," which in fact had been so. Certain ministers in the Cabinet called this astropalmist every day to see whether today were a good day to approach the President, or embark on a new project.

One way and another, Punitham came to know all the servants in the Residence. She was able to get the cook admitted to a crowded hospital and to find the right doctor for one of our houseboys. After we left Sri Lanka, our servants continued to see her.

Since Punitham was forever being generous to others, I was pleased when she asked me one day if I could do something for her. Would I be a godmother to her new grandson, Dushi? "We will go together to my temple and you can be the one to buy the baby," she said. "Janaki and her husband have already given him to the temple, and you must buy him back so they can bring him up." The ceremony is actually called "Buying the Baby."

So one steaming hot morning we all went together to a Hindu temple surrounded by palm trees and hanging vines. Clusters of families were sitting or standing in the courtyard in front of platters piled high with fruit and green leaves. Black images adorned with orange garlands, some of them dressed in faded pink shirts and dripping with flowing ghee, or clarified butter, stood in small temple enclosures. Fleshy priests wandered about, naked to the waist. They were very unlike the suave gurus we knew in the West. To me, it seemed a long way away from the exalted Hindu philosophy found in books. I felt apart, foreign, white-skinned, more than usual like the pale underside of a white fish.

Then I looked down at Dushi, with his snapping black eyes and head of bushy black hair, lying quietly on a small pink pillow on the ground. The feeling of distance vanished. I was closely tied to Dushi through Punitham.

We offered a platter of papayas, orange mangos and yellow plantains to a priest who came toward us. He put a paste of sandalwood on our foreheads. When the auspicious time came to buy Dushi for his parents, Punitham whispered, "Some people give thousands of rupees to the temple." Her eyebrows drew together the way they often do, and then she relaxed. "But you know, Sally, Dushi is *so* valuable that he has no price. Just give five or ten rupees." She laughed. "The priests won't like it but go ahead." I did as she said, producing a rumpled note worth about two U.S. dollars. I liked the symbolism of the baby belonging to the temple and the small ceremony that restored a baby to its parents for upbringing. It was the way I had always thought about children: their belonging to life or to God, with their parents bringing them up "in trust" until they went off on their own and themselves became parents—and the cycle continued.

Sri Lankans—and not just Punitham—have a beguiling way of including friends into their families. Even on the first meeting, a friend of the parents is introduced to a child as "Aunty" or "Uncle." This custom makes it much easier for the child to relate to the grown-up and for the adults to feel close to the child.

I valued my tie to Dushi and remembered that Punitham had been close to our children. During our first stay, Punitham had often come to see me when Jenny was a baby. When we left, she gave eight-year-old Dinny a pink sari with gold edging. Dinny was thrilled. Jenny, a tall grey-eyed senior at Yale in 1978–79, had come to Colombo for a short stay with us. We had been preoccupied by the visit of several American Congressmen, and Jenny arrived exhausted. Her journey half-way around the world had been very scary, especially at the end when a faulty door seal on the airplane had to be stuffed with blankets to keep the air seal tight. Punitham saw what to do, and immediately whisked Jenny off to her house to rest for a few days. Jenny returned with newly-pierced ears, dressed in a shining malachite-green sari which Punitham lent her, and wearing a new ring. I was very grateful that Punitham took her off, for I wanted Jenny to know her without my being around, and to appreciate Punitham and love her in her own way. I was glad she came back looking so beautiful, too. I have a mental picture of the two of them, Jenny towering over Punitham as she towers over me. Punitham also found an astrologer for her. Jenny's horoscope could be cast with certainty, for Punitham knew the exact moment of her birth.

Before she left, Punitham gave Jenny a batik shirt which she had purchased for her husband for his birthday. He had died before Punitham was able to give it to him. That Punitham could give away something so precious on an impulse was very moving to Jenny and, indirectly, to me. Punitham was like that.

Sometimes she pressed too hard for us to accept a gift. Years ago I refused to take a stuffed leopard she offered me as a farewell present. At a Tamil New Year's celebration at her house, she urged us to take every delicacy so that it became a contest of wills, and it was too much. But other times it was just a game. When Jenny and I were with her once, that is exactly what happened.

"Won't you have a glass of coconut milk?" she asked Jenny.

Jenny had already finished one glass, and declined. "Please drink the rest of mine."

"No, thanks, really."

"It is so good for you, and you don't have it very often." Finally Punitham had run out of reasons but she went on. "I don't really like liquids"—as though Jenny would be relieving her of a burden if she finished her coconut milk.

Jenny laughed at the ridiculousness of this latest argument, saying, "Oh, you don't like liquids? Certainly. In that case . . ."—suggesting that she knew as well as Punitham that it was not at all that she didn't like liquids.

I noticed that Punitham gave her a very playful but somehow deep look. Jenny took this as a recognition that she had caught

Punitham at her own game. Jenny had always liked a contest of wills more than I did, which may be why she became a lawyer who loves to litigate.

Jenny drank the coconut milk. It was a kind of Asian charade, an almost transparent pretense, but Punitham's special stamp was that she could often create exchanges which led to greater closeness and not more distance.

Several times Punitham took me to the famous Buddhist temple at Kelaniya for special festivals, in the company of one of her friends, a handsome judge who intended to become a Buddhist monk. He was one of the many, an endless variety of people who sought her out.

I don't know whether they ever talked about what Kingsley de Silva, Ceylon's leading historian, has called "the inferiority complex" of the Sinhalese people. The fact is that the Sinhalese, although an overhelming majority of the population on the island, nevertheless have a minority complex vis-a-vis the Tamils. They feel encircled by the more than fifty million Tamil speakers living in present-day Tamilnadu in Southern India and in Sri Lanka. In Sri Lanka, Sinhalese outnumber Tamils by more than four to one, but they, in turn, are outnumbered more than five to one by the Tamil-speaking peoples of South Asia.

"Is it true, Punitham," I remember asking one time as she and I walked around the temple courtyard, "that everyone seems better off now than when we were in Sri Lanka before?"

"It's hard to say. Many people are, but not everyone." She smiled.

"There are wonderful vegetables in the market, lots more than there used to be," I said, enthusiastically thinking of the fresh beets, okra, onions, green beans from upcountry.

She cut in. "If you can afford them." In that moment we both looked at a young mother in a sari cradling such a small baby in her arms that it seemed to be more like a child's doll than a human being. In my mind's eye I can still see that tiny head, its doll-like arms and legs. "It's so little." Punitham's eyebrows were pinched with concern. "But let me take you to some of the Colombo slums."

"Just the way you used to?"

Then she was silent. A dark cloud seemed to envelop her.

"But you know, Sally, the city boys in the north are increasingly unhappy. The government's policy has made it so much harder for them to get into the university. Recruitment for the government service has almost stopped. I am worried about the number of young Tamil boys who say they want independence. They feel their career chances are being blocked by a succession of Sinhalese governments; and in the last election they supported only those Tamil politicians who said they favored independence. I worry that it will come to violence unless something is done."

"It is so discouraging. I remember years ago when you told me about the rape of Tamil women physicians in hospitals after the 1956 elections."

"Then there were the 1958 riots after you left. Some said over one thousand people died. Twelve thousand became refugees."

"And 1977?"

Her eyebrows pinched together with concern. "That was much worse than it was in '56. Twice as many refugees, people killed, looting, arson, crimes."

"What made it worse?" I asked. "False rumors? I don't know, maybe envy, fears? Or a downward spiral of mutual suspicion?"

"Yes, and the 1972 Constitution. The 1956 Sinhalese Only legislation was put into the Constitution. Buddhism was made into a state religion. Sri Lanka used to be a secular state in the old days."

"So Tamils lost hope, especially young people."

We climbed into my car to go home. "And when people lose hope—" She paused. Her voice fell to a whisper. "Desperation sets in. I'm terribly worried. I'm afraid something awful will happen."

I had never seen Punitham so distraught. I suspected she was thinking about some of the more zealous Tamils Howard had told me about, the ones who were threatening a war of "national liberation" if they didn't get their way. Things had gotten so bad that the Tamils were sending youths to PLO camps in Lebanon, for training in guerrilla tactics. The name Prabhakaran had not become prominent but he was beginning to organize Tamil Resistance movements in 1975 when he assassinated the mayor of Jaffna.

Several Sri Lankan women and I had lunch or tea together every few weeks in Colombo to air our spiritual concerns and to talk about differing ways of meditation—Hindu, Buddhist, Christian. I modeled this gathering after the Lady Philosophers in New York, a group to which I had belonged for a decade. I could only make a beginning for such a group in Sri Lanka. Interestingly enough, Punitham said little on these occasions. Why this was so, I am not sure.

Once I took Punitham to a Buddhist temple to listen to the American Buddhist philosopher, Dr. Joanna Macy, talk about Buddhism and science. In an effort to be closer to her audience, Dr. Macy sat on a railing near the front of the temple. Punitham listened very intently but didn't say anything at the end of the talk. I never could decide if it was simply that she preferred not to criticize my compatriot, someone she knew I had known slightly. Could it have been Dr. Macy's informal American style, or perhaps that her ideas were too far removed from Punitham's own loyalties? Punitham was President of an organization called the Bhakti Maram Society; I still have a devotional poem of hers about Meenakshi, Mother of Love. I don't remember talking to her about the poem or the particular kind of Hinduism which had meaning for her. At the time, I concluded that Punitham was more interested in a variety of people than curious about a variety of religious beliefs and practices.

The heat of the tropics didn't always agree with me, and there was a time when I couldn't sleep at night because of excessive thirst. My physical ailments drew me closer with Punitham, who was suffering ill health herself. "No one ever says hello to me anymore," she said when she came up to my bedroom one morning for a visit. "They want to know whether my temperature is up and whether my pulse is down. Am I plus two or minus two today?"

She sat at one end of my bed and we both laughed. "Is your urine dark or light? And tell me, what is your sedimentation rate today?" The air conditioners banged away and we laughed some more. Implicit was the feeling that the doctors might regard our bodies as mere chemical solutions in two test tubes for their analysis. We knew better. They housed our souls and our laughter.

Punitham's illnesses were much more serious than mine. I often wondered how she could do so much, when the asthma attacks seemed to come more often and her fingers were in pain from a complication of diabetes. Yet she seldom complained and always brushed aside other people's worries about her.

Toward the end of our stay she was appointed to the State Film Board to monitor films of Tamil origin (which usually came from India). She used to laugh about how Indian films not only lasted for hours and hours but their romantic themes were always the same. Nonetheless, she enjoyed this opportunity. Sometimes it took her to India, and she appreciated her colleagues. She continued her work with the International Red Cross and the several international associations for the blind, and she helped a Sri Lankan blind woman to become a practicing lawyer. I knew less about her promotion of Tamil culture, but it was obviously important since, after we left Sri Lanka, a portrait of Punitham was unveiled at the Tamil Women's Center.

Our assignment in Sri Lanka ended and we arrived in America in January 1980. Punitham and I continued to correspond with each other. On March 22, 1981, two months before she died, she wrote:

> From the 23rd of January I have been in and out of the intensive cardiological unit. . . . Two months is a long time to be hovering between life and death. In this intensive care unit one's heart is constantly monitored, and I have drips and a million wires all over my body. You are not encouraged to read. After much pleading I have been allowed to, but I must be careful that the stuff I read is not exciting. . . . TELL ME SALLY WHAT ON EARTH CAN EXCITE ME AT 62? I am bubbling to say so many things but my hands are weak being on a liquid diet for two months and also the nurses are screaming at me for sitting up and writing.

Sally dear, there are moments in one's life when something seemingly quite ordinary happens, but in some inexplicable way, it changes a dimension in one's perception. A hidden capacity for awareness suddenly opens up, and you are not the person, the same one you were. That is what I feel with you.

Anyway Sally, there has been such an affinity of love, interest and affection that I never experienced with others.

If by some fate, I should die, don't be sad. Please remember that knowing you has been one of the most enriching experiences of my life and I pass away happy. I love Jenny and tell her that for me.

Then, typically, Punitham thinks of something quite practical. She wonders why the two of us didn't pose for a grand picture together when there are two such excellent photographers in my family, Chris and Howard.

Punitham said it all, and so much better than I ever could. We were completely different in birth, nationality, culture, education and experience, and we had come together from opposite ends of the earth. To me the mystery of our intuitive closeness remains. I still wonder how it is that we were so closely bound up with each other, Punitham and I.

Once she told me that she had always wanted to be a doctor. When she was a little girl growing up in Jaffna, she was fascinated by all forms of animal life. She took care of the bird that broke its wing, the small animal that hurt its back. This matured into her strong desire to help the blind, the deaf, the poor, any child that was handicapped. When Punitham was telling me about her love of little creatures, I kept thinking of Dr. Doolittle and his hospital for animals, all the animals who came to his doorstep to be made whole.

Something like that happened at Punitham's funeral. She died May 20, 1981. According to the newspaper accounts, the blind with their white sticks, the mute, the disabled with their crutches all found their way to pay homage to this incandescent spirit that had been released from the frail body. I am so thankful that she died before 1983, which many people think of as the beginning of the civil war in Sri Lanka.

I found that I have a record of Punitham's family tree, showing that one of her forebears was one of the first students to attend a school founded by American missionaries in 1823! Her great-grandfather was a distinguished astronomer, her grandfather taught mathematics, and her mother opened a college for teaching English near Jaffna.

"The world stands out on either side / No wider than the heart is wide."[14]

I suppose the missionaries who went forth in 1823 in their sailing ships to Ceylon hoped that this would prove to be true. Punitham showed me that it was.

Chapter 9

BUDDHIST TUTORIAL

I began to have fantasies of changing the names on place cards at the elegant twenty-four-guest sit-down dinners at the Embassy. I knew this was a bad sign, indicating boredom. I considered inventing names like Mrs. Smiling Teeth or Mr. Gritwell, or giving everyone names like Robin Hood or Alice in Wonderland.

Did other Ambassadors' wives chafe as I did, when the driver quickly removed the American flag and the Ambassador's flag on our limousine as soon as the Ambassador stepped out of the car? Was it only his seeming haste that I minded? Or that the flag on the Residence was taken down when Howard was out on a field trip somewhere on the island? Was there no one sitting at a desk doing Embassy accounts while he was gone? Or was it that when the leading women of Sri Lanka, preparing to set up a Women's Bureau, came to lunch, I had to foot the bill as a personal expense because it was not considered official entertaining unless the Ambassador put his head in the door?

Writing was impossible because there were so many interruptions. I felt useless and unhappy. I kept waking up at night with an insatiable thirst. Clearly I needed help of some sort. Later an image formed in my mind in which I was standing on the shores of a shining sea, when someone called me away. The image of standing on the shores of Sri Lanka was always accompanied by a wrenching feeling, the sensation of being summoned away from what I really wanted to do—writing.

Then I came down with a mild case of dengue fever. This was a little like flu with its aches and pains—but in addition it was accompanied, as is typical, by a severe depression. I was more depressed than I have ever been. That first day when we got up from our midday siesta, I cried out to Howard, "I can't stand it. I can't stand it. I can't stand it!" Howard was sufficiently concerned that he took the afternoon off and Miranda drove us to the wide beach at Negombo. We just sat and watched and watched the waves rising, cresting, falling back on the shore. We listened to the ocean's primal rhythm without saying anything. We stayed there watching the waves for several hours, with only a few words between us, and I was strangely comforted. It is still a vivid memory. I often wonder how Howard knew what to do with me—but he did.

Perhaps if I could achieve a state of mind where "I like this," or "I do not like that," or "I am happy," or "I am unhappy," had become irrelevant, the two years ahead would not seem so endless. Could Buddhism, with its emphasis on detachment, provide some guidance?

The spareness of Buddhism had always appealed to me. When we lived in Sri Lanka the first time, I had liked the clean-swept floors of Buddhist courtyards, the pure lines of their white bell-shaped shrines, the sacred Bo trees with their grey trunks and overarching limbs decked with orange and yellow flags. Although the temple interiors looked garish to my Western eyes, the Buddha image, seated or lying down, was always comfortingly serene.

To be sure, I had read a few Buddhist books, mostly on my own—but some I had read with that small group of women in New York whom I called the Lady Philosophers. Sally Kerlin had introduced me to these women; her husband had dubbed them "The Deep Group." They were extraordinary women who were searching for meaning in their lives, particularly in the areas of philosophy and religion. The founder was Margo Wilkie, who brought together her friends, many of them writers: Nancy Wilson Ross, who had grown up in Seattle and had written a fine book on Buddhism; Evelyn Ames, a writer and poet; Anne Lindbergh, the author of *Gift from the Sea*. The group included an artist, Emmy Maxwell, educators like Sally Kerlin, a textile designer named Mary Strudwyk who I think was a practicing Buddhist. They had begun their explorations in the 1950s. By the time I joined in the early 1970s, our afternoons together began with tea, followed by twenty minutes of silence, and then we adjourned, usually to another room, to discuss contemporary religion, particularly Eastern thought. Several of the women were experts on Zen and the philosophies of India. We returned periodically to secular philosophers or the Bible. At Christmas we turned to poetry, each of us reading something we had discovered. Other times we had special visitors. Some of them were Zen Buddhists and later Tibetan Buddhists, but there was also a wonderful Benedictine monk, David Steindl-Rast, and two young Theravada Buddhists who sat on the floor and described the extraordinary discipline of Vipassana meditation. We treasured the quality of those afternoons.

So I guess I thought about a Buddhist tutorial, not so much as a continuation of the Lady Philosophers' searching together, not so much as a source for the kind of stimulation gained from being with these extraordinary women—but as a way of providing myself with an intellectual and spiritual challenge and a renewed sense of purpose.

In March 1978 I went to the head monk of a well-known Buddhist temple in Colombo, in search of an adventure of my own. I shared with him my interest in the seventh-century Chinese pilgrim Xuanzang, the one who went to India in search of the true Buddhist texts to take back to China; the head monk thought "the China connection" could be a link for me with an elder Sinhalese monk there named Kheminda Thera. And here he was, with his luminous brown eyes, thick glasses, slightly pointed ears and a dome-shaped head that, until I got to know him better, made me think of the Wizard of Oz.

On the afternoon of my first lesson in March, as I was driven in the Embassy's plush maroon car through the gates of the Buddhist compound, I saw a young man in a saffron robe standing in front of a small building.

"Kheminda Thera?" I inquired somewhat hesitantly of the young monk. "Where may I find him?"

"He is behind the library. That is this building," he said, pointing to the one directly ahead of us. "There is a quadrangle with a garden. His room is the last one on the left-hand side."

The swept courtyard of the quadrangle contained a few pink bougainvillea bushes, palm trees, a rubbish heap, and a tree with tiny sun birds—almost as small as hummingbirds—flitting from one branch to another. A covered veranda was in front of the monks' rooms; between its posts hung a clothesline with saffron robes drying in the sun. No monks were to be seen.

As I slipped off my sandals on the porch steps, I felt myself embarking into unknown territory. There would be no prescribed agenda; instead it would be an exploration into the mind and spirit of a Buddhist monk as well as into new parts of myself. I did not plan what I was going to say.

When Kheminda Thera came out of his room, he was wearing a saffron robe, his left shoulder bare, as is the custom for Ceylonese monks. He bowed, his palms together in front of his chest in a Namaste greeting. I did likewise. Outside his room on the veranda was a table piled high with musty Buddhist texts. An adult-sized chair stood on one side and a kindergarten-sized chair on the other; my sitting lower, in the small chair, was a sign of respect. I liked that reversal of my usual role as the one to whom deference was given.

Usually when I went to see Kheminda Thera, he was standing in his saffron robe on the veranda near the bird-filled tree. Often he was reading the newspaper. Once he was pacing the covered veranda from his room to the far wall, a distance of twenty-two steps.

Wednesday at three p.m. was our appointed tutorial hour. What Kheminda Thera said that first afternoon in March 1978, I don't remember. I sensed that he was learned, and very gentle; a suggestion of humor often played around his lips. His skin, a light brown, was almost free of wrinkles in spite of his great age. His thick glasses, which he took off now and then to rub his eyes, intensely magnified his brown eyes. I found that I looked mostly at his left eye which was kindly, deep and penetrating. Before I left he apologized for being groggy. "I have to take some medicine and it makes me sleepy." When I got up from my small chair, I was surprised to find that he was almost shorter than I am.

All too often, as I sat in my kindergarten chair and the monk in his saffron robe sat in his large one at Vajirarama courtyard, I listened to the sun birds singing in the crimson tree. I found it difficult not to watch these tiny birds darting among its branches. One time the monk was reading from a sacred text:

> The foundation of mindfulness which begins with the long incoming breathing and the long outgoing breath is reviewing the body.

[I wanted so much to see the sun birds with their lemony breasts and curving long beaks as they came out from amongst the crimson blossoms after drinking their fill of nectar.]

> That which begins with the renewing of joy is the renewing of feeling.

[My tutor told me that the Indonesian people think that the crimson *Hamelia patens* tree is inhabited by deities, so they call it the spirit tree.]

> That which begins with experiencing the mind is the renewing of thought.

[I could almost see the sun birds out of the corner of my eye.]

> That which begins with the discernment of impermanence.[15]

My attention faltered for a second, and I had to ask my Buddhist tutor to repeat the last part. He was patient; always he was patient, no matter how many times I asked him the same questions. The sun birds I kept seeing out of the corner of my eyes were like the insights at the edge of my consciousness which I knew to be there but never could quite grasp. "Quick," called the sun birds. "Find them, find them."

Find what? I didn't know exactly. I knew that Buddhism was a way of life and thought, and that Buddhists believed that life is full of suffering. The Buddhist's task was to eliminate the cravings which contributed to suffering. Buddhists addressed themselves to trying to achieve detachment and dispassion. What they strove for was Enlightenment, and this was achieved by right views, right thoughts or motivation, right speech, right action, right livelihood, right effort, right mindfulness and right concentration. This was the Noble Eightfold Path which the Buddha enunciated in his First Sermon. This was the so-called Middle Way between severe asceticism, which the Buddha had tried and found wanting, and self-indulgence.

At first glance, it was deceptively simple. But the meditation practices of Buddhist monks were clearly very sophisticated, the product of centuries of practice and profound insights. What were some of the insights?

The kind of Buddhism practiced in Sri Lanka was called Theravada Buddhism and had as its ideal the Arhat, a Holy or Enlightened One who occupies himself with his own salvation. As our Buddhist tutorial progressed I realized that Kheminda Thera was steering me toward the very ancient texts, the ones "free from all the later corruptions," as he put it. Because he was a purist, I struggled with manuals from the first century C.E. The words were difficult, and the lists, oh, those lists of the thirty-eight subjects of meditation, the eighteen principal insights, the five aggregates, the seven enlightenment factors, the five hindrances, the thirty-seven subjects partaking of enlightenment, and the law of dependent arising! Yet he gave me a clear sense that the mind is a gifted and supple instrument.

I was fascinated by the old-fashioned values of Buddhism. Energy was important. Will was paramount. Habits were vital;

many of the admonitions we heard from our parents while growing up were significant. Most of these virtues have long since gone out of fashion in America. Now that I was based in Colombo, I could see on my occasional visits to the U.S. that an emphasis on the will seemed to be coming back, in such diverse enterprises as running, bio-feedback and meditation.

Each week I looked forward to my conversations with Kheminda Thera. But on one Wednesday afternoon when I approached the sun bird-filled tree, the Buddhist monk was not there. Surely someone would have told me if something had happened. Was he ill? His room looked just as it always did, with the picture of Soma Thera, whom he admired so much, on the wall, and his desk piled high with books. Where was he? His library, at which I had only glanced before, contained Pali-English dictionaries (Pali was the language of the first Buddhist canon); a German-English dictionary; rows and rows of leather volumes which were most likely ancient texts; Edgar Cayce in paperback; Moody's *Life After Life* in paperback, *Twenty Cases Suggestive of Reincarnation* by Ian Stevenson, and a few issues of *Reader's Digest,* which I had procured for him from America.

He had spoken the first time we met of the medicine that made him groggy. Had something dreadful happened? I stopped at the library on the way out, where a monk told me that Kheminda Thera was "in hospital." It seemed indelicate to inquire how serious his condition was, so I went to see him in the hospital as soon as I was able. No doubt he didn't have many female callers. Still I believe he was genuinely surprised and pleased to see me.

After some weeks he was allowed to return to his temple, and when we were back on the veranda again, I asked him about something we had touched on before, psychic research in the Soviet Union—psychotronic exploration, I believe he called it.

"You believe in mind control, don't you?" I asked.

"Oh yes, the mind does many wonderful things."

"Can an arhat determine his life's end? Surely that is the ultimate control of the mind?"

"There is a story concerning a very holy monk who attained complete extinction while walking to and fro." He paused significantly. "Yes." And he read a passage from "Mindfulness of Breathing"[16] about an arhat who drew a line on a terrace saying that he would attain extinction on reaching that line. And did so.

Once, perhaps in response to my testament of some small progress made in meditation, he was quite joyful. He spoke of Buddhist themes in a flowing cadence, of the importance of inquiry, intellectual study and practice. "Always it is the same." His face and especially his eyes glowed. "Once one is going up the ladder, unskillful and unwholesome thoughts go away. It is like that. There is no guilt. Virtue abides and because of this, there is happiness. Happiness brings calm, calm brings concentration, concentration brings insight and wisdom."

The first book I read under Kheminda Thera's tutelage was *The Path of Freedom*,[17] which he had translated as a young man when he was in Japan.

"I wanted to go to China," he explained one afternoon. "This was in the 1930s. There were no airplanes in those days." He laughed his quiet laugh. "So I went with Soma Thera, mostly on foot."

"How did you go?"

"Oh, we walked over the misty Dawna mountains across the border into Thailand, and then we went by bus and by boat to Hong Kong and to Shanghai. There were no facilities to study in China at the time so we went on to Tokyo. Someone at the university heard we were from Ceylon and asked us to come to Jozaiji." He took off his glasses and rubbed his eyes as he often did. "The head of the temple was a Reverend Ehara. He put us up at his guest house, Lion Hall, I believe it was called. The earliest Buddhist texts were first written down in Ceylon so he thought we should help him translate into English a first century meditation manual, even if it was in Chinese. Ehara knew Chinese and we worked twenty hours a day on it for four months."

"You mean it had never been translated into English before?"

"Never."

After their journey, Kheminda Thera and his friend went to Burma for their ordination. He was instructed in a kind of meditation which emphasized "the four awakenings of mindfulness." Then they came home by way of India.

I didn't think much then about the parallel between Kheminda Thera's journey to Japan and his translating of Buddhist scriptures, and the Chinese pilgrim Xuanzang's journey to India to find the true scriptures. It seems more obvious now. Maybe this was yet another example of not appreciating the significance of something while it is going on. Perhaps it was because I was too filled with my own malaise and trying to find a practical way of meeting it.

"Were you always a Buddhist?" I asked him on another afternoon.

"No." He paused. "My grandmother knew the Sutras by heart and she often used to recite them. I must have picked them up from her as a child, so when I grew up I knew I wanted to become a Buddhist."

"Your parents?"

"They were Christian. I was brought up a Christian but there is nothing to do in Christianity."

What did he mean? That there was no emphasis on strict meditation practices? That all one did was to go to church? There were so many things I wanted to ask him about. Always I was afraid that he might have to return to the hospital, or that we would have to stop our conversations.

We both liked similes and I copied this one into my notebook from *The Path of Freedom*:

> As in a pool of water with a spring into which no water flows from the four directions, nor rain descends, the water wells up cool and pure from within, saturates the entire pool, and overflowing spreads afar—even so joy and bliss, cool and pure, welling up from concentration saturates every part of the bhikku.[18]

Kheminda Thera's voice was soft. One time the monsoon rains pounded so hard on the veranda roof that I could hardly hear him. I don't know whether he could hear me either. I was trying to tell him that my every attempt at Buddhist concentration was hard work, like writing. "I can sharpen pencils endlessly, balance my checkbook, or invent twenty excuses to avoid it." I kept pulling my kindergarten chair nearer to his knees. Up close I said, "The breathing exercises of Anapanasati are very helpful." We finally went inside his room to talk. I remember feeling that the noise of the downpour didn't matter because the intent of what I had to say was more important than any string of words I might utter.

What was Anapanasati? Mindfulness of In-Breathing and Out-Breathing relating to the body, to feeling or one's emotions, to the mind; and recollections on Impermanence as part of life. The first recitation is from the Path of Purification:

(i) Breathing in long, he knows, I breathe in long; or breathing out long, he knows, I breathe out long.
(ii) Breathing in short, he knows, I breathe in short; breathing out short, he knows, I breathe out short.
(iii)Experiencing the whole body (of breath) I shall breathe in, thus he trains himself; experiencing the whole body I shall breathe out, thus he trains himself.
(iv)Calming the bodily-formation, I shall breathe in, thus he trains himself; calming the bodily-formation, I shall breathe out, thus he trains himself.[19]

At my best I had a clear sense of the in-drawing breathing as being like a violinist drawing his bow slowly, surely, perfectly across his violin in one direction, and then on the out-breathing, slowly, surely, perfectly drawing the bow (breath) in the other. I liked the other recitations and practice pertaining to one's emotions and one's mind. Feeling happiness . . . Feeling joy . . . Experiencing the mental formation . . . Calming the mental formation . . . Experiencing the mind . . . Gladdening the mind . . . Liberating the mind . . . Concentrating the mind.

However, after my brush with death from the pulmonary embolism, I could not experience the recitation relating to impermanence . . . detachment . . . relinquishment . . . and cessation. I wanted to live; I could never be a good Buddhist.

The first year with Kheminda Thera was a year for questions. The second year was a time for at least a few answers. I began to connect a few ideas and could say Anapanasati without being too self-conscious. In time I began to put on dark glasses for many long trips as I was being driven to the airport to greet visitors or old friends, so that I could keep my eyes shut and practice in-and-out breathing along the way. I finally learned to practice concentration while I sat on a public platform, with my eyes closed behind dark glasses, during those long afternoon speeches in Sinhalese. I learned more about myself; that I could indeed carry on this public life, unless I was ill with fever, even if my heart was not in it.

And I picked up fascinating details, such as the story of Kheminda Thera's robe, which I always thought was a single piece of saffron cloth. He got up from his chair one day, very slowly, and shuffled to his room, his sandals slapping the cement floor. He returned with another robe in his hands just like the one he was wearing, explaining that the saffron material was patched together because the robes were a symbol of poverty. After unfolding it in its entirety, he showed me that the patchwork of yellow-gold cloth was roughly the size of a double bedspread.

"It is stitched together. You see, it is like a rice paddy field. Here is the bund or the ridge that separates one field from another and keeps the water from running off while the paddy is growing, and here is the ridge on my robe."

I liked that, the closeness to the soil and to the work of so many in his country. He told me, too, that a walking meditation, which he does very often, is more lasting than a seated meditation.

I was just beginning to gain some feeling for the Buddhist view of life as being intrinsically full of sorrow, of the impermanence of all life, of all worlds, when I happened to read *Moments of Being,* one of Virginia Woolf's last autobiographical sketches.

> Many bright colours; many distinct sounds; some human beings, caricatures; comic; several violent moments of being, always include a circle of the scene which they cut out; and all surrounded by a vast space—that is a rough visual description of

childhood. . . . But somehow into that picture must be brought, too, the sense of movement and change. Nothing remained stable long. One must get the feeling of everything approaching and then disappearing, getting large, getting small, passing at different rates of speed past the little creature . . .[20]

Here was a Western perception of the Buddhist doctrine of impermanence. I read it aloud to Kheminda, my teacher, wondering what he would say. "It is very good writing. But space is changing too. The universes are evolving and dissolving. Nothing is still."

"She has a sense of the sorrow of life, too," I said.

I handed him her book and he began to read. "But here she says that we are the Thing itself. So she introduces the self, and that is false. Because the world and everything in it is impermanent and because there is only suffering, there can be no self."

"But she brings a sense of order and beauty," I said.

"Oh, this is all false. All art is whitewashing. There is no order, there is only chaos. Everything devours everything else. There are many forces which destroy. They are all around us. It is for this reason that we must meditate on the Buddha, on loving kindness, on the foulness of the human body, on death."

"But music takes you to a higher plane, doesn't it?"

"Maybe so, and then it drops you down and you are even more discouraged than before."

"Doesn't meditation or concentration do the same thing?"

He waited, something more than a pause, before replying in his gentle voice. "No, concentration shows you things as they really are. First must come virtue, then concentration, then wisdom."

I like that view of meditation, I thought to myself, but what an inhospitable world to live in! Had I only imagined the time that we stopped talking to watch three small kittens playing on the veranda steps? After a few moments, he commented that they seemed to be playing happily. "Usually you go up to them, and they start back in terror. They are so afraid. They have to live and die and be born over and over again. It is awful."

126

I didn't challenge him when he said this, nor did we talk much about one of the less appealing parts of Buddhism—the "blood, guts, pus and bile" syndrome. I assumed that this demeaning of the body and its natural functions was used to combat lust among the monks probably in much the same way that it was employed by Christian monks in the Middle Ages.

This approach may be even more pervasive in Buddhism than in Christianity, but I don't know. For example, in order to break down the sense of "the self," Buddhism atomizes experience. Take eating. Enjoying one of Crooz's delicious meals at the Residence is not just savoring texture and taste: one should also recognize that eating is digesting, bile, eliminations, etc. In order to combat drowsiness or torpor during meditation, one should either "gladden the mind" by thinking good thoughts, or think on the foulness of the human body. Much more congenial to me was the Psalmist who declared that "our bodies were fearfully and wonderfully made." Perhaps as a woman who had been blessed with three children, all born by Natural Childbirth, I felt differently about the human body.

Part of the background of this often elusive philosophy has to do with the doctrine of Not-Self, the idea that my personality is not as solid as I sometimes think. It may be a simple stream of phenomena. My "I" is in fact just a collection of attributes known as Aggregates—forms, feelings, perceptions, mental formations (wishes, dreams, ideas) and consciousness.

In a famous passage called "The Questions of King Milinda," a wise monk asks a second-century Greek Bactrian ruler to explain what a chariot is.

"Is the pole the chariot?" — "No, reverend sir!" — "Is then the axle the chariot?" — "No, reverend sir!" — "Is it then the wheels, or the framework, or the flag-staff, or the yoke, or the reins, or the goad stick?" — "No reverend sir!" — "Then is it the combination of pole, axle, wheels, framework, flag-staff, yoke, reins, and goad which is the 'chariot'?" — "No, reverend sir!"

After all these questions and answers, they finally conclude that "chariot" is only a designation with no innate reality.[21]

Only twice in the years I had been going to my tutorial had I seen other pupils coming to Kheminda Thera. Both were young Sri

Lankan men in their thirties. I took courage and stopped to talk to one who was making obeisance before the Bo tree in the front courtyard. I waited until he turned in my direction.

"How is it going?" I asked.

"Oh, fine."

"How often do you go?"

"Oh, lately I've gone every day. I have some problems. He is such a good man," he said enthusiastically. "I am sure he will become an arhat."

If Kheminda Thera attained the highest enlightenment, I wondered, would he wish to die like the arhat who determined the moment of his dying? I decided to ask him the question in my next visit. When I did he rose slowly and gathered his robe around him, and returned with a leather book from his room. "Ah, here it is," he said softly, putting his finger on the appropriate passage. "It is like the worker who has finished his work and who has not yet gotten his wages."

Was he saying that his destiny or his Karma was incomplete? I wasn't sure what he meant. As I thought about it, I concluded that though Kheminda was clearly fascinated by psychic powers, they were not to be used lightly; he himself would not do so. So many harbors of the mind—his and mine. So much to ponder that I began to wonder how insight and understanding happened at all.

As the time of our departure from Sri Lanka crept upon me, I knew that I didn't want to be caught in the trap of "pride of achieving," and yet I wanted to feel that I had made more progress than I had indeed made. Sometimes after a few breathing exercises and focusing on the tip of my nose and between my eyes and gradually moving to the top of my head, there came a change of focus. I no longer had to try to direct my attention to a still point; a lambent awareness was present. Measured by Theravada Buddhist standards, this achievement scarcely approached the first rung of the ladder of real concentration. Kheminda Thera didn't say this, but I knew it to be true.

Several months before we left Asia, we flew to the Maldive Islands. After Howard's exit on a speedboat to make his official calls on Male, the capital, I sat down on the beach of the island where we were staying. With no purpose in mind, I began to listen to the waves roll out and in, hearing the rise and fall of my own breath; I was in tune with the ocean's rhythm, the pulsating movement of in-and-out breathing; the plangent sounds from the waves coming in and the waves going out were the same.

This was not a blinding insight; it seemed very natural. Not at the time, but much later, I began to wonder whether our Buddhist tutorial had any connections with this feeling of deep resonance and connectedness with the ocean's rhythm. Was it a preparation? Possibly. Yet our lively conversations stood on their own, and the image stayed with me of a venerable man with a light smile playing on his lips.

PART FIVE
EXPANDING MY HORIZONS

Chapter 10

TRAVELING WITH JEANNETTE MIRSKY IN BURMA

By January of 1978, I was stale and the hands of my clock stood still. I didn't know what was wrong exactly, but a dream gave me a clue. In it I was playing tennis and the space to play on my side of the net kept getting smaller and smaller; large packing cases kept cutting off more and more of my side of the court. It was as if I had no place to move or to swing my racquet.

It felt as though I had been in Sri Lanka a long, long time, but the reality was quite different. We had arrived in Colombo in August. In November I had been gone for almost a month on a long-dreamed-of expedition to China. Howard had agreed that I could go with Jane Brown, an art historian friend from Riverdale. Because Jane had been the wife of the Consul General in Chungking, we were able to go to China two years before it was recognized by the United States in 1979. Jane was not only very knowledgeable, but very able as well. I met up with her group in Tehran and we flew over the Pamirs and the Gobi Desert by moonlight.

Part the First:
'The Voyage Out'

Lured by the same irresistable call which brought Marco Polo, Sir Aurel Stein and countless others, Sally bids a nonetheless reluctant adieu to hearth and home.

As the plane skims above the swaying tops of the small pear-shaped island's palm trees, Sally does *not* wonder if she has left the stove on.
Here are some of Sally's monkey friends who saw her off at the airport.

FIRST STOP, **KARACHI**

Dreams of strange albino monkeys, and of the great wall turning into a dragon kite are a little unnerving. But next day is the plane to <u>Teheran</u>, Desert Oasis, Jeweled City.

Here, Lucky Riverdalians
are soon reunited with
their missing, and sorely
missed, member

But Soon, They're Off!
— To Exotic Peking!

All during that trip, Monkey danced ahead of me in puppet shows, on calendars, in paper cut-outs, on sandalwood fans, in comic books, on movie marquees and in outdoor theaters. I saw murals illustrating some of the chapters of this Chinese classic, high up on the walls of the Summer Palace outside Beijing. I saw Monkey as a superman in a TV film called *Uproar In Heaven*. What a shape-shifter he is, I thought. It was almost as if he were saying, "What shall I do to amuse them now?"

In contrast to this ever-present figure of popular culture, the Monkey I knew as a Western reader was the creation of scholars. He was a Trickster archetype—part human, part divine, able to change his shape at will—a sort of adolescent hero described by Jungian writers. He was the central figure in *Journey to the West*, the 2,000-page Chinese epic whose translator, Dr. Anthony Yu, describes Monkey as embodying "an underlying vision which was drawn from . . . the major religions, Buddhism, Taoism and Confucianism."

This Monkey I knew was an outgrowth of thousands of years of tradition—an ancient lineage for one mischievous Monkey. I had already learned that the Monkey story was inspired by Xuanzang, an *actual* Buddhist pilgrim who had lived in the seventh century. I am not sure I had realized, before then, that the pilgrim had made a 10,000-mile journey from China to India in search of Buddhist scriptures. His sixteen-year pilgrimage was celebrated even during his own lifetime, but after he died the stories took on a life of their own. Something about this Chinese pilgrim and his journey had stirred the Chinese imagination, and mine.

His seventh-century exploits had become folk tales, part of a living oral tradition, told first in Chinese monasteries. "Do you know how the Chinese pilgrim subdued the demon in the cave?" The stories grew bigger and better as each storyteller added something. Finally, in 1592 C.E., all the tales were put together in one gigantic narrative.

By this time the Chinese pilgrim had been renamed Tripitaka, which refers to the "three baskets" of Buddhist wisdom. Also by this time the actual pilgrim had slipped into the background and

Part the Second:
THE ARRIVAL

A top cultural affairs minister meets the Riverdale group at 'Ah-so international Airport.'

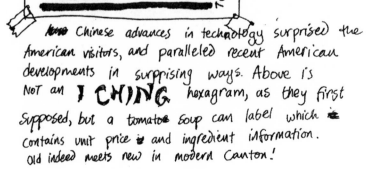

Chinese advances in technology surprised the American visitors, and paralleled recent American developments in surprising ways. Above is NOT an **I CHING** hexagram, as they first supposed, but a tomato soup can label which contains unit price and ingredient information. Old indeed meets new in modern Canton!

WINED and DINED with extraordinary
lavishness, everyone soon becomes an
expert with chopsticks. At the
feast above, the only dish left untouched
was the sharks-fin soup,* because
someone made a joke about JAWS.
 *top right

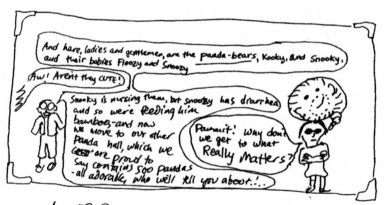

A TRIP TO THE ZOO

had been upstaged by a mischief-making Monkey and two companions, the greedy Pigsy and Sands, who appears to be a fearful monster. They were the ones who slew the demons and the dragons. They took care of the Chinese pilgrim on his journey.

So I had started with the Monkey, Pigsy, Tripitaka and his fantastic companions. While I was organizing my Monkey exhibition, I had become intrigued by the actual Chinese pilgrim who lived so many centuries ago. But I wasn't sure I could find much about him, until I remembered that ancient map I found in Oxford, dated 630 C.E., that showed exactly where the pilgrim had gone. It would be perfect if I could have it enlarged five or six times so that people could see his itinerary on his 10,000-mile journey in Asia. I also obtained from Audrey Topping a picture of the Wild Goose Pagoda in Xian. This was the pagoda that Xuanzang had asked the Tang Emperor to build to house his precious scriptures after he had brought them safely home. When I visited Xian in November 1977, I climbed to the top of the Wild Goose Pagoda. I talked to a guide who gave me a small map, a replica of the large map of Xuanzang's travels that I had found. I saw a rubbing of the pilgrim, made from a tombstone in a nearby village. It was like tracing clues in a mystery. The guide told me that Xuanzang had come from this very village; he knew where to find his burial site, "half way up a hill on a site of favorable influences." I wrote to my old friend Ethel Grant, "Who knows, maybe I will come back to Xian some day?"

It was hard to come down to earth upon my return to Colombo. Not long afterward, Howard and I went to India for a Regional Ambassadors' conference in Nepal. I had just been up-country in Sri Lanka for a week at a hill station, where I did some writing and revisited the putting green, my symbol of British influence in Sri Lanka. Soon we would meet Jeannette Mirsky, an American writer friend, in Singapore, and from there would fly with her to Burma.

The trip to Burma with Jeannette offered a release, a draught of fresh air. Jeannette was unconventional. Diplomats are seldom unconventional. Jeannette liked to shock people. Diplomats make it a point never to shock people. There was a part of myself that reacted to the very thought of diplomatic life by wanting to acquire a mynah bird. A talking mynah bird would rescue me from dull, diplomatic conversations by screeching something inane, unexpected, bizarre; a mynah bird might suddenly cackle, croak, swear or do something unpredictable.

In Burma we would be free to be ourselves. Jeannette belonged to my world, or rather—I didn't know her very well—I wanted to belong to hers. We were both members of the Society of Women Geographers in New York. What drew me to her was her book on Chinese travelers, which included the Chinese pilgrim Xuanzang. She had also completed a book on Aurel Stein, who had made many Silk Road expeditions and had written numerous scholarly volumes about them. Later on she read my Monkey book for children, and was enthusiastic. "Monkey's role and his universality keep sneaking around the back of my mind," she said. I wonder if she responded, as I had, to the playfulness of Monkey and the wild imagination that went into his creation. She thought my exhibition on the history and background of Monkey had wide appeal. She suggested it be shown at the Gest Oriental Library at Princeton University, or at Princeton's town library.

Before we met Jeannette for the first time, Fabio Coen, who was the editor of my Monkey book and a good friend of Jeannette's, told me about her. "Jeannette is quite a gal," he said. "She's written about Sir Aurel Stein, about sea-going frontiers, and about explorations on at least four continents. She's been everywhere: Asia, all over Turkey, Finland, Africa, Soviet Central Asia. You'll recognize her right away," he added, "all the exotic necklaces, the gold, dangling Indian hairpieces, the silver bracelets up to her elbows. Oh yes, and all the rings."

I had spotted her before at the Explorers Club where the Lady Geographers met, a short, older woman with warm, brown eyes that contrasted with her barley-colored hair piled on top of her head—and, yes, the bracelets up to her elbows, and one of her long silver necklaces. I didn't notice the rings on her pudgy hand until we were actually on our flight from Singapore to Burma. She told me about each one: the largest, twelve turquoise stones in three rows mounted in silver, was made by the Zuni Indians of New Mexico. The second, a large star sapphire from Sri Lanka, was a gift from her husband who had died some years earlier. She proffered me her left hand, the one with the rings. "This lovely pink coral ring I'm very proud of. A Tibetan gave it to me when I was in Manali, in northern India."

"Oh, I've been there," I said, remembering how Chris, our son, discovered Manali in the wonderful Kulu valley in the Himalayas on our family trip in 1969.

"Let me tell you something," was usually the beginning of her storytelling. "You're interested in Xuanzang, so you must be interested in caravans," she said in her husky voice. "Some camel drivers had a load of Mediterranean coral stones. I don't know where they were, maybe on the way to China on the Silk Route. They came to a frontier post, and didn't want their coral to be confiscated, so they mixed the branches of coral with the camels' usual feed. After they had crossed the border they collected the coral from the droppings."

"Now, Jeannette, where did you get that story?"

"It's from *An English Lady in Chinese Turkestan*. You know, Lady Macartney, wife of the Consul General in Kashgar in the early nineteen hundreds."

"I wonder if that is what drug dealers do today."

We sat with this learned, earthy and zestful woman in the airport in Rangoon, waiting for our bags to come off the plane. We speculated as to why the Burmese government had relaxed some of its very strict travel restrictions. Tourist permissions had recently been extended from a forty-eight-hour stay to a week. We had been granted a few extra days, which would give us time to see both Mandalay, the last capital of the last dynasty in Burma, and Pagan, which is filled with examples of religious devotion—over 2,000 temples stand in an area of twenty-six square miles.

The next afternoon we drove to the Irrawaddy River near Mandalay with John Flynn, the Consul General there. Howard announced that the traffic jam we found ourselves in was like the ones he had seen in 1956 when he visited Burma. Little had changed in twenty-two years. Converging on the Irrawaddy river was a streaming confusion of horse-drawn carts with large creaking wooden wheels; chickens scurrying across the road; the bulky bodies of aimlessly wandering bullocks; hundreds of bicycles, and tri-shaws, bicycle contraptions with side-cars providing two extra seats and carrying six or seven people. "Glorioso!" exclaimed Jeannette.

As we got out of the car Jeannette said, "I must fix my sandal so I don't disgrace my age group." She was seventy-five. "Ask me where my hat came from."

"Okay, where did your hat come from?"

"From Central Asia. Beyond the Caspian Sea in Turkmen USSR."

At the periphery of this flux was a young man on his bike heading toward the river; behind him, sitting regally side-saddle on the back fender, was an old woman with a black cheroot in her mouth, blowing clouds of smoke in the air. "Granny out for a ride with her son! She's seeing and being seen." Jeannette's trained anthropologist's eye caught it all. "God, don't you love it? I can't get enough of it."

In a flat-bottomed, two-cylinder launch with a roof and open sides, we headed for our destination, the great bell at Mingun, across the river seven miles north of Mandalay. A bamboo raft the size of a city block floated down the river just a few feet away from us.

"Glorioso!" exclaimed Jeannette again.

I shared her joy, for I loved being on a river. Beautiful Burmese girls giggled, pounded their laundry at the raft's edge, tittered, poured water over themselves. Skinny naked boys with pipe-stem legs chased one another up and down the raft, in and out of the water. Farther upriver we chugged past low-lying boats piled high with dried corn husks that are used to wrap the cheroots or cigars of Burma.

Before we reached Mingun, Jeannette looked a little green. At breakfast that morning she had said that burnt toast and charcoal were good for her upset stomach. Maybe she had a heart problem. As we returned in our launch to Mandalay, Jeannette still looked rather pale. I realized, as I gazed at the Mandalay hills with the many white stupas (which the Burmese call pagodas) catching the light of the afternoon sun, that we knew nothing about her medical history.

It was hard to tell, with someone as artful as Jeannette, just how she felt. That evening we wandered around Mandalay's night market, patrolled by police at its outskirts. There Burmese wandered among open stalls that overflowed with textiles from Thailand, bottles of iodine and penicillin, automobile parts, batteries, radios and ten-cent-store notions. The black market by now had become the principal public market. Other sources of consumer goods had long since dried up because the government, having nationalized business activity including retail trade, was never able to develop its own commercial channels. We stopped before a table with little packets of needles and thread.

"Let me tell you something," Jeannette began again. "Whenever I see needles in little packets like that I think of my father. He had come over from Lithuania, did well and then lost his money and was a peddler in New Jersey. He used to go up and down the streets selling needles and thread. One night he was about to go out of his apartment when he noticed a suspicious-looking group of boys at the street corner who were holding icy snowballs. He suspected they were out to get him, so he turned up the gas in the stairwell so they could see him clearly. He pretended to be looking for something on the staircase and on the landing. Three times he came near the gas light, looking, looking, looking." She paused for effect. "When he finally reached the ground floor he still kept his head down on his chest. He walked a few steps, then gave a searching glance. The boys came up to him and one of them snarled, 'Hey, Jew, did you lose something?'"

"Yes, I lost fifty cents."

"While they were all looking down at the snow on the ground for money, he beat it."

"What a fascinating story," I murmured, realizing that our days listening to Jeannette were like listening to Scheherazade.

Jeannette seemed better the next day, so we flew to Pagan, the medieval capital of Burma. We had already decided that we would call the Consul General if there were a real medical emergency. We checked into our hotel. Jeannette tossed her room keys on the floor just as she always did, while we looked around her room to make sure she would be comfortable.

I couldn't help asking. "Why do you throw your keys on the floor?"

"Oh," she said in her husky voice. "This way I never lose them and I always know where they are."

We hurried to get to the Gawdapalin Temple before dark. In the quiet of a sunset evening we looked down from a terrace 150 feet above the ground to an unbelievable sight. Scattered across the plain were thousands of small red-brick bell-shaped stupas, white-washed stupas, and massive square temples with gleaming gold spires rising above their white-washed terraces. Why did they build so many? Who were the builders? Why did the dynasties die out? I had so many questions..

As I walked around the crowning terrace and gazed down on all the stupas and temples in the early evening light, I couldn't help thinking of the white shining stupa domes of Sri Lanka.

Several of those at Anuradhapura were built centuries earlier than these, probably from the first to the third century. The Sri Lankan stupas—one of them 400 feet tall—seemed almost as large as some of the Egyptian pyramids. These simple white austere domes—called "dagobas" or "stupas" in Sri Lanka and "pagodas" in Burma—became the most important symbols in all Buddhist lands, as well as their chief architectural form.

Just as the cross became the symbol of Christ and, centuries later, the form of vast medieval cathedrals, these mounds, with their spires pointed toward heaven, kept evolving in the forms and meanings attached to them. The form reached its highest development in the Great Stupa of Borobudur in Indonesia, I thought, still looking at the stupas below me. There a pilgrim climbs the World Mountain, looking at the bas reliefs on its terraces that dramatize the major events in the life of the Buddha. A Christian views the Stations of the Cross; a Buddhist relives here the Buddha's life through an art rich in symbolic meanings.

I watched as the sky, awash with golds, crimson and blues, turned quickly from dusk to darkness. When the thousands of temples disappeared in the night my mind began to fill with wonder at the many, many ways in which people have sought to express their deepest religious feelings through architecture, man's sacred geometry. I wish I had known at the time that Jeannette had written a book called *Houses of God*. Her grandfather had been a distinguished rabbi from St. Petersburg. Her father was interested in ethical culture. Jeannette rejected the beliefs of both her grandfather and her father and, although she was interested in religion, subscribed to no particular religious or moral beliefs..

Howard touched my arm. I jumped. "So many thousands of temples," I murmured. "What happened to them?"

"The Mongols, old Kublai Khan, attacked and destroyed them in the thirteenth century. Your friends from China, I am afraid, are just like everyone else," he teased. "Strange, for reasons we don't know, both the kingdoms of Pagan here and Polonnaruwa in Sri Lanka seemed to have disintegrated in the thirteenth century."

That night Jeannette looked pale again, but she was dressed like a femme fatale from a sultan's harem—heavy African jewelry, a gold-edged flowing scarf from India, a scarlet and orange embroidered caftan, and dangling earrings. Jeannette could carry off this harem costume. Later someone told me that for several years she had been a buyer at Macy's. An expert in buying, with a keen sense of drama and an anthropological interest in the clothes people wear? What a combination!

Jeannette's colors were bright reds, yellows, vivid oranges and purples like those of Van Gogh, colors to suit her personality. The colors of my landscape were soft blues and greens, Cézanne colors—colors that reminded me of the blues of Puget Sound or the Atlantic Ocean and the dark greens of northwestern forests and the sunlit greens of the shallow waves around Little Cranberry Island before they break on the shore.

Howard interrupted my reverie by asking Jeannette how her book on Stein had been received.

"My old friend, Paul Fussell, was supposed to review it for the *New York Times* and didn't get around to it." She pursed her lips. She was annoyed, but she didn't stay cross for long. Then she laughed. "Have you ever heard the story about how Sir Thomas Beecham got a lousy book review from the *Times Literary Supplement*? Well, he replied to the reviewer as follows: 'I was sitting in the coldest room in the house when I read your review. I immediately put it behind me.'"

Somehow it didn't surprise me that Jeannette could be vulgar. She was vulgar enough to be amusing, but she was never offensive. I was sure she could also be feisty on occasion, although she was usually very gentle with me, and I with her. However, once back in America, I made a semi-facetious remark on my third or fourth visit to her small, museum-filled-to-overflowing apartment in Princeton. She had a collection of primitive spoons made of wood, bone, brass, inlaid shells from Africa and the South Pacific; Tibetan begging bowls and textiles; pots, pans, Finnish designer glasses, Asian carpets; hanging beads from one continent; dolls from another; slightly lewd African paintings; Indian sculpture; gaudy lamp shades; South American wall hangings; masks, baskets, pictures, plates, bowls, sculpture—and, of course, books.

"Why do you have so much stuff?" I asked, my Quaker beliefs ("'Tis a gift to be simple") coming to the forefront.

"STUFF!?" she roared. "THOSE ARE ARTIFACTS!"

However much it showed my lack of appreciation for ethnographic materials, it was a moment I treasured.

Jeannette collected objects and she collected people. She had many circles of friends. She was a good cook and she delighted in bringing them all together; her "salon" in Princeton was famous.

Howard and Jeannette shifted from the politics of book reviews to Sri Lankan politics. The two of them discussed political institutions, and then, as one often does in Asia, they shifted to more subjective realms. Why was it, they wondered, that Sri Lankan people were so afraid of others' hostility? Often it was very subtle, but there was the clear sense that other people could do one harm, perhaps calling on the supernatural to cause one trouble. People went to Kataragama as pilgrims to pray. Or they might even ask their extended families to do their dirty work.

"Like the gardener we have?" I put in. "The one who was getting even with the man who ran off with his sister."

Jeannette closed her eyes to narrow slits and leaned back, her face revealing an amused detachment. I found myself envying her flamboyance and her way of dramatizing both herself and whatever she was talking about. Howard offered Jeannette one of his little black cigarillos and lit it for her. She took a puff and blew smoke in the air near me. "It took me twelve years of writing and research to do my book on Sir Aurel Stein, and this trip is a present to myself. The book has been nominated for a Pulitzer, but I am not going to sit around waiting for it."

The two of them switched back to politics, to problems of succession and monogamy in Burma, in Turkey, in Greece, and I don't know where. I didn't care. Jeannette was, after all, my friend, not Howard's, and we wouldn't have much more time together. I decided that I had to ask her more about the subject of her new book. My interest was in Aurel Stein's work as an archaeologist and historian who was inspired by Alexander the Great, Marco Polo, and Xuanzang. Stein had followed in the footsteps of this Chinese pilgrim 1,300 years after his trip to India; as he traveled on his Central Asian expeditions, Stein felt that Xuanzang was his patron saint. For Xuanzang's report to the Emperor was accurate and richly informative, and became recognized in modern times for the light it cast on Asian geography.

Sir Aurel Stein's patron saint was none other than the Chinese pilgrim whose journey to India had inspired the Chinese classic *Monkey* or *Journey to the West*. Jeannette had even written a book, *The Great Chinese Travelers*, which included Xuanzang. She also knew about the literary tradition relating to Monkey.

I cut into their conversation. "Jeannette, aren't all the history and legends about Xuanzang, and the way they grew in China for centuries, rather like those of King Arthur and the Arthur stories and legends in England?"

"No, not quite, because your monk left behind writings and many translations. King Arthur never did. He's—" . . . Then she said loudly, "He's just a legend."

"Xuanzang represents a kind of legend too, and the first part of his journey when he crossed the desert, well, it embodies the classic elements of a hero's quest. And the time period of both their—"

"You know, Sally, when you talk about Xuanzang your eyes light up and you really get excited," Jeannette said, looking at me intently.

147

"Do I?" I asked, feeling very stupid yet knowing that she was right. I hadn't realized until that moment the depth of my feeling for Xuanzang. I had been working on an article about him for *Orientations* magazine, but this was more than just an intellectual interest. Why was I so intrigued? It is true that he was a bridge between the two major cultures of Asia—India and China.

All the traveling I had done on the Indian subcontinent related to Howard's world of diplomacy and politics. But I had always been drawn to Chinese painting, Chinese literature, and Buddhist sculpture. Perhaps it was my deepening interest in Buddhism that led me to be captivated by a Buddhist monk called, by some, the Prince of Pilgrims.

"So?" She shrugged her shoulders. "Why don't you write a book about him? He's China's Marco Polo. He traveled thousands of miles to India in search of Buddhist scriptures . . ."

"Well?" I heaved a big sigh. "Where do I begin?"

"Start with my book on Chinese travelers. It would be fascinating." Jeannette said "fascinating" a lot, always pronouncing it with a strong "F." Whether Jeannette knew it or not, for me traveling with her would be much more than one trip to Burma. I knew this in some strange, intuitive way, like a hunch, that here was something very important.

The next day in Pagan, Jeannette seemed to be feeling good as we walked and rode among the grand sweep of thousands of medieval shrines on the Irrawaddy River's dusty plain. Among the hundreds and hundreds of smaller temples was a blazing white mountain of masonry, a series of white tiers with a golden spire on top—the Ananda Temple.

We went inside to see four deep niches in its dark vaults, each with its gilded figure of the Buddha. Standing on their lotus pedestals, these figures seemed taller than their actual height of roughly thirty-five feet. A shaft of light fell dramatically on their bland faces, cascading down on their foreheads, their heavily-lidded eyes and cheeks, even catching a dimple on the Buddha's chin. The dramatic lighting made them seem as if they were designed as theatrical sets by someone without Buddhist wisdom or understanding.

Suddenly I realized that their graceful emptiness was almost saccharine; it made me long for the purity of Buddha statues in Sri Lanka. I tried to picture in my mind's eye the powerful stone Buddha at Anuradhapura. I loved the massive triangular base formed by the locked legs, the folded hands and the calm face. This same power and serenity is at Polonnaruwa, Sri Lanka's medieval capital. You see it in the standing Buddha figure and the reclining stone body there. Thomas Merton, the Trappist monk, had been so moved by these Buddha forms in stone that he felt his Asian pilgrimage had somehow become clean and purified by his seeing them.

As we jeeped home that night, I was still trying to recall the setting of these stone-cut figures at Polonnaruwa, a wide, quiet hollow on the hillside, graced by frangipani trees with their shiny dark leaves and waxy white blossoms. There was a gentle slope on one side, a path dipping down to a low-lying cliff with a cave cut into it. The standing figure was strong and serene, arms folded and one leg slightly bent at the knee, near the head of the reclining form. And that Buddha, in Nirvana beside him, in his moment of dying revealed a fine, supramundane peace which was very moving.

Howard and Jeannette, who ate heartily and was fully recovered despite my concern, were busily talking about why the Burmese had built so many stupas and who the builders were. But I was far away, remembering how, when I was sixteen, I used to walk five miles uphill to visit the Seattle Art Museum, to stand rapt before the mysteries of a Khmer sandstone head of an inward-looking Buddha. Its face, with its slightly-open downcast eyes, had that same otherworldly quality.

Soon enough, the next morning in fact, we left Burma. Back to the strength and purity of the ancient stone Buddhas and the shining white stupas of Sri Lanka. Back to the diplomatic round, in which nearly everyone was skating between a cliché and an indiscretion. Part of me accepted the restraints, and how little was asked by way of individual response. Another part of me missed having a dinner companion who might talk about camel caravans in Asia, or describe a little boy as being called "Ten of Six" because his head was always tilted to the left. Or who began by saying, "Let me tell you something. . . ." I would miss her—not just because she was amusing or because she talked brilliantly about a wide variety of subjects, but because she could teach me so much about exploration, about Asian history, geography, literature, Asian religions, myth and tradition—the subjects I cared most about. More than this, Jeannette had showed me that the adventures of a Buddhist pilgrim on the Silk Route were beginning to fill the Eastern horizon of my mind.

Chapter 11

DISCOVERING A SILK ROAD IN PAKISTAN

Whenever I think of Betty Lou Hummel, I see her surrounded by Burmese, Thai or Vietnamese women at our Asian American Forum meetings in Washington, D.C., where I first met her. In my memory she is wearing a distinctive handcrafted metal pin, a blue handwoven jacket from Burma and a matching skirt. I always admired her taste and evidently Asian women did as well. Betty Lou was a small woman with sandy-colored curly hair and porcelain skin. *Sympathique*, warm, she was the perfect fit for her husband Arthur, whom someone described as "unloquacious." He was an angular, reserved, plain-talking man who wore black horn-rimmed glasses. He had the reputation of being a very tough negotiator; he was famously adept at using a poker-faced silence to elicit concessions from the other side.

Betty Lou and I shared a love of Asian art and often went to art museums together. This was always a treat because she absorbed so many details—it would take her two hours to look at an exhibition that I would have covered in an hour. Howard and I often saw Betty Lou and her husband when we all lived in Washington, D.C. Over the years Howard and I had also visited them in the countries where Arthur had been posted as Ambassador—Ethiopia and Pakistan—and we had tried to see them in Burma, but our passports had expired.

In the 1940s I had heard Arthur's father, who was then head of the Orientalia Division of the Library of Congress, speak about the Buddha (he pronounced it "Budddha") in Quaker Meeting in Washington. Arthur Hummel, Sr. had been a missionary in China, where Arthur, Jr. was born and lived until he was eight years old. As a young man, the younger Hummel had escaped from a Japanese internment camp and had became a fighter for the Nationalist guerillas in China during the Sino-Japanese War.

A few days after we arrived in Pakistan to visit the Hummels, on October 2, 1978, we went with them as part of President Zia ul-Haq's official party to Gilget and Hunza in northern Pakistan. We were, therefore, along with a dozen Ambassadors to Pakistan, the first foreigners to travel down the newly opened Karakorum Highway. As Howard and I boarded the C-130, a military transport, Arthur looked down at me with his slate blue eyes and remarked, "All the diplomats in Rawalpindi have been angling for months for just such a trip."

"I can't believe it, I mean—" I mumbled, overwhelmed by this sudden opportunity for adventure. When I was growing up, it always seemed to me that my two older brothers had a monopoly on exciting trips—skiing at Mt. Baker, hiking on Mt. Rainier, even staying in a cabin that had been built for the movie *Call of the Wild*—and I was too little to go. And now I was on my own adventure. Betty Lou had told us that there were huge glaciers in the Karakorum mountains, surpassed in size only by those in the Arctic Circle. Here I was seeing them with my own eyes.

The windows in the C-130 were high up on the walls of the plane. By standing on the make-shift seats, we could peer down on snowy peaks misted over by filmy clouds, gaining only an occasional glimpse of mountain crags and glaciers. Then the clouds became truly opaque. Down below us was the massive

Nanga Parbat, 26,650 feet high, wreathed in a bundle of clouds so thick that they hid both the central massif and the mountain's crown. Had the clouds allowed, we might even have seen K2, the second highest mountain in the world, in the distance.

Clouds hovering over mountains was something I knew about, although once when I was sixteen I had been granted an extraordinary experience. (The painter Isabelle Bishop, when I tried to tell her about it, called it "the gift of space.") I had stood at the top of Mt. Constitution, a tiny, tiny mountain in the San Juan Islands near Canada. The atmosphere was pure as crystal—unusual for the Northwest, where usually either the clouds hover over the mountains, or else it rains. That day the sky seemed to be transparent; the horizon stood back. It was so clear I could see five mountains of the Cascade range, many of them a hundred miles apart: Mt. Baker, Mt. Rainier, Mt. Adams, Mt. St. Helens and even Mt. Hood, almost 300 miles away. Each rose up majestically from the low foothills. It was like a vista from an airplane, but I was standing on a mountain less than 2,000 feet high. It had the feeling almost of a vision. I have never forgotten it.

Underneath the cloud's blanket in Pakistan also lay the Karakorum Highway, which began sixty miles north of Islamabad, the country's capital. The highway climbed to Thakot, where it joined the old road that followed Pakistan's greatest river, the Indus. Always accompanying the rivers that cut through the high mountains, the highway climbed up and up, eventually running beside the immense Batura glacier before reaching the Pakistan-China border at 16,000 feet.

At Gilgit, where our C-130 landed, a military band clad in Black Watch kilts and white leggings was playing skirling bagpipes for the president's arrival—the Gilgit Scouts. The very name evoked the era of what the British dubbed the Great Game—the long and shadowy struggle for political and economic supremacy in Central Asia—when British-trained Indian agents eyed Russian moves beyond the Pamirs and the Himalayas. In this sensitive area, Russia, Pakistan and China lay near each other. "Just feel that cold air!" I exclaimed as we listened with pleasure and stamped our feet on the ground to keep warm.

Landslides on the highway in the previous twenty-four hours prevented our driving from Gilgit to Hunza, so we flew in two helicopters, feeling ourselves to be giant birds winging our way up the narrow river gorges. I thrilled to the sight of pure white snow after the tropics. I craned my neck to peer down at a gigantic snow glacier from which a huge black thrusting snout emerged. Flying at only 2,000 feet above the valley, I couldn't see the tops of the mountains, for they were much too tall. I looked down again. On the left side just in front of our helicopter were more glacial ice masses and moraines, dark and forbidding. Another glacier thrust its black ugly snout of ice and from it issued a tiny river of shining water.

Such a rush of feelings! I was intoxicated. Should I look up? Down? Behind me? Ahead? The sight of glaciers took me back to trotting behind my mother and father over the dirty moraine of Nisqually Glacier on Mount Rainier, near our home in Seattle. I remembered thinking then that glaciers ought to have a shiny blueness of ice and snow and not the blackness of piles of ice-looking-like-coal that I saw around me. Mother had told me that glaciers moved several feet a year, which didn't seem like much to me as a seven-year-old. Here, now, I grabbed my knees for something to hold on to as I looked down on vast glacial masses that seemed to grow larger and larger. They were of a different order of magnitude than any glacier I had ever seen.

Later I learned that Nisqually Glacier on Mount Rainier is only a few miles long. The largest glaciers in the Swiss Alps are ten and a half miles long. In the Karakorums, they may extend to thirty, fifty and even seventy miles! About fifty-five million years ago, there was a collision of two continents: South Asia, moving north until it hit a central land mass, produced mountain ranges spreading from Nepal to Afghanistan. The subterranean plates still press against each other, making for occasional devastating earthquakes, like those that struck Pakistan in 2005.

As we flew farther up the river gorge, I spotted a tiny ribbon of highway penciled in a steep escarpment sometimes on one side, sometimes on the other, of a torrent of grey water. That tiny smooth black ribbon was the result of the efforts of 15,000 Pakistani and 10,000 Chinese workers, for the highway was a joint effort against this phalanx of mountains, this collection of threatening glaciers.

Down below me a few minutes later were brown and yellow fields among scattered stretches of tableland, two and three hundred feet above the Hunza river. An army officer leaned over my shoulder and pointed to a long canal, or kul, marked by fringes of green, half way down a steep slope. "Some of those aqueducts were made as early as 1860 without iron or steel," he said proudly.

We were approaching the district of Hunza and the town of Baltit with its flat mud houses, tall Lombardy poplars, smaller apricot and peach trees. Our helicopter landed nearby at the Ganesh helipad, at an altitude of roughly 8,000 feet. Then we transferred to a row of waiting cars and jeeps. Howard and I snuggled close together in our open jeep, part of the President's convoy.

"Just feel that freezing cold air," we repeated happily to one another. I put my hand on his cold cheek. "A jubilation of air, that's what it is." I took a long, deep breath and let it out very slowly.

Legend has it that Hunza was founded by the soldiers of Alexander the Great who took Persian wives and settled there 2,000 years ago. As if this were not romantic enough, Hunza is the likely model for James Hilton's *Lost Horizon*. The Shangri-La of the novel was reached by flying beyond Nanga Parbat, just as we had done. As the hero flew toward the Tibetan plateau, his plane crashed and he was led to this isolated paradise beside a cone-shaped mountain.

After a short drive, our convoy stopped near a wedding-size marquee tent. Pakistani soldiers deposited the Ambassadors under this flamboyantly designed canvas with its red stripes, purple hexagons and green and yellow triangles, and escorted the women a short distance to the unpretentious white-washed bungalow of the District Political Officer. We were six: the wife of the former Mir of Hunza; her beautiful daughter-in-law, Rani Atiga Ghazanfar Ali; Begum Shananwaz, the wife of the Secretary of Foreign Affairs; Theodora Bushell, the wife of the British Ambassador; Betty Lou Hummel; and myself as the wife of the American Ambassador to Colombo.

"Two years ago when Bhutto took over," the sophisticated young Rani told us, as we sat in comfortable wicker chairs inside the bungalow, "everything changed and the police came in. Before that my father-in-law ruled. We had no prisons, no crime, and no taxes." Her jet-black eyes were solemn as she spoke in flawless English. "When the people had a problem, they came to my father-in-law and in two hours it was settled." She sighed. "Now they have to wait for some decision from Gilgit. We have so many problems now. Some say the police tease the people. They were happy before," she concluded wistfully.

The Rani, who couldn't have been much over twenty-eight, was a graduate in political science from Lahore University. Apart from the way she was dressed—a yellow georgette scarf loosely draped around her head, the two ends falling down her back over a long peach-colored tunic, pantaloons and embroidered slippers—she seemed very Westernized. Maybe it was her British accent.

She sighed again. "Before, we had no market. People just bargained if they wanted something."

"You mean they didn't have any money?"

"Yes. Nowadays everyone is buying things. The stores of Hunza are filled with Chinese goods. Mao caps, silks, porcelain." She paused. "You know, Chinese acrobats came to Hunza to entertain the people who were building the highway."

"And the people of Hunza, do they still live to be a hundred? Is it the wine?" All of us had heard that medical specialists from many countries had studied Hunza's elderly people but couldn't agree on why they lived so long.

"Oh, I don't know," she laughed. "Maybe it is, for our wine is delicious."

"Was it their vigorous life? Hunzukuts can walk sixty miles and still not be tired."

"Was it all those apricots? Their vegetarian diet? Oh, but the people do eat meat at festival times."

"Could it be the heavy concentration of minerals in the silted water coming down from their glaciers?"

"The Mir thought it was because no one was very rich or very poor and his people had no worries."

An awkward silence fell, for we had run out of ideas. "Could we perhaps see Mt. Rakaposhi?" Betty Lou asked in her low, pleasing voice.

Our Pakistani hostess took the cue and ordered the servants to move our wicker chairs outside on the lawn beside a garden filled with orange marigolds, pink cosmos, peach and apricot trees. As we talked, the grey glacial water in nearby irrigation ditches trickled softly.

Far above was Mt. Rakaposhi, all of its 25,510 feet, sometimes behind a cloud, sometimes—but not often—revealing its icy crest. Mt. Rainier hid like that, too, I thought to myself, smiling inwardly. Mt. Rainier was the mountain my father had climbed as a young man, and had slept in the crater on the top. That feat had seemed unbelievably wonderful to my young ears.

A light rain drove us inside. The Rani wanted to show us her home, which was the fabled white castle at the head of the valley, but we were the guests of President Zia ul-Haq and had to be on call until his return.

Three hours later the President arrived and we finally joined the men in the banquet tent. The Rani's young husband, the present Mir, was introduced to the officials and diplomats. Instead of the rich turban and flowing robes of another era, the Mir was wearing a brown pin-striped suit with a gold watch chain across his chest. His eyes were cobalt blue and his hair a light brown. "He is a very twentieth-century Mir with a string of guitars at Hunza House in Rawalpindi," Betty Lou whispered. "He himself plays in a rock band."

With Hunza now governed as merely another administrative district in Pakistan, the Mir's position was purely ceremonial. In 1974, his father was put on a pension along with all the other Newabs, Khans, the Wali of Swat, and other rulers of the ancient principalities: a glorious era was at an end.

Long reception tables were piled high with cold meats, chicken, mounds of rice, bowls of dal and delicious curd, tempting grapes and apples and what a polite officer told me was "army cheddar." I ate ravenously as I looked at President Zia ul-Haq, a square-shouldered, unassuming man of medium height in an army uniform, mingling and talking with everyone. I had watched him earlier in the C-130 plane and noticed how tender he was with his young daughter, who appeared to be mentally retarded.

Some of the older diplomats, standing around in clusters, were recalling the days when the former Mir, Mohammed Jamal Khan, wore a robe of gold brocade and carried a gold-hilted sword in a scabbard of ivory at the spring planting festival. In even earlier times, it was believed that the Mir could make the rain to fall. He ran his kingdom, they said, "by telephone and his council of elders."

"You should have seen his guest book," Ambassador Hummel said, with an appealing glint in his eyes. "It reads like a Hall of Fame for Central Asian explorers—Lord Curzon, C. P. Skrine, Sir Aurel Stein, Sven Hedin, Theodore and Kermit Roosevelt, members of the Citroën-Haardt Trans-Asiatic Expedition."

"Or what about more recent travelers? Lowell Thomas, Franc and Jean Shor, Peter Fleming, Eric Shipton, the Michauds," I put in. "They all contribute to the Hunza mystique." These were the authors I loved to read because they also described the deserts of Central Asia and the Himalayas, the terrain of the Silk Roads where Xuanzang, the Chinese pilgrim who had inspired the Monkey story, had traveled.

*****

On our drive back on the highway to Gilgit, where we would spend the night in the Rakaposhi Inn, Pakistani soldiers stood beside the road, often in front of wide talus slopes in the midst of nowhere, saluting smartly as we passed. Work crews cleared landslide debris in at least four places as we drove along in our jeep. The road, nonetheless, was a smooth, two-lane, asphalt highway. The way was marked by road signs with little black autos mounting a steep hill, that looked exactly like English country road signs. Modern. Incongruous, really.

We were descending a very ancient caravan route. One branch which the Karakorum Highway followed was along part of the Indus River. Two thousand years ago there had been a path along the Indus River. The fourth-century Chinese traveler Faxian had noted that the tracks were "difficult and broken with steep crags and precipices along the way." Another branch of the Silk Road went farther north, up the Wakhan Corridor in the Pamirs and along the upper reaches of the Oxus River. Xuanzang took this route. Even as early as the first and second centuries, Khunjerab and Mintaka passes in Pakistan were subsidiary routes of the Silk Road. Caravans carried tea, porcelains and silks westward from China to be exchanged for gold, ivory, spices and jewels from India and Asia Minor. The Silk Road's trading network stretched from Rome to China; it was a conduit not only for trade goods, but also for the flow of ideas between the lands of the East and West.

At dawn the next day, as our convoy started for home alongside the Gilgit River, the sun flecked Mt. Rakaposhi's white crown. Once again the sound of the river sprang open a trap door into my childhood. I closed my eyes and found myself lying in a sleeping bag on the ground next to Toto Ohata, my Japanese-American friend, under tall Douglas fir and spruce trees, listening to a rushing river in the Olympic mountains. I would be weak with laughter as Toto told me about the way a funny old woman used to sneeze; after much gasping and sputtering, she could only utter a tiny "peep, peep." We loved Spoonerisms and used to recite them by the hour: "Mardon me, Padam, but this pie is occupued. May I sew you to another sheet?" "Mes, yedam, some people tink so, do you?" We spent hours on our hike trying to learn how to burp. We wanted to be able to say "watermelon" in one long burp the way my cousin Norrie did, but we never could. Poor dear, I recalled how Toto wanted to be a dancer; the shock of her parents going to a Japanese internment camp during World War II split her mind in two. Here I was on the roof of the world while she had ended up in a mental institution. What an ache that leaves in my heart.

I wondered how different the sights and sounds of my friend Punitham's childhood would have been from this. They must have included the dry, clacking noises of the dark green palm trees in the wind, and the cries of sea birds in the Jaffna lagoon. I don't remember that she ever spoke about the landscape of her childhood: clearly this didn't have as much meaning for her as it did for me. She had talked much more about the little creatures she had cared for, the ones who had been hurt and needed help, than about her Jaffna birthplace. And now she was worried about racial hurts and violence and how it was getting worse and worse.

Gorges of awesome desolation, grey crags and dun-colored slopes strewn with boulders the size of houses, and even cathedrals, pulled my mind away from Sri Lanka and its plight. Rough, gravelly surfaces, pock-marked and striated rocks, Bryce Canyon-type fissures, pillars, and rock faces, as individual as the aged men of Hunza, told of awesome natural forces.

We slowed down for shepherds with small flocks of goats that wandered along the highway. A two-foot snake slithered off a rock. Arthur Hummel, a good hunter, spotted wood pigeon and wagtails. I always suspected that Arthur enjoyed his tour in Burma partly because there was such good hunting there.

"Ten or fifteen years ago, before all the blasting, there were markhot, ibex, snow leopards and Marco Polo sheep," he said ruefully.

We broke our fifteen-hour jeep ride with stops at some of the Chinese bridges, with their white marble balustrades consisting of smiling lions and lattice designs underneath, which Arthur translated as "hsi," or Double Happiness signs. Such a nice touch of fancy in the midst of so much that was grey and grim.

I remembered that Arthur had gone to Westtown School, a Quaker boarding school, but hadn't been allowed to participate in the Commencement exercises. Why not? A few days earlier he had set off an alarm clock in Quaker meeting. He had also dropped out of Antioch College and for two years had worked as a hospital orderly, a sales clerk and a detective. Clearly he had been much happier when he returned again to China. I finally asked Arthur about his life in China. "Oh, I was teaching English in Beijing when the Japanese bombed Pearl Harbor in 1941. I was interned for two years."

I moved over for a better view of his steely blue eyes and the expression on his face in the rear-view mirror. "How, ah, did you escape?" I asked tentatively.

"Well," he replied with a cryptic smile, "the guerrillas helped me. I fought with them for fifteen months in a three-cornered war against the Japanese, their Chinese puppets and the Chinese Communists. We hid from the Japanese in the daytime and ambushed them at night." He talked about his experiences in a restrained way and with a marked economy of words, though he did admit that it was exciting and that he had enjoyed it immensely. His face lit up and, I thought, assumed a greater zest the tougher the situation he was describing.

Several years later Arthur clearly enjoyed facing down Henry Kissinger in the State Department. "To this day," Arthur was quoted in the *Washington Post* as saying, "Henry likes to tell people that I'm mean to him. I'm proud of the fact that I'm one of the few Kissinger subordinates who, after one of his statements, looked him in the eye and said 'bullshit.' Four or five times he directed me to do things I just thought were wrong. In a shouting match, I insisted that he at least listen to me."

Kissinger never fired Arthur, but he sent him to Ethiopia as Ambassador, a difficult assignment at the time, with the leftist government gradually shifting toward the Soviet Union. What his reactions were on November 21, 1979, when his Embassy in Pakistan was burned down, I don't know. Betty Lou, I am sure, was a source of strength. She was always poised, and always seemed to look on life with quiet eyes. All these qualities showed themselves during the necessary evacuation of American wives and children. Their flight to America took twenty-four hours. Later Betty Lou's account of the evacuation was reported in the *Christian Science Monitor*:

> "It was the day before Thanksgiving. We had a turkey so I just told the cook to go ahead and prepare the food." [Betty Lou elucidated the situation later in a letter, indicating that embassy staff from Lahore and Peshawar were assembling at the residence, and so she had the cook fix turkey sandwiches and the usual trimmings. She thought these might be welcome on the plane, even in the

middle of the night.] . . . Before and after the attack, she continued to wear the *shalwar kameez*, the long tunic that Pakistanis wear. "I didn't want to stand out. . . . We'd been in the foreign service long enough [that] it was my feeling that we were guests in these countries, and we do what is appropriate in their country, according to the custom."[22]

Howard felt that Arthur's assignment in Pakistan, at the time of our visit, was also a hard one. President Carter's concern for human rights meant that President Zia ul-Haq's coup was in bad odor with the United States. His predecessor, Mr. Bhutto, had set Pakistan on the road to acquiring a nuclear device, declaring that "Pakistan would eat grass" if necessary in order to develop a nuclear program to match India's. Our cutting off economic aid to Pakistan left Zia little room for maneuvering. Perhaps difficulties like these account for Arthur's characteristic gesture of shrugging his shoulders as if to say, "Nobody ever said a diplomat's life would be easy."

Several cars of our convoy had halted by the side of the road. We stopped to see what the trouble was. The British Ambassador's car had broken a fan belt. His wife recalled that on a similarly isolated road, the ingenious wife of another Ambassador had substituted a pair of panty hose which had held up for forty kilometers.

"I don't know if mine are strong enough," she said, as she searched for a place to take hers off. A suitable fan belt turned up, so we never had the chance to whiz past their car and ask, "How are your tights holding up?"

As we crossed the graceful suspension bridge at Thakot we realized that we were going away from the Indus River, and that we would be leaving the Karakorum Highway before too long.

"Why build a highway in such a hostile environment?" I asked these knowledgeable men.

Howard responded, as I knew he would. "Well, for the Chinese, the highway was their first land link with Western Asia and the Arabian Sea. It symbolized their political support for

Pakistan, and it could be useful if the Chinese felt impelled to come to the aid of Pakistan in the event that it had to face the Soviets in Afghanistan or India."

*****

At the dedication ceremony of the Karakorum Highway a few months earlier in June, 1978, President Mohammed Zia ul-Haq had said, "Just as the Great Wall was regarded as an extraordinary accomplishment in ancient times, the Karakorum Highway will be considered a wonder of the present ages." The comparison to China's most famous strategic bulwark was surely more than a casual turn of phrase, but I preferred to conjure up in my mind's eye that tiny ribbon of a highway on the steep defiles of the Indus River, and the black snouts of mighty glacial dragons.

PART SIX
CHINA, INDIAN SUBCONTINENT, JAPAN (1980-2002)

Chapter 12

THE OPENING UP OF CHINA

In 1979, just as our diplomatic tour in Sri Lanka was ending, Ben Booz asked us to come and spend Christmas with her in China. "What fun we would have, what a lovely repetition of the Christmas of 1969!"—Ben wrote, referring to the time Howard, Chris, Jenny and I visited them in Indonesia ten years earlier on our way around the world.

The Cultural Revolution, launched by Mao Tse-tung in 1966 and carried forward by the notorious Gang of Four (Mao's widow and her close associates, who were brought down a decade later) had brought China's educational system virtually to a halt. Many intellectuals had been sent to rural labor camps and factories. Countless ancient buildings, artifacts, antiques, books, and paintings had been destroyed by the Red Guards; Communist dogmatism prevailed. Ben told us that not a single course in history or geography had been taught in Chinese secondary schools. Then in 1976 when Chairman Mao died, the Gang of Four were overthrown and, after years of cultural isolation, the Chinese began trying to catch up with the outside world. In 1979 the United States finally established diplomatic relations with China.

Ben, along with her son Paddy, had been teaching and developing curriculum materials in China's Southwest, at the Yunnan University in Kunming, the capital of Yunnan Province, in the aftermath of the Cultural Revolution. The students of Yunnan University embodied China's awakening with their brightly-colored shirts and pants—so colorful after the drab uniforms of the Cultural Revolution—and with their eagerness to learn. It would be an exciting time to visit.

Though I had visited China in 1977, Howard had not. We didn't need much persuading to accept Ben's invitation, for our families had been very close over the years, ever since the famous summer when Ben took care of her five children and our three on Little Cranberry Island. As I had not been able to do on my first trip, we would be free to determine our own itinerary. Because Howard was still officially Ambassador to Sri Lanka, we would be traveling in China with diplomatic privileges. Chris would meet us in Colombo and we would fly together to Rangoon and over the hump of mountains to Kunming.

First I had to consult my doctor, for I had had a pulmonary embolism a few months before, the result of a long flight without stretching my legs. "I wonder, Dr. Buehl, if we shouldn't fly straight home and not run any medical risks?"

"You're fine. Just keep up the Coumadin blood thinner as you travel. Stop in a few hospitals on the way to check it out."

Dear man. I could have kissed him. So Howard sent out some cables to Rangoon, Kunming and Beijing, explaining that his wife would need a blood test called "prothrombin time and content test." We stopped in each of those places, and I was tested, although we were never sure that the tests were accurate.

On December 17, 1979, we flew together to Kunming in China with our son, Chris. When he joined us in Colombo for the China trip he was sporting a mustache. Then in his late twenties, he was tall like his father, although his curly black hair was much darker than Howard's. He possessed the same large capable hands. After graduating from Bennington College, he had adopted an unusual lifestyle: summers he built houses in Maine and in the winters he went trekking in Nepal, or as close to Tibet as he could get.

In the plane together, Chris and I couldn't help recalling that 1969 Christmas with the Boozes in Indonesia. Jenny was along that time too, and we had spent several weeks in the Boozes' bungalow in Djakarta. At that time Ben's husband, Paul, was still alive.

169

Their house was filled with animals. "Wasn't there a cage for their lemur, a slow loris, in the dining room?" was the first thing that popped into my mind.

"And after he had several babies, they changed his name to Doris?" Chris chuckled.

"Or what about their bright crimson parrot named 'Snivers' that used to swoop down and steal everyone's bacon at breakfast?" I added.

When we arrived in Kunming, we discovered that this Gerald Durrell family was still flourishing in a kind of joyous, spontaneous chaos. Ben, for some inexplicable reason, loves the element of surprise and creativity that can flow from disorder and chaos. I always suspected that this was the result either of attending a very strict English school, or of having an English nanny, for Ben had been brought up in London by her American parents.

Ben's red hair was now a little greyer. She and her son, Paddy, with his hair cut short because the Chinese complained that he looked like Beethoven, greeted us with much slapping of backs and warm-hearted laughter. I almost said, and then didn't, "Where's Boris, I mean Doris? Or the monkey, or the boa constrictor?" The Booz family has always had a menagerie wherever they lived. Because Paul was with the United Nations and the Harvard Development Group (later renamed the Harvard Institute of International Development), they had a number of overseas assignments, so that Miche was borne in France, Mamoo in Jordan, Paddy in Lebanon, Rustam in West Pakistan and Katherine in East Pakistan. (Ben had written and illustrated children's books about their family both in France and in Pakistan.) Paul died suddenly on June 17, 1971, and Ben brought her family to Sandy Spring, Maryland. She worked for the *National Geographic*, spending six months of the year in Yvoire, France and six months in Sandy Spring.

Ben had come to Kunming because an old friend of hers heard that China wanted to recruit fifty foreign language teachers from the United States to teach in Chinese universities and foreign language institutes. Although Ben had been teaching high school history at Sandy Spring Friends School, her friend believed that

Ben's graduate studies in Switzerland, her published books, and her experience living in Asia would qualify her for one of these positions. This friend suggested that Paddy might apply as well, since he was about to graduate from the University of Wisconsin and spoke Chinese quite well. A mother-and-son team might appeal to the family-conscious Chinese.

The Boozes each taught five courses: Spoken English, Composition, Literature, Grammar and a survey course, "The History and Culture of the English-Speaking World." In this course, which was wildly popular, Ben gave a three-and-a-half-hour lecture on "American History from Columbus to Carter." She wrote four textbooks, two of which were still being used in China long after her teaching ended.

Throughout China, temples and historic places defaced by the Red Guards were now being repainted and restored. Since foreign language books had been destroyed during the Cultural Revolution, Ben asked all her friends in America to send books for a library. Booklift sent over 2,000 books. One of the university's prized possessions was a 1964 *Encyclopaedia Britannica*, which only the faculty were allowed to use. The Boozes also introduced the university to social dancing, Western style, and all manner of "evil" Western ways.

One of my most vivid memories of the university was seeing the 1,500 students walking along in their brightly-colored clothes in the cold air, dipping into their bowls of noodles with their chopsticks as they went. Were there no dining halls in those early days? Or was that simply the way students and faculty were fed in China?

One of our first excursions from Kunming was to the Western Hills high above Lake Dian. To get there, we climbed a steep rocky path and passed under a Dragon Gate, reaching up to touch the highest part for good luck. At the foot of the climb was a large Buddhist temple where Ben engaged one of the monks to tell us about the fish drum, a brown carved wooden collection box at the entrance. Here one could donate money to buy new scriptures to replace the ones that Xuanzang lost in the river on his way back from India to China. Losing the scriptures is a famous incident of his journey that is referred to as well in *Journey to the West*. The Bamboo Temple—farther up the mountain—had Monkey figures, as well as a sculpture of Xuanzang with a shining golden crown, sitting on a white horse. Clearly the monkey and the monk were part of the folk culture of southwestern China.

We had a grand Christmas dinner, Chinese style, thanks to Ben's excellent cook, a rotund little man with a huge cleaver. We had brought the Boozes many practical things like scotch tape, rubber bands, paper, erasers, band-aids—luxuries in many Asian countries, but especially in China. We had also brought along the box of fancy Cuban cigars which the President of Sri Lanka had given Howard, as presents for Chris and Paddy. Each had a glorious time, puffing and blowing clouds of smoke in the air. The Boozes in turn presented us with hot water bottles and exotic, fur-lined Mongolian caps.

We were thankful for both the hot water bottles and the warm caps after we left the Boozes and made our way to Chungking, where we embarked on a river steamer, named *East is Red #36*, to travel down the Yangtze River. The hot water bottles were our constant companions day and night. Often the January days were so cold that we just stayed in bed, hot water bottles at our feet. While Chris made architectural drawings on a small envelope, and Howard read, I worked on a journal, trying to set down a flood of new impressions. When we did get out of our beds for meals, we walked on long narrow outdoor passageways jam-packed with families, their live chickens tied to the railings ready for the next meal. We were the only foreigners on board. Our Mongolian caps had long flaps covering our faces, so we could hardly see the steep cliffs rising on either side of us in the spectacular Yangtze River gorges. Men and women wearing Maoist blue suits and blue caps—China was still very much Maoist China—were also on deck. At one point, the crowds became very excited. They began to shout, pointing to three odd rock formations high above us. "Monkey! Pigsy!" they cried. The characters in the rock formations were the well-known figures from *Monkey*. Just as Anne Goodrich had told me, these were as dear to the Chinese as Paul Bunyan and Mickey Mouse are to Americans.

Shortly after docking in Wuhan I happened to look out a second story window and saw a smashed violin, a moving reminder of the determination of the Cultural Revolution to wipe out bourgeois influences. The violin made me recall the very young man who had been our guide on our 1977 visit to China, when the Cultural Revolution was barely over. The glory days of his youth had been spent with the Red Guards, and he might well have engaged in this very type of destruction. On this trip our guide was very sophisticated, much smoother and less dogmatic than the guide of only two years before. However, she still clung to the belief that China had liberated Tibet and brought enlightenment to the Tibetans. This didn't sit very well with Chris, who loved Tibetan folkways and culture. Later he went with Ben to Tibet when she was gathering material for a guidebook on Tibet that was published in 1986. At an exhibition of propaganda art, with giant idealized bodies of workers—I think it was in Chungking—Chris had had enough propaganda about China liberating Tibet; he exploded with rage. The words were flying from his mouth and his voice shook, for he had seen the terrible destruction of monasteries wrought by China.

We left *East is Red #36* at Wuhan to go to Xian. For me, this would be the high point of our journey, for the Wild Goose Pagoda is there. Xuanzang had asked the Tang emperor to build it to house the Buddhist scriptures he had brought back from India. He hoped the Emperor would build it of stone like the buildings he had seen in India. The Emperor compromised: it is made of yellow brick. Various explanations had been offered for its name, the most imaginative of which has to do with a meal of roast goose that was miraculously dropped on a community of starving monks. The first time I saw the Wild Goose Pagoda in 1977 I rejoiced in its austerity and simplicity, after the lavish and overly-ornate palaces of Beijing. I climbed its squeaking wooden steps to the top. The view from there was panoramic—a grey city with well laid-out streets surrounded by green fields in a wide, wide valley. In medieval times Xian had been a model for Nara in Japan and for cities in Korea.

In the seventh century Xian, then known as Ch'ang-an, had been the greatest city in the world, with a population of two million. In physical extent, it was twice the size of Rome, five miles by seven miles. It is, of course, the beginning and also the end of the Silk Road and, like Constantinople, had been a thriving imperial center of commerce, administration, religion and cultural splendor, especially during the Tang dynasty (618–907 C.E.).

On this visit, at the end of 1979, the Wild Goose Pagoda still seemed to me a plain and somehow elegant seven story building. It had been rebuilt many times since the seventh century and was very nearly destroyed during the Cultural Revolution. In 1958 the Abbot was forced to leave, and had to make a living selling coal in a handcart, an example of the general persecution of Buddhist monks. Later the Red Guards stormed the pagoda and burned many of the scriptures that Xuanzang had translated.

When we visited, there were very few tourists and no monks in evidence at the pagoda, which stands in what was formerly the temple of Great Maternal Grace. It was, in short, a far cry from what a Chinese friend of ours would later experience in 1999: queues of people waiting to light candles and burn incense to the sounds of chanting monks, broadcast through the loud speaker in a temple gift shop. A rubbing of Xuanzang, the familiar portrait of him with a fly whisk and a kelty pack, stands on the temple grounds. I hadn't known that it came from a stele near his burial site. But I remembered that my first Chinese informant had told me that the place that holds Xuanzang's ashes—the Temple of Flourishing Teaching—was located half way up a hill on a site of "favorable influences." He had often run past it as a boy.

We drove into the countryside outside Xian to see the burial site; we climbed up the hill, paused before the terra cotta wall and tall gate to the temple grounds, and went in. No one was around; not even a monk to be seen. We didn't know what all the buildings were and there was no one to tell us, no guidebook to inform us. I recognized the Temple of Flourishing Teaching—a smaller version of the Wild Goose Pagoda—that contains Xuanzang's relics. I gazed up at its five stories, to see the grass growing on the roof. We were just reflecting on this example of neglect when we noticed that Chris was no longer with us. Earlier we had passed by some underground houses on the way to the temple. They seemed to be open-air pits. Twenty feet below was an open courtyard, some with a tree, some without, and on all four sides were rooms opening on to the courtyard. With his interest in architecture, we knew that that's where Chris would be taking pictures.

Our final stop in China was Beijing. Here, of course, the Forbidden City, the beautiful Temple of Heaven, the Summer Palace and the nearby Great Wall of China had all been beautifully repainted and restored.

*****

My next trip to China was in 1981, organized again by Jane Brown. The group included many of the Riverdalians from the first trip and a few art historian friends of Jane's from San Francisco, where Jane once had lived. I was delighted that Anne and Carrington Goodrich were along this time. We began our journey in Hong Kong and then flew to Beijing.

I was able to meet up with Betty Lou Hummel in Beijing, where Arthur had been appointed Ambassador. She had only been there about five weeks. I was shocked to find the American Residence in Beijing was about half the size of our Residence in Colombo, and the staff was also about half as large; they worked an eight-hour day and were employed by the Chinese Government. Betty Lou was philosophical about the many constraints to the running of her Embassy Residence.

Instead of sightseeing around Beijing with the group, I was going to go with the Goodriches as Carrington searched for his father's grave in Tongzhou, a town twelve miles outside Beijing. I have to confess that I was dreading what might have happened to Tongzhou in China's rush to modernize. Would we be tramping around rows of tall apartment buildings or a factory? What if nothing remained, nothing at all? How could I comfort the Goodriches, who had been through so much already? As we drove out on a modern four-lane highway from the city, I grew more uneasy. So did Anne, for she kept rubbing the joints in her arthritic hands.

A soldier stopped us at the historic Marco Polo Bridge, where a famous battle in 1937 marked the beginning of the Sino-Japanese War. A sign near the bridge noted: "Foreigners with Special Permits Only." Carrington and Anne didn't have their passports. I did, but I was also the problem. Anne explained to the officials that I was not their real daughter; I was a "dry daughter," which is something like her goddaughter.

The soldiers let us through. We drove around until Carrington spotted a medium-sized pagoda. He recognized it immediately. As a boy, he used to count the number of stories. He counted them again then: thirteen, just as he had remembered. Seeing the pagoda gave us hope, so we kept driving around asking questions until finally we found the college where Carrington's father had taught. His father, who was interested in astronomy, had mounted a telescope on the roof of a tall building with a crenellated roof. During the Boxer Rebellion the Chinese thought it was a cannon, so they didn't fire on any of the academic buildings! We wandered around and finally found the large grey houses where the faculty resided. There among them was the very house—now undeniably shabby—where Carrington had lived. It now houses four or five families. Carrington didn't want to go in.

Crowds of people had gathered around us by this time; very often on our trip, the Goodriches attracted lots of people. Was it because the Chinese venerate age and wisdom, or was it Anne's nimbus of white hair? Anne was born in 1895, and so she must have been 86 years old at that time. Carrington was a year older. We didn't have time to see the school that his mother had established in memory of his sister, who died at eleven. The cemetery where his father and sister were buried was gone, but we did find out from someone in the crowd that the school was still going and was known as the Goodrich School. Alas, it was time to leave.

Although at the end of each discovery Carrington said, "I am very satisfied," it was clear that he was churning inside. As we waited for the elevator in our Friendship Hotel, he said softly, "I am afraid my emotions have been through a wringer." His eyes misted over for the first time.

The next day I went with the Goodriches to search for the house where they had lived in Beijing. It was in the neighborhood of the Peking Union Medical Center, near the hospital for foreigners where Howard had taken me to check my blood. Well, we found their old house—"the one we lived in when we were first married," Anne said excitedly in her deep voice. The red gate to their compound was still there, but we didn't go inside. On the street near Carrington's old office was the church where Sun Yat Sen, leader of the 1911 revolution, was buried. We stopped to watch a man making little figures out of flour dough with a twirl of his wrist and thumb. Anne was thrilled, for it was just the way it used to be in the old days, when there were camel caravans bearing coal, donkeys with jingling bells, and low-lying shops made of wood. Anne asked him to make a dough figure for me. Guess what it was! Monkey, of course.

That night I woke up at 2:30 a.m. to the sound of a snapping whip and faint bleating noises. It turned out to be 800 sheep, in groups of a hundred, being herded down the streets of Beijing—to their death? For someone's dinner the next day? A cheap way to transport food to meet the needs of a more affluent city?

Anne used to tell me that Beijing was the most beautiful city in the world. "It was a place of *power* and *dignity*," she said with emphasis. Well, the old walls and the famous gates had gone, and the tall apartment buildings and four-lane highways were unimpressive to me as an American.

Our tour of the Yungang Caves in the far north of China, near Mongolia, was a good introduction to the next leg of our journey. These ancient caves are largely Buddhist. Our principal destination, however, was the Dunhuang Caves in China's Far West. In order to get there, we flew from Beijing to Lanzhou and then to Jiayuguan Pass, then took a seven- or eight-hour bus ride across the desert to the town of Dunhuang. We were traveling the very desert Xuanzang had crossed alone with his scrawny horse. His guide had abandoned him. He had lost his way, then he had spilled his water bag, so that for five days he was consumed by hunger and thirst as he made a desert crossing of some 300 miles.

First Xuanzang was in the Gobi Desert, then the Taklamakan Desert. I had read so much about them in books, and now I would see these places for myself. I'll never forget our flight from Tehran over the Pamir mountains, and looking down on the desert by moonlight. Yet now, on the ground, I was surprised. The desert didn't look like the undulating sands of the desert in the Middle East around Dubai—the way I thought deserts are supposed to look. Sometimes the Gobi resembled huge mounds of "black coal." Or was it like a field of very rough gravel and filled with salt-encrusted hummocks? On one of our stops I remember lying down on my stomach on the sand just to feel it. Another time we stopped to see herds of camels, not the one-humped scraggly Dromedary camels of our zoos, but two-humped Bactrian camels with shorter legs and bushy, thick brown fur. (To remember the difference between a Dromedary and a Bactrian camel, Nick Middleton suggests laying the first letter of each word on its side, and you have the number of humps.)[23] Such a vast expanse of sand dunes! Taklamakan in Turkic means "Where You Go In and You Don't Come Out." This was a desert that sometimes swallowed up travelers—or whole cities. Right in the middle of the Taklamakan were the Dunhuang Caves, at the juncture of the Northern and Southern Silk Roads. An art gallery in the desert—ten centuries of Chinese art!

Xuanzang had resisted stopping at the Dunhuang Caves on his way to India, but he did stop there on this return. That Lone Ranger of archaeology, Aurel Stein, by invoking Xuanzang's name, was able to persuade Abbot Wang to open Cave Seventeen, sometimes called the Library Cave, which had been sealed up since the eleventh century. We approached a mile-long cliff honeycombed with caves. Beyond the abandoned ones on the eastward-facing slope was the spire of an orange pagoda in the midst of three or four tiers of caves. Winds from the Gobi desert brought a steady shower of sand over the lip of the caves, piling up on the higher cement walkways; men in blue overalls swept it off, the sand hitting the ground with a resounding whack. The only other sound was that of young attendants locking and unlocking the brown padlocked doors. No one could enter a cave unattended.

I ran ahead to see what for so long I had only imagined, the paintings and sculpture of the Cave of a Thousand Buddhas, as the Dunhuang Caves are sometimes called. I couldn't believe what I saw. Instead of badly chipped and faded colors, the walls shimmered with warm reds, blues, emerald greens—myriads of Buddhist figures; strong friezes of men and animals in Chinese landscape; tier upon tier of paintings from the floor to the ceiling. Looking up, I saw more graceful designs and whirling shapes high above those statues which had been painted to fit with the decorated walls. The extreme dryness of the desert had preserved them.

There are 492 caves, which are estimated to contain over eleven acres of wall paintings and more than 2,000 sculpted and painted figures. In spite of the devastation of barbarian invasions and the ravages of wind and sand, the grottoes embody the work of seven Imperial Dynasties from the fourth to the fourteenth centuries. Chou En-lai, the Communist leader, is reputed to have been responsible for saving them during the Cultural Revolution.

We had asked to see Cave Seventeen first, because this sealed-up cave was the very one that opened up the eyes of the world to the long-forgotten caves of Dunhuang. Not unlike Angkor Wat, which had been swallowed up in the jungles of Cambodia, Dunhuang had been ignored. Inside Cave Seventeen, along with literally thousands of Buddhist scrolls and silk banners, was a copy of what is regarded as the world's earliest printed book, the Diamond Sutra, dated 868 C.E. Thanks to Aurel Stein, the original is now in the British Museum, not far from the Gutenberg Bible.

At sunset that first day, we climbed up the steps at the open face of the Dunhuang Caves right to the top, as was possible in those early days of Chinese tourism. We stepped out onto a flat expanse of desert leading almost to the horizon. The sands were now golden. Shadows grew longer as we explored the vast expanse of sand on top of the caves. The smallest dunes made entrancing patterns with the coming of night. We saw a herd of wild camels running across the desert.

As it became darker, I walked back to the edge of the caves, and what a panorama I saw. From Mt. Mingsha where the caves are located, the earth spread out below us. I could see the wide valley and could gaze across at a gnarled chain of mountains. I could almost see where we had come from, the small village of Dunhuang, sixteen miles away.

On that steep climb up the stairs to the top of the caves, I was huffing and puffing, breathing so heavily that Bob Stratton, one of our Riverdale travelers whom I scarcely knew, said, "Sounds sort of like a pornographic phone call." Well, this knocked all sense of the sublime out of me, all right!

Visiting Dunhuang was surely the high point of that China trip. The low point was meeting Howard at the end of it. Some of our group were flying straight to New York instead of stopping over in San Francisco. But I needed to rest, so I spent the night there after the long flight across the Pacific. Word of my change of plans did not reach Howard, so he waited at the airport where he found I was not among the group. Howard was understandably furious, and his anger was not easy to assuage.

There were other problems I needed to address, and I concluded that I needed some help. I consulted Dr. Edith Wallace, a Jungian analyst. This opened up new horizons for me and helped me to explore my feelings and Howard's more directly. Dr. Wallace also urged me to concentrate less on pure scholarship and to investigate my feelings about Xuanzang.

*****

My last trip to China, in 1985, was run by the Kuo Feng tour company and called "Unexplored Silk Road and Kashgar." Howard and I would be going together to explore China's Far West. Kashgar is right up against the Pamir mountains where the China/Pakistan Karakorum Highway begins. It is in the heart of Islamic China, and is the largest oasis city in Central Asia. The highway we had traveled with the Hummels in Pakistan had been extended, opening up India, Pakistan, Afghanistan, Russia, and Persia to China. What is more, Kashgar would be of special interest to Howard, as a student of international politics, because of its role in the Great Game, the rivalry between Soviet and Western Powers in Central Asian politics. Of course what could be more enticing for me than going so far west—along the Silk Road in the footsteps of Xuanzang? I had already written ahead for permission to take photographs of a very special cave that we would be visiting at Dunhuang.

Our tour began in Shanghai. The old Peace Hotel stood on the Bund, Shanghai's economic and financial center. Inside the hotel we found the famous jazz bar, where a band—whose average age must have been sixty—played "Blue Moon," "Over the Rainbow," "Alexander's Ragtime Band," all the old chestnuts of the thirties and forties. What a great beginning for Howard, who loves jazz. Were they just catering to Western tastes? Or did their choice of music show how far behind they were? We never found out. But we had a hunch it was the former.

Again Betty Lou Hummel's contacts were invaluable. We stopped to see the American Consul General and his wife, Stan and Claire Brooks, in Shanghai. We were having lunch with the Brookses when Howard turned to me and said, "Tell them what you are doing." (I often play this game with Howard, and this time he turned the tables.) So I began with the Monkey story, and was beginning to talk about the pilgrim Xuanzang whose journey inspired this epic. Claire interrupted:

"I can take you to meet Elizabeth Boulton, who would be happy to have somone with whom to discuss Xuanzang. She is the wife of one of our staff members. She wrote her thesis about Xuanzang and Chinese travel writing."

After a three-hour conversation with Elizabeth Boulton, I emerged with a grateful heart—I had been working alone for so long—and with my head spinning. She told me so much about the traditions of Chinese historical writing, Chinese strength and weakness; how no Indian had ever provided such precise historical information as Xuanzang. How, as a writer, he had made a significant contribution to Chinese literature, incorporating new themes, new legends, descriptions of Buddhist heavens and hells; recording his reaction to Indian excesses. In our discussion, Elizabeth and I touched on Silk Road geography, Buddhism, Xuanzang's dying wishes, and his appearance. Of course, I procured a copy of her thesis, *Early Chinese Buddhist Travel*

Records as a Literary Genre, from Georgetown University. I had a fine new source to work from.

From Shanghai, we were scheduled to fly all the way to Urumchi, a large commercial entrepot in Western China. We would be traveling under the guidance of Dr. Victor Mair, a vigorous scholar from the University of Pennsylvania. Victor knew many Central Asian languages, but he carried his erudition lightly, with a kind of boyish enthusiasm. His long face was animated, his eyes especially were bright, sparkling. His voice carried, for it had a slight nasal twang. Even though I was not a scholar, he treated me like one, sending me his articles and books on a wide range of subjects. After that I often saw him on television, telling people about the remarkable mummies—4,000 years old—which have been preserved by the dry sands of the Taklamakan Desert.

Victor Mair came to China scholarship as an adult; he did not even think about China until after he had been to Nepal with the Peace Corps. There he became interested in Buddhism and, eventually, Sino-India studies. Victor has been "running" ever since; the sheer quantity of pages he has written or volumes he has edited is immense.

Victor also had the largest curiosity and thirst for knowledge of anyone I have ever met. His field is Central Asian studies and its relation to Chinese studies, and includes Iran, but he's also written or edited large volumes of Chinese literature and has translated Lao Tzu. His drive and colossal energy are not just intellectual; when we finally got to Kashgar at the very end of the Taklamakan Desert, he scrambled like a mountain goat up the steep cliff in front of the Cave of the Three Immortals.

In Kashgar, we were surprised actually to be staying at the residence of Nikolai Petrovsky, the famous Russian Consul General of the early 1900s. We knew that the Russians had been spying in Kashgar, but we hadn't realized that a Russian trading mission reached China as early as 1858. This residence is now the Semen Hotel, with several outbuildings, but it is still the same old colonial stucco building with high ceilings and tall, narrow windows.

The British Consul General lived just down the street at Chini Bagh, The China Garden. George Macartney, the Consul General in Kashgar from 1890 to 1918, was posted here to strengthen the British position against the Russians in The Great Game. Both diplomats had also been instructed by their governments to acquire whatever ancient manuscripts they could from local treasure hunters. Macartney's Residence was a haven for all the famous explorers of the early twentieth century; they came here exhausted from their lonely mountain treks in the Pamirs, or weakened by long marches in the desert. They all loved it and they all wrote about it: Aurel Stein, Sven Hedin, Peter Fleming, Ella Maillart. Macartney's wife planted an unusual garden with pear and apple trees and flora brought from India and England. Chini Bagh has come down in the world, now a shabby hostel for long-distance truck drivers, and a multi-story modern hotel has been built over the famous garden.

As I went to sleep our first night in Kashgar, I didn't think about whether the mattress was lumpy. I was remembering that Jeannette Mirsky had told me Lady Macartney's story about traders smuggling coral over the border by mixing it with the camels' feed.

There were very few Buddhist sites around Kashgar, so the next day we went to the Kashgar bazaar with Victor Mair and our local guide, Sultan. We passed by Uighurs, Tajiks, Kyrgyz people on the way to the bazaar. Howard took my arm and held me back for a moment. "Whatever you do, don't be enthusiastic about a rug. Pretend that you don't like it. Feign indifference."

We browsed around among the piles of carpets, but kept returning to one that was unlike the others, and unlike anything I have ever seen before or since. This one had stylized leaves and flowers. Surely this carpet was a hybrid—part Chinese, part Indian, part Central Asian—and very mysterious.

"Good price. Very good price," the rug merchant said, smiling. A crowd began to gather. The excitement mounted. Someone had told us that you should pour water on a carpet to see whether the colors held fast. First Howard poured a few drops, and then the whole cup. Howard conferred with me and we conferred with

Victor. The merchant and his cronies put their heads together too, with much pursing of lips and scratching of heads. A bystander, who wanted to sell us two plastic bags to wrap the carpet in, joined the other team. More and more visitors came to watch, until perhaps fifty people had gathered.

The guide's voice grew louder. So did Victor's. They scowled, pursed their lips once more. Then they whispered to one another. It was a grand ritual, with a rising intensity of emotion. Victor bargained. The merchant shook his head. We pretended to leave. The merchant started after us. Victor shrugged his shoulders. The owner threw up his hands. Finally we bought the rug for 340 yuan, or 100 U.S. dollars. Howard bore it home triumphantly, balanced on his shoulders in its plastic bag. When we got back to our hotel, we arranged to have it vacuumed. Clouds of dust rose in the air, revealing much brighter designs and a vivid ruby red background.

We hauled the magic carpet on the plane with us back to Urumchi. From there we had to take a five-hour bus trip down the mountains to Turfan. The oasis was 260 feet below sea level. One of our group had bribed our driver with tapes to induce him to transport us so late at night, and to help him keep awake on the drive. I slept much of the way, but I awoke about 1:00 a.m. to Bruce Springsteen belting out "My Home Town" as we approached Turfan and the desert.

The 1980s

The ends of the Earth

Of special interest to me was the ancient town of Gaochang outside Turfan, where Xuanzang may have preached to the people. I was also interested in the remains of Buddha images still quite visible high up in the niches of crumbling buildings built by the King of Turfan. But far more dramatic were the setting and the monastery itself at Bezeklik. Xuanzang didn't write about Bezeklik, but he surely visited there. When I have seen Victor in recent years, he always recalls our visit to the Bezeklik monastery in the Tien Shan mountains, above the Turfan oasis on the Northern Silk Road. Victor was afraid that I might fall into Murtok Gorge: Howard and I had to climb far out on a promontory in an effort to get a picture of the monastery that would show its unusual location. Like the builders of temples in Greece, the Buddhist monks had a genius for place.

After the Turfan oasis and exploring the caves at Bezeklik, we flew to the Dunhuang Caves. I was glad that Howard was with me this time. Our local guide told me that he had made two trips following in the footsteps of the Chinese pilgrim; so Xuanzang meant something to him, too.

Cave #103 (from the first half of the eighth century) contains a mural of Xuanzang. I had never received permission to photograph it, although I had written months ahead of time. The guide didn't have a key for Cave #103; but on this felicitous day the cave door was open. Victor jumped in. I slipped in and so did Howard. Some of the walls were in quite bad shape. But the representation of Xuanzang and his elephant, the one an Indian king had given him to carry his scriptures, was just as I had hoped. Then Victor peered around behind a statue in the left hand corner to see what he thought was Xuanzang. The bottom part of the painting was a burnt sienna color, and then what seemed to be a torso, and finally a finely drawn upturned head. I had never read about it or seen pictures of it, didn't know of its existence. I couldn't believe it. Was it Xuanzang or another monk? Who was it? The question continues to haunt me.

By great good fortune, later on Victor went with us to the Temple of Flourishing Teaching outside of Xian; this is the tomb pagoda we had seen on our way home from Sri Lanka in 1980, that had been so neglected. The five-story Temple of Flourishing Teaching covers the ashes of Xuanzang. The Tang Emperor wrote two characters, "Flourishing Teaching," on the pagoda, which meant that Buddhism would flourish by inheriting Xuanzang's achievements. The three pagodas on either side are dedicated to two of Xuanzang's disciples. On this visit two abbots, one of them fingering his beads, saying "Amitabha, Amitabha, Amitabha" (Buddha of Light), conducted us around the walled compound. The famous stele of Xuanzang with his big kelty pack full of scriptures was housed in a new wooden building to protect it from the rain. I bought several rubbings and a modern scroll of Xuanzang from a new store for tourists.

At the very end of our visit, Victor and I went back to the store to buy two incense sticks to place in a receptacle full of sand on an altar. Because my right hand was holding my new scroll, I tried to place the incense with my shaking left hand. The incense stick didn't want to go in. I kept trying to plant it in the sand, but it broke part way in. "I hope this isn't a bad omen," I said to myself. What I meant was, "I hope I have a chance to finish my biography of Xuanzang."

I did, of course, and ten years later my new scroll—a lively portrayal of Xuanzang and his pack—adorns the cover of my book about him.

Chapter 13

LEARNING TO READ XUANZANG'S REPORT TO THE EMPEROR

W hen Xuanzang returned home from his sixteen-year journey to India, the Chinese Emperor asked him to write a report about the countries, peoples, rulers in the West. Xuanzang did so, in his *Record of the Western Region*. This, along with an admiring biography of him written by a contemporary Buddhist monk, was the major source material for my book. But reading the account, with its archaic language, obsolete terminology, and obscure content—even in translation—was like beating my way through the dense undergrowth of virgin forest.

I vividly remember the setting: I, sitting in a rattan chair in our chilly bedroom cabin on Little Cranberry Island, a portable heater at my feet, blanket over my legs, trying to decipher the *Record of the Western Region*. How I struggled over the pages, and fell asleep trying to make sense of the strange words in front of me. And then gave up.

I pored over these ancient texts, stumbling over one long unintelligible word after another. I scratched my head over medieval maps in old books and contemporary maps in modern books, in futile attempts to follow Xuanzang's journey. There were many different names for the same places. Which was right? Khotan, Hotan, Hetian, Ho-tien. Were they all the same place? Very different places? Even Xuanzang's name appeared in English translations with about six different spellings.

Yet another word with lots of syllables. I skipped it. Figured it must be a Buddhist term. I stumbled and groaned over passages like this one: "In a mango wood east of Shoslaran were the foundations of a house in which Asanga P'usa composed his Hsien-Yang-Sheng-Chiao lun." I tried to get some sense out of the paragraph, and failed. Later I remembered that Zhu Fang, a Chinese student who had lived with us while studying at Columbia, told us that during the Cultural Revolution he had tried to learn English from a copy of Dickens's *A Tale of Two Cities*. Surely if he could do that, I could slog along, trying to master these seemingly impossible texts.

I tried again and again to read the nineteenth-century translations by Thomas Watters and Samuel Beal of Xuanzang's report and Hui Li's biography. I fell asleep in my chair. It was too much. Why had I gotten interested in this impossible subject? Why something so obscure, so hard to master? I didn't know, but I was driven. By what?

I skipped page after page until I came to a word I recognized. Like most mornings, it was cold. Fall was coming. I turned the electric heater up higher. The beginning of the *Record of the Western Region*, where Xuanzang is still in Western China, was the hardest—though I grew to love the sound of place names on the Silk Road like Bezeklik and Dandan Ouilik. I thought I knew something about China from my four visits there, but there was still so much more to learn. After this difficult section, the text of the *Record of the Western Regions* became easier because I knew a lot about India from Howard's work and my own travels. Ah, Taxila, the Ajanta caves, were places I recognized, for I had been there. Gradually I became familiar with Xuanzang's itinerary. I knew the direction he was heading. The biography of Xuanzang was helpful. I tried to put the biography and Xuanzang's report to the Emperor together in my mind. More Sanskrit words, Pali words, Chinese. Oh dear.

I don't know why I struggled so. "In our darkness, you kindle a fire that never dies away." In French this is "Dans nos obscurités."[24] I like it that darkness and obscurity are equated.

People who can do jigsaw puzzles—which I cannot—start with a few pieces. They work with jagged, squiggly shapes and gradually put small clumps of puzzle together. Yes, that is what I was doing. Puzzle people stare at all the crazy shapes. They combine one or two, then more. They complete whole sections of the puzzle so that it makes sense. I stared at all the new-to-me words, looked some of them up in Buddhist dictionaries. Whole parts of a page began to have meaning, then a few pages, then a whole chapter.

Along with descriptions of the geography, the major products, the customs, the strengths and weaknessess of the rulers, Xuanzang always included a great deal about Buddhism. That meant that part of learning to read the *Record of the Western Region*s was mastering Buddhist nomenclature—Yogacharabhumishastra, Prajnaparamita Hridaya Sutra, those long names took a long time. Elizabeth Boulton's thesis *Buddhist Travel Writing*, happily, had a good appendix on Buddhist schools and religious leaders. I audited a course on Mahayana Buddhism given by Robert Thurman at Columbia University. (On occasion, his knowledge, wit and electrifying mind at play made his seminar seem more like a conversation in an Irish bar.) My tutorial with Kheminda Thera in Sri Lanka so many years earlier had given me a feel for Buddhist ways of thinking as well as Buddhist practice.

The legends connected with Buddhist monuments and holy sites were a very important part of Buddhism. Xuanzang encountered many such stories on his journey, and loved to repeat them. He must have seen them represented over and over again in the bas reliefs of Buddhist monasteries or in Buddhist wall painting in ancient caves. The birth of the Buddha, his miracles, stories of his preaching, the story of his First Sermon, tales of the former

Buddhas—Xuanzang saw them everywhere. So I began putting words and pictures together in my mind.

Along with studying Xuanzang's record for the Emperor, I kept poring over books like Grousset's *In the Footsteps of the Buddha*, which I had first read a decade before. This proved to be a very important book for me because of Grousset's wonderful way of capturing the spirit of the Buddhist Middle Ages, as well as the broad canvas of cultural history with its strong emphasis on art.

But this precious volume with its warm burnt sienna covers is badly damaged now, with big toothmarks in the back cover, pages 157 to 160 missing, illustrations falling out. I know when most of the damage was done, and by whom! Before our 1981 China trip, I had been sitting in a chair in our enclosed side garden, trying to look up something, when our Bouvier puppy jumped up on my lap, knocked my copy of Grousset out of my hands, and played with it like a ball before I could get it back. Howard had to take care of this same frisky puppy, only four months old, when I was out in Western China.

Over the years I did research in the many libraries around New York: the inimitable Explorers Club where a huge white polar bear stands on its hind legs at the top of the stairs; the New York Public Library with its famous lions guarding the entrance; the Metropolitan Museum library with its giant editions of Aurel Stein's work. Best of all, I loved Columbia's Kent Library of East Asian Studies with its nineteenth-century feel—mustiness, dark walls, cases filled with Chinese or Japanese treasures. Exploring the stacks showed me what other books were being written in fields related to my study of Xuanzang. Oh, and those rickety, creaky elevators with metal grills and sliding doors, that took me four or five floors down into the bowels of the earth. Whenever I got lost, some kindly Asian student would help me find the book I was after or the place I was trying to go. This world of research has now given way to computers, and is hard to imagine for anyone born after 1980.

My adventures researching my book were not always intellectual. I had found a scroll with a rubbing of an inscription that detailed the major events of Xuanzang's life. This inscription is from the Temple of Flourishing Teaching, where Xuanzang's ashes are buried. I needed someone to translate it for me. To my delight, Anne Goodrich referred me to a Buddhist nun who was doing graduate work at Columbia. S. Heng-ting Tsay had a ravishing smile and shaven head, and wore a grey habit. I had lunch with her several times at the Faculty Club, where she told me that she was translating *The Twenty Verses*, a book that Xuanzang had translated. She had visited a Xuanzang temple in Taiwan, where she grew up. She had gone four times, and each time she had wept and wept—she didn't know why. She then vowed to bring Eastern thought to the West the way Xuanzang had brought Buddhism to China.

One day when we were walking across campus together, I tried to enlist her services. "So you think you can translate the inscription for me?"

"Yes, but it will be very difficult. It is in medieval Chinese, for it is from the Tang era." She smiled. "I may not do it very well."

We both noticed that the grass beside the walk under a row of maple trees had suddenly become an eerie green. There was something unnatural about it. "Yes," she said smiling, "it is the day of the eclipse. We had better not look up at the sun."

We stared at the strange color. It was dark for a minute, but not completely dark. "No wonder ancient peoples were afraid," I continued. "Mystery and magic often go together."

She laughed. "I know."

"Look," I said, "each leaf is reflecting the coming back of the sun. But each leaf looks as though someone has taken a bite out of it." I was one who stated the obvious.

Unfortunately this was the last time I saw this charming nun. She had to go back to Taiwan because a family member was ill, so she couldn't finish her translation. Did she remember seeing the eclipse with me? I hope so.

Bit by bit, I was beginning to get a pretty clear sense of Xuanzang's journey and some insights into him as a person. I wrote an article for *Orientations* magazine, "A Monk's Journey to the Buddhist Holy Land."[25] This ended with the sentence, "It was the combination of exotic travel, religious fervour and the reaction of a noble mind and a lively personality to danger that excited the Chinese imagination." I thought of it as providing background for *Journey to the West*,[26] the literary classic which was then being translated in four volumes by Anthony C. Yu, a professor at the University of Chicago. His first volume of this work had been published the same year I mounted my exhibition "The Nine Lives and Ancient Background of Monkey" for the New York Public Library. Glen Dudbridge, our friend the China expert in Oxford, had told me about Anthony and his work. When I finally did meet him, he told me that his grandfather had told him the Monkey stories when he was a small boy in Hong Kong. It was serendipitous that he made his translations when he did, because these classic stories were hard to find in English. Arthur Waley, the great Sinologist and linguist, had translated only about a third of this epic.

I hadn't even begun to think about writing a book on Xuanzang when Dr. Frieda Murck, a friend of Jeannette Mirsky's, asked me to talk to some of the staff at the Metropolitan Museum about the Dunhuang Caves.

Very few people had yet been to Dunhuang in 1981. It was not long afterwards, in 1983, that the exhibition "The Silk Road and the Diamond Path" opened at The Asia Society in New York. I was asked to speak there, along with Jeannette Mirsky and Morris Rossabi, a professor of history at Queens College and the City University of New York. The author of the standard biography of Kublai Khan, Morris turned out to be very helpful in getting my book published twelve years later.

Howard helped me immeasurably with these slide presentations, by expertly photographing images from the books in my ever-expanding library. Along with studying Xuanzang's report to the Emperor, I was collecting slides and photographs of the art in Buddhist caves, photographs of the Gobi Desert, and views of the Tien Shan mountains separating China and Russia, as they would look from a monk's cell. What was truly extraordinary: in one of the oases where Xuanzang had rested, I was able to obtain a copy of a painting of the King and Queen of Kucha, whom Xuanzang surely had met. I was beginning to *see* his journey.

While my China trips enabled me to see many of the landmarks in Xuanzang's life, artifacts from this period are in museums all over Europe. In the early eighties I went several times with Howard to Europe, once to an academic conference on South Asian studies, in Sweden. In the Museum of Antiquities in Stockholm were beautiful Wei Buddhas; and Stockholm's Ethnographic Museum owns artifacts from Sven Hedin's explorations. Unhappily, most of them were in locked trunks in the basement, for Hedin's pro-Nazi views had alienated his countrymen. In Uppsala, I picked up copies of some of his splendid maps of the Gobi and Taklamakan Deserts and the Silk Roads.

We made a special trip to St. Petersburg in Russia to visit the Hermitage Museum, where I expected to find some Central Asian paintings and sculpture—for the Russians had also explored the Silk Road in the early twentieth century. On a cold morning, we walked up and down the vast corridors of the Hermitage in our overcoats, waiting for a door to open or a museum official to appear—for there seemed to be no information desk. At length, a young woman came forth, papers in hand. This looked promising. Her only foreign language was German. I tried to draw on my high school and college German, to no avail. Howard tried his German/Yiddish, learned in his years of working with refugees in Europe, and she understood immediately. She guided us to Dr. Lesnichenko, the Silk Road scholar. When we met him, we gave him Jeannette Mirsky's greetings. He turned out to be a charming man with a dark moustache and a splendid goatee. His Old World courtesy instantly made us comfortable. Dr. Lesnichenko toured us through the Silk Road galleries and engaged one of his staff to show us two of the Hermitage Museum's treasures: the Pasyryk carpet, the oldest known knotted carpet; and the locked Treasure Room of Scythian gold.

This was certainly exciting, but even more so was a frieze that had been found near Termez in Afghanistan, where I knew Xuanzang had been. The Airtam frieze had been found in the Oxus River, which forms the border between Afghanistan and Russia. Its origin was possibly a Buddhist monastery. We gazed at three

Grecian-looking lady musicians separated by acanthus leaves. Yet again we were discovering the fascination and beauty of statues executed in Greek style, Hellenistic influences dating probably from the first century.

And Berlin? Howard wanted to visit the distinguished political scientist Karl Deutsch in Berlin and to see Checkpoint Charlie, the garrison that divided East and West Berlin. I was eager to go to the Dahlem Museum in West Berlin because of their collection of evocative frescoes from the oases of the Northern Silk Road in China. We saw on the ceiling a hauntingly beautiful rondel of Thirteen Goddesses of Mercy. How to convey the feeling of intense religious devotion of the Buddhas, their disciples and the apsaras (flying angels) in fresco after fresco? I learned that the museum was about to send some of the frescoes to the Metropolitan Museum of Art in New York for an exhibition the following year (1982), called "Along the Ancient Silk Routes: Central Asian Art from the West German Berlin State Museums." This exhibition did indeed come to New York, and Dr. Frieda Murck, Jeannette Mirsky's friend on the Museum staff, took me around the exhibition before it opened. I was thrilled. This was the first showing of Central Asian Art in America, and it gave me the feel of wall painting in monasteries on the Northern Silk Road.

Howard and I often stopped in London or Paris en route to Asia, and this meant that I could spend time in the British Library with its collection of Buddhist scrolls, and the British Museum where the world's first printed book, *The Diamond Sutra,* was on exhibit in the same room as the Gutenberg Bible. Howard loved to go to Paris, and there I could visit the Musée Guimet, one of the best museums of Asian art anywhere. In each place I went, I bought slides, photographs and books for my slide presentations. Later, much later, I would write to museums to request professional photographs for my book.

As I came to know Xuanzang's *Record of the Western Region* better and better, I could skip over some of the pages and reread others. Seeing his travels through maps and artifacts enabled me to recreate some of the scenes he was describing. It was almost like making a documentary film. I could show where Xuanzang is believed to have lost his elephant in a particular gorge in the Pamir mountains; I could display a statue of King Kanishka, a great patron of Buddhist, and especially Gandharan, art that Xuanzang saw; the pass he crossed to get into Russia; an Asoka pillar of polished chunar sandstone in India, a famous icon which even today is used on the Indian flag and Indian currency. I had become engaged in the cultures of both India and China, and found Xuanzang to be my point of reference for these two cultures. His *Record of the Western Region* was detailed, specific and largely accurate. The art I collected reinforced this view. I could also use the wonderful stories his biographer told about him to make the account of his journey exciting. I had found a treasure trove.

And I still had so much to learn.

Gradually over the years I came to know Xuanzang as a devout pilgrim; as a linguist and intellectual *par excellence*; as a first class trekker who crossed the Tien Shan mountains, the Hindu Kush and the Pamirs; as a clever diplomat—in short, a man for all seasons.

Today I look at Thomas Watters's and Samuel Beal's English translations from the Chinese of Xuanzang's *Record of the Western Region*—those books I found in Oxford so many, many years ago. The volumes are tattered, the bindings collapsing, the fly pages missing, sheets falling out. It makes me realize how many years I had been working and thinking about Xuanzang.

Chapter 14

THE BUDDHIST HOLY LANDS IN INDIA AND PAKISTAN

There are four places, Ananda, which the believing man should visit with feelings of reverence and awe. Which are the four?

Lumbini, where the Buddha was born

Bodh Gaya, where the Buddha received his Enlightenment

Sarnath, where the Buddha preached his First Sermon

Kunsinagara, where the Buddha died

> *Paraphrased from the Mahaparinibbana Sutta,*
> *or the Sutra of the Glorious Decease, V. 16-22*

I had been waiting for several years to go to the Buddhist Holy Land in India and Pakistan to follow in Xuanzang's footsteps. This time I would take with me two five-by-seven notebooks, my "journal of the head" filled with names, sites, institutions (such as the Indian Archaeological Survey and the Nalanda Institute) that I wanted to see, and a blank notebook for a "journal of the heart." In the end I kept only one journal, but I had become much more sensitive to Xuanzang's religious feelings as well as my own.

My opportunity came in 1984 when Howard was invited to a conference in New Delhi. While Howard was conferring with Indian leaders and scholars in the capital, I arranged to travel with Maya Sen to Benares, one of the poorest regions of India. Barbara Harrison, a friend of many years both in Washington and Little Cranberry Island, had known her for years. Maya could help me, for unlike New Delhi, where many Indians spoke English, Benares was home to many who spoke only their native dialects. Maya Sen was Hindu, but she had been once to Sarnath where the Buddha delivered his First Discourse—which suggested to me that she was broad-minded. Like me, she was a grandmother and not very tall. Maya wore glasses and often seemed to lean her head forward as if she wished to see even better than she did.

Maya had never flown before. Our plan was to fly to Benares and visit Sarnath. We would then drive to Bodh Gaya, where the Buddha received his Enlightenment under a Bo tree. Next we would visit Nalanda, the Buddhist monastery where Xuanzang had stayed and studied for several years. Historically, it was also the most famous Buddhist monastery in all of Asia. Finally we would drive to Patna and fly back to Delhi, where Maya made her home, and meet up with Howard—all in the space of about ten days. Exactly where the Buddha died is uncertain, and it is difficult to get to his birthplace in Nepal, so I decided to skip Lumbini and Kusinagara, the alleged places of his birth and death.

Benares with its burning ghats, terraced stones which go down to the Ganges River, is the holiest of places for Hindus. To die there guarantees a Hindu immediate entrance into Heaven. A teeming city of a quarter of a million people, located between the rivers Varana and Asi, it is sometimes called Varanasi. It is ageless. Five miles away is the Buddhist site of Sarnath.

At the Sarnath Museum I looked up at the brilliant highly-polished Asoka pillar near the entrance and was entranced. Xuanzang, who had seen this very pillar in the seventh century, said, "It is as bright as jade. It is glistening and sparkles like light." It still does. Highly polished pillars like this one were crowned by animals, recalling the pillars of the Persian empire. Its cream-colored chunar sandstone gives lie to the many, many centuries that have passed; it was made around the third century C.E. for King Asoka, one of India's most famous Buddhist rulers. I have trouble believing it is so ancient. At the very top are four splendid lions standing back to back, with curly manes covering half their bodies; below them are an elephant, a bull, a horse and a lion separated from one another by wheels. Finally at the bottom is a bell-shaped base in the shape of an inverted lotus flower.

But I was eager to see the Buddha Turning the Wheel of the Law, which is also called "the Buddha preaching his First Sermon." This has long been regarded as one of the masterpieces of Indian sculpture. I stood in awe before the luminous softness of its sandstone. I focused on the Buddha seated in a yoga posture, with his hands in the Turning the Wheel of the Law pose. His eyes are lowered, his gaze turns inward. On the large halo behind him, two celestial beings are worshipping him. The proportions of the figure are perfectly balanced; the whole has a quality of unparalleled spiritual poise and equilibrium.

I was drawn to the Buddha's face, which expresses such wisdom and infinite compassion. It speaks of overcoming suffering and of inner peace, the very heart of Buddhism. The Buddha seems to exist in a world of perfect spiritual awareness, embodying the paradox of spiritual calm and the body bursting with a kind of contained energy. I recalled the lines from T. S. Eliot's "Burnt Norton":

> At the still point of the turning world
> Neither flesh nor fleshless
> Neither from nor towards
> At the still point there the dance is.[27]

Is the Buddha's face the still point in Eliot's poetry which is both "still and moving"? No, there is more—for it embodies that extraordinary combination of the sensual and the spiritual that the Indians do so well. For the purpose of Indian art, I take it, is to lead from the concrete form to the abstract realm of the spirit. The sacred image points beyond itself. Words go only so far. They must needs reach into silence. As I stood before the Buddha, time stopped.

Later on, Maya and I explored the Deer Park, where we found the Buddha Walk. I saw two Sri Lankan monks in their yellow robes, lighting candles at the Dharmajika stupa. Outside the Deer Park it is very different. As we traveled toward Benares I was in another world. What struck me, though, about this part of India is not its spiritual qualities but its physicality; people urinating anywhere, animals defecating, men soaping themselves as they bathe in the river, men squatting by the roadside in different postures. Bright purple brinjal, cauliflower in carts, dung, dirt and more dirt, muddy wells. And in a boat trip on the nearby Ganges River at Benares our guide rowed us past the ghats where bodies wrapped for burial are burned. Actually, burning bodies seems like a sensible clean way to handle one's eventual demise. I was shocked, however, to see a baby wrapped up like a mummy being thrown in the Ganges. (Babies apparently don't have to be purified by burning because they haven't sinned)

It was a six-hour drive through flat country from Benares to Bodh Gaya. We drove at harvest time, when many people were gathering rice in the fields or sifting grain on threshing floors. Hundreds and hundreds of antiquated trucks lumbered along, belching black smoke, in front of us and behind us. Terrible roads, grungy-looking towns, huge dry river beds. Egrets, kingfishers and a few herons in roadside ditches. Many hawks soaring, circling overhead. Three overturned trucks, two with piles of black coal in them, and one seemingly dead dog lying there, three vultures waiting, waiting. Villages with small tea stalls and innumerable men in loose shirts and baggy trousers—never women—sitting on charpoys (flat beds) with ropes strung across the frame. Some palm trees, mostly paddy-rice fields. We'd come due east from Benares and only headed north at the end of the journey. We saw more stone stupas, brick shrines, and monuments erected by kings, patrons, believers.

Bodh Gaya is a very holy place where the Buddha achieved Enlightenment under the Bo tree. I felt its sanctity immediately. Pilgrims come from all over the world. A young Tibetan prostrating himself; he had two wooden blocks, one in each hand, on which, when he had cast himself to the ground, he slid a few feet forward. Then he rose to repeat the same prostrations. He had been prostrating himself 2,000 times a day and planned to continue this practice for two more months. I am not sure why he did this—perhaps to atone for something he did or, as the Buddhists say, "to gain merit."

Under the wide spreading branches of the Bo tree, there was constant quiet devotion. Bodh Gaya, as Les Hixon once put it, is "a place of power." Japanese monks in their black robes along with Sri Lankans in saffron, Tibetans in deep red robes, a Burmese in copper, some Westerners meditating, smiling at each other as they rose from their meditations. Like climbers who have reached a summit of 18,000 feet, there is a kinship, a sense of exaltation, of peace.

Maya and I walked inside the Mahabodhi Temple and then around and around it, circumambulating with the smiling Tibetans, chanting monks, a beautiful young woman carrying a baby on her hip, wonderful old women with leathery faces. Everyone smiled and made eye contact, even the prostrating monks. Even Maya, a Hindu in a Buddhist temple, acknowledged how peaceful and holy it was. The temple is in a large garden among little bell-shaped white stupas, with beds of flowers nearby. The Bo tree is behind the Bodh Gaya temple, the same temple Xuanzang described with such accuracy in his *Record of the Western Region.*

As we were leaving Bodh Gaya I stopped before a large bell and rang it twice, once for me and once for Xuanzang, for it was here that he discarded his intellectual self and his reserve. He got down on his knees and wept. "In what cycle of life was I when the Buddha lived?" he asked himself. It is the only place in the record of his sixteen-year journey from China to India and back in which he shows any real emotion. This remains, therefore, the most moving part of his biography. I rang the bell for me too, perhaps out of a sense of inadequacy, of being always a seeker and not someone who has found. If only I were a better meditator than I am; the Buddha's message is to get at the root of one's own mind, because all action is based on thought and the quality of thought is based on the quality of the mind. Meditation is the tool.

201

We undertook a two-hour drive from Bodh Gaya to Nalanda Monastery, where Xuanzang stayed and studied for about five years, and later to Rajgir, a nearby city; both are in Bihar in northeast India. What Cluny and Clairvaux were to Europe, Nalanda was to Asia, the most distinguished of all its monasteries and universities. As we approached the town of Nalanda, we came to a fork in the road. Two young men in white shirts and slacks stopped the car. Was I the American lady? They had been waiting all morning long for us. I assumed that they were on the staff of the monastery. It turned out they were scholars, and I was never sure just how they learned that we were coming. We were well-guided by these two, Dr. Prasad and Dr. Singh, on a tour of the wonders of Buddhism's most famous monastery.

Together we visited the Nalanda Museum and climbed Stupa Three, the tallest building in the monastery. We could look down and see the monks' cells on one side of the monastery and several lecture halls and five temples on the other. At one time the compound also held spacious libraries, an observatory and ten ponds and garden courts. Dr. Prasad thought there were no community kitchens, and that the places we saw that we thought were for ovens might instead be for sauna baths. We did much tramping up and down, and our guides kept talking about layers, how the monastery had been built up over centuries. I asked one of them how tall Stupa Three was, and he didn't know: "Archaeologists don't talk about heights, only about layers." For Nalanda is very old. No one knows exactly when it was built, but it has existed for at least a millennium.

During the five years he stayed here, Xuanzang, when he wasn't studying and preaching, went around the countryside on an elephant. He was a highly honored guest. Of course he visited Vulture Peak, the place where the Buddha gave some of his most famous sermons. The place is like the mountainside at Capernaum where Jesus is said to have delivered the Sermon on the Mount. So we climbed the giant rough-cut stone steps of the Bimbisara Road, just as Xuanzang had done. The peak is not very high, and the countryside with its striated rocks reminded me a little of our Southwest. Nonetheless, it commands a fine view of the valley and is said to be shaped like a vulture. The peak is very famous. (Curiously enough, we were followed on this walk by a soldier shouldering a gun—was I still a diplomat's wife?)

We also visited a Xuanzang Memorial Hall nearby, which Chou En-lai had dedicated in 1956. It was built to house collections of Chinese Buddhist scriptures and significant relics from China. At that happy time, the Indian Prime Minister received financial support for this hall from the Dalai Lama and the Panchen Lama of Tibet. The hall is a beautiful Chinese-style building with graceful eaves, that stands beside one of the largest irrigation tanks in the area. But Chinese-Indian relations were severely strained by the Chinese invasion of 1962, and the relics promised by Chou En-lai were never sent. The shell of the building was empty in 1985 when I visited. Chinese leaders since Chou En-lai have been much more insular and were not at all interested in improving China's cultural relations with India.

I had been looking forward to hearing Rajiv Gandhi give a political speech in a neighboring town that night, but he made his appearance an hour early. By the time we got there the crowds were dispersing. I was so disappointed, for I had hoped to report on politics in Bihar state for Howard.

Before we left, we visited the Nalanda Institute with its accumulation of ancient manuscripts—a huge collection of Korean, Tibetan, and Cambodian works, all of the Chinese Tripitaka, plus all of Xuanzang's works in Chinese that had been presented by Chou En-lai in 1956. It was a scholar's dream. As a parting gift I was given a fine book on the history of Nalanda.

I was sorry to leave this peaceful countryside near Nalanda, where the noises are those of men shouting at their cattle, the jingle of bells on the little cart-horses, and the birds singing. The peasant women had spread their harvested grains to dry on the cement driveway in front of the Rest House. The next morning when we left our lodging in the Rest House, we skirted the harvested grain in the driveway.

We drove for two hours to Patna, a large city on the Ganges River. Ted Riccardi of Columbia University had arranged for us to meet with the eminent Dr. Gustav Roth, head of the Nava Nalanda Mahavihara.

This is an Institute for postgraduate teaching and research in Pali language, Literature and Buddhist Studies, functioning under the Department of Culture. After our first bath in a week—pleasurable albeit in cold water—Maya and I had tea with Dr. Roth. What a charming, erudite spell binder he was! Trained at Göttingen University, he knew dozens of languages. He was perfectly charming to Maya, saying how great Indians are because they are tolerant of all religions and because their religious temples are still alive.

Dr. Roth's ideas and queries came forth at two hundred words a minute. Their range and depth blew my mind. "How had the monks and monasteries gotten started in Christianity?" Then he answered himself, "They came from Tumshuk and Kizil on the Northern Silk Road in China. There were Christians there, and they brought the ideas of shaven heads, ringing of bells, communities of monks to the West." Near the end of our visit I learned that as a child after World War I, Dr. Roth had been fed by the Quaker Speisung feeding program. I was intrigued by this, since Howard had also worked with refugees in Europe for the American Friends Service Committee during World War II.

At a final dinner on the last night of our travels together, Maya and I discussed her children and mine, the next generation and their values, our generation and its values. She had a married son, an engineer in Bombay, whose wife worked, and had young chidren and no help, just like my daughter and son-in-law. Both of us regretted the dispersal of extended families under pressure of modernization.

It was several years before we were able to go to Pakistan. During that time I wrote an article for *Archaeology* magazine on Xuanzang's journeys on the Northern Silk Road in China. This article was a landmark for me, and I remember Howard saying when it first came out in 1987 that I must feel like a young doctor who has gotten a first article published in the *New England Journal of Medicine*.

On this 1988 trip we went to Pakistan first, then to Sri Lanka, and finally spent a few days in New Delhi at the end. Howard has always insisted on going into the field to get the feel of things, what people are thinking, and this is true for me too.

Since Pakistan is sometimes called the second Buddhist Holy Land, I was delighted when I could join Howard on another trip to Asia. Photographs and pictures were an important part of telling Xuanzang's story, so I wanted to take pictures of the sites, the stupas, the ruins of the monasteries that I know he visited or might have seen. Then, too, I needed to keep haunting the museums, for many of the ancient monasteries were in ruins; in museums were the bas reliefs and statues that Xuanzang must have seen, especially at Lahore and Peshawar.

The Lahore Museum is the House of Wonders that Rudyard Kipling wrote about in *Kim*. The first page begins with Kim sitting (illegally) on the ancient gun, ZamZamma, outside the House of Wonders. Kim befriends an ancient Tibetan lama fingering his rosary, and takes him inside the museum:

> Kim clicked round the self-registering turnstile; the old man followed and halted amazed. In the entrance hall stood the Graeco-Buddhist sculptures done, the savants know how long since, by forgotten workmen whose hands were feeling, and not unskillfully, for the mysteriously transmuted Grecian touch. There were hundreds of pieces, friezes of figures in relief, fragments of statues and slabs crowded with figures that had encrusted the brick walls of stupas and viharas of the North Country, and now dug up and labeled, made the pride of the Museum. In open-mouthed wonder, the Lama turned to this and that, and finally checked in rapt attention before a large alto-relief representing a coronation or apotheosis of the Lord Buddha. . . .
> "The Lord! it is Sakya Muni himself the Lord," the Lama half sobbed.[28]

And then Kim introduces him to the white bearded Englishman, Director of the Museum (who is based on Kipling's father, Lockwood Kipling). Together the ancient Tibetan lama, with his yellow wrinkled face, and the museum director tour the museum. They gaze at the very Gandharan art that I came to see, the Buddhist art of eastern Afghanistan and Pakistan that shows Greek and Roman influence. I was as excited as the Tibetan lama, because in the middle of the Gandharan room was a partially reconstructed stupa, a bell-shaped structure which is the principal form of Buddhist architecture all over Asia. Originally stupas were burial mounds or sepulchers and contained holy relics or scriptures. An elaborate symbolism grew up around the stupa; its form and meanings have continued to evolve. The symbolism varies, but it has come to be known as a cosmic diagram in which the dome represents heaven sheltering the interior as a world mound. The stupa also stands for nirvana, the ultimate goal and highest consummation of all Buddhists.

I had known white shining stupas in Sri Lanka, and had never forgotten the Shwedagon Pagoda, the gilded spires of the huge stupa looming over Rangoon in Burma. On the Indian subcontinent, stupas are usually earth-colored. Halfway down this particular huge bell-shaped stupa, which is at least twenty feet tall, were bas reliefs at waist height depicting the life of the Buddha. So a pilgrim like Xuanzang would circumambulate just such a stupa looking at each scene—His Birth, His First Sermon, His First Miracle—just as a Christian at Easter time would contemplate and pray before the Stations of the Cross as he moved around a cathedral.

I too could walk around, examining each of the stories relating to the Buddha's life. I knew many of them from Xuanzang's book, for he retells these stories with relish. Buddhists all over Asia know them too, just as a Christian knows the Flight into Egypt, the Birth of Christ, the Crucifixion or the Resurrection. These stories about the Buddha I had seen on the walls of monasteries on the Northern Silk Road and in the Dunhuang Caves.

Before we left the museum, a young public relations girl in a red sari told me that she had majored in English and loved the odes of Keats and Elizabeth Barrett Browning. "How is it that you like such Romantic poets?" I asked. She smiled and said, "Isn't there a love of the romantic in everyone?"

Our next stop was Taxila, which we had visited before. I remembered the figure of the Double Eagle among the ruins of one

of the ancient cities. On our previous visit we had just come from
Russia, where we had seen the Double Eagle as part of the
Romanov coat of arms. So I knew a little about Taxila and its
archaeological remains of three very ancient cities. Alexander the
Great had been here in 316 B.C.E. Taxila is located in a eleven-
mile-long valley, enclosed on three sides by mountains but open on
the fourth, the west—the direction from which the White Hun
invaders came. This time I was interested in the Buddhist
monasteries. I learned that Jaulian, one of the best preserved of
them all, crowns a 300-foot hill above the ancient cities.

I climbed up to Jaulian, where I found myself trying to
imagine robed monks quietly going about their devotions in the
monastery, with its golden domes and spires. Then they would
descend to one of the ancient towns to beg for alms. Perhaps as
they made their way down, they could see roads filled with horse-
drawn carts; occasional donkeys bearing farmers kicking their
flanks; grazing cows. They would pass by women grinding spices
in mortars; shopkeepers squatting by their stalls on the main
streets, haggling with their customers; or heavily-laden nomad
camel caravans winding their way through the streets. So too,
Xuanzang, after staying in the monastery, would descend to one
of the ancient cities to talk with traders about the price of food,
where they had come from or where they were going, who was
running things, the legends of the place. Did he pick up the story
of the local dragon in the bazaar or in the monastery? How did he
know how large the kingdom was? How did he learn what there
was to know so that he could write about its size, its rulers, its
principal crops, its people?

I had written ahead to Dr. Fidaullal Sehrai, the director of the
museum in Peshawar, whose fine reputation preceded him. This
was our next stop. I was looking forward to our meeting. I had
brought along my *Archaeology* article to give to him. Howard
came with me to the museum to meet him too. We discovered that
Dr. Sehrai had been to Sri Lanka and America: a well-traveled,
well-spoken art historian. Howard left, and as Dr. Sehrai glanced at
my article, I began to feel that he was taking me seriously; I was
not just a white-haired old lady in tennis shoes.

Dr. Sehrai was a very erudite man who spoke fluent English as well as many other languages. He is a boldly handsome Pathan, a famous tribal people of both Pakistan and Afghanistan who are noted for their bravery and their self-confidence. His face was animated as he he talked about how, in the Gandharan art that flourished in Pakistan and Afghanistan, it was the life of the Buddha from his birth to his death that was distinctive. This is a historical Buddha, whereas the Indian Buddhas tend to be idealized Buddhas. Dr. Sehrai had written an excellent pamphlet for the general public called *The Buddha Story in the Peshawar Museum*, an enterprise rare indeed for a museum director anywhere, let alone in Asia where, although erudition and scholarship are stressed, little attention is devoted to the ordinary museum goer. When I commented on how useful his pamphlets were—there were others on Buddhist monasteries around Pakistan—he said that he had gotten the idea from "those very useful little pamphlets you Americans have on the Wild West and the Indians."

Before I left, he leaned forward. "Interesting," he began, "we've just had Takada Koin, a Japanese monk visiting from the Yakushiji temple in Japan. He was carrying the relic bones of the Chinese pilgrim in a little box around his neck. I believe he was following in his footsteps around Pakistan and India."

I didn't think much about it at the time, but eleven years later I would go to Yakushiji temple where the Japanese monk had been an abbot. Subsequently, too, I would learn what an extraordinary man Takada Koin had been.

There are several schools of thought about where the making of Buddha images may have originated. Some are sure it is Gandhara in Pakistan, but others claim that the practice really comes from Mathura in India. So after we returned to New Delhi, I thought I ought to go to Mathura to learn more. I also wanted to go where Xuanzang may have gone. A friend lent me his driver and car. Himani Lal Khanna, who has the innate dignity and grace of many Indian women, went with me. She had been a student of Howard's at Vassar many years before. On our three-hour drive we swerved around camels, donkeys, mopeds, horses, bicycles, buses and trucks, lurching every which way so that we were slightly carsick on arrival. We found the director of the museum sitting in an inner garden courtyard, reading reports by daylight: the electricity was off in his office and the museum.

It was noon time, so we had a picnic on the lawn in the front of one of the museum buildings. We were joined by Mr. Misra, a young photographer, slim with the narrow hips young Indians sometimes have. He showed us a cardboard box filled with his photographs, many of them of a very high quality. The red sandstone Buddhas were so beautiful it was hard to choose, and I took many more than I would use just because I liked them so much. I also bought a photograph of a statue of King Kanishka of the Kushan dynasty, one of the great patrons of both Buddhist and secular art in the second century. It is a splendid statue which shows him with his powerful hands resting on his sword and his mace. The king is clad in a long-skirted coat and heavy padded boots; after all, he was a nomad from the North. The inscription on his skirt says "King Kanishka, King of Kings." His farflung empire had three capitals, in Mathura, Peshawar and Begram. Xuanzang had seen the remains of Kanishka's famous stupa in Peshawar.

As we were leaving the Mathura Museum grounds, we passed by part of a railing with pillars of the kind that sometimes surround a stupa or relic mound in a sacred enclosure—only these pillars were carved with very voluptuous ladies standing in evocative poses. One of them was a Yakshi (fertility goddess) with full rounded breasts "like a heavily laden fruit tree," broad hips and a slim waist. She was bedecked with earrings, a necklace, a broad hip band, bracelets, biceps ornaments and anklets. Himani inspected the Yakshis closely and exclaimed, "I have some of the same jewelry!" I couldn't believe it, for the sexy ladies are usually thought to have been carved around the second century.

Before we left, Mr. Misra stopped and said, "I always ask people why these pillars were part of Buddhist monasteries, just to see what they will say."

Himani Lal Khanna had an answer while I was still trying to think of one. Then Mr. Misra answered his own question. "To tempt the monks? No, because we are human and must overcome all our desires."

These yakshis not only have a long and remarkable past, but some art historians feel that they represent the Indian ideal of feminity. Bare-breasted courtesans were carved on ivory coffers discovered in the excavations of the Kushan capital. The poses, the clothing and jeweled accessories of the female figures in these archaeological finds were identical to those of the Mathura railings. I saw them when I visited the Kabul Museum in the 1970s.

Would Xuanzang have noticed these worldly ladies on the Mathura railings? Probably not, because he always seemed to be totally absorbed by his Buddhist studies wherever he went.

Chapter 15

XUANZANG: A BUDDHIST PILGRIM ON THE SILK ROAD

I and Pangur Ban my cat,
'Tis a like task we are at:
Hunting mice is his delight
Hunting words, I sit all night.

Tis a merry thing to see
At our tasks how glad are we,
When we sit at home and find
Entertainment to our mind.

'Gainst the wall he sets his eye,
Full and fierce and sharp and sly;
'Gainst the wall of knowlege I
All my little wisdom try.

So in peace our task we ply,
Pangur Ban, my cat, and I.
In our arts we find our bliss,
I have mine and he has his.

Like Pangur Ban, the cat in the traditional Irish poem,[29] I do my best hunting in the middle of the night. I usually work with my mind in the daytime doing research, and at night I seem to be drawing on my unconscious feelings. I wake usually around 2:00 a.m. and order what I have done according to intuitive principles. What seemed dry and intellectual during the day is now enriched. Long sentences grow shorter, my mind makes connections, sorts out ideas and feelings in a way that doesn't happen during the day. Creative energy seems to flow and I jot down words and ideas for deciphering the next day.

This doesn't always work. After chiseling each word in a preface I was writing, I had the feeling that I was trying to create a person, draw a person, write about a person, without really writing about a person. The only thing comparable I can remember is when I took a painting class from Ben Summerford at American University in the sixties. The assignment was to build up the reality of a still-life without *outlining anything.* A bottle had to be a bottle not by drawing its outline but by darks and lights and by creating space around the bottle to suggest its shape. I had the feeling that I was trying to do that in writing, not by drawing the outline—that is, by *telling*—but by showing masses next to it. But it was even more complicated, more difficult than that. The thing had to emerge out of three-dimensionality, the way a sculptured form emerges out of a piece of wood, as Ben Booz told me years ago.

I am sure that when I started I wasn't writing both day and night. I was a late convert and had a lot to learn. The fact is that I didn't start writing until I was in my fifties. We had just moved to New York after ten years in Washington, D.C. I joined the Bank Street Writers' Workshop while I was working on the Monkey story. I sent one of my first efforts to Ben Booz, who has been endowed with extraordinary artistic abilities, whether in painting, writing or sculpting. She replied:

> Writing a book is very like the creation of sculpture. First you make an armature, as notes in a card file or your head if you are a writer, with wire if you are a sculptor. This allows you to see and adjust the parts in relation to one another, look at

the thing as a whole. The second stage is to cover with an abundance of material—words if you are an author, clay if you are a sculptor. It is very hard work. When I am at this stage, beating away endlessly at the typewriter, I can clearly visualize myself standing in a pit, shoveling the heavy, set clay and throwing it by the shovelful onto the metal skeleton. When the skeleton is all covered, it will retain the proportions and the thrust of the underlying armature. The third stage is to work over the entire surface, cutting away, refining, clarifying, occasionally embellishing, rewriting if you are an author, modeling, molding, tooling if you are a sculptor.[30]

A decade later, I was at the second stage in the Xuanzang book when a chance meeting with Dr. Fritz Mote changed my book, my attitude toward Xuanzang, and my life. In May 1983, I sat next to Dr. Mote at a Princeton-in-Asia dinner, an organization that sends eighty students each year to Asia. Howard was on the board, our brother-in-law Bob Atmore ran it, and we had many friends in Princeton. I had never met Dr. Mote before. I bless whoever was in charge of seating that night.

For some reason, I didn't try to reach out to learn about him or about his interests in Asia. Almost right away I began talking about what a great man Xuanzang was. Once I sensed that he knew something about Xuanzang and was receptive, I kept going. I could feel my excitement rising. Usually people's eyes glaze over. And when this didn't happen, I went on and on. I didn't want to stop.

Perhaps if I had known then that he was a distinguished professor of Chinese history at Princeton who had written many books, I would have been more restrained. He was such a good listener that I didn't find out until later that he had a deep personal interest in China. He had met his wife, Hsiao-lan, in Nanking. She was a superb cook and an accomplished potter. I didn't even realize, until we were getting up from our chairs, that he was a good friend of Jeannette Mirsky.

Fritz kept asking me questions, so I also didn't find out until much later that he had served in Burma and China during World War II. He had had army interpreter's training and spoke Chinese, but he first started reading the language on a long, slow transport voyage to India. Chinese fellow passengers lent him a novel by Pa Chin and helped him with it. In China, he graduated in 1948 from Nanking University, where he was the first non-Chinese to be elected to the Chinese equivalent of Phi Beta Kappa. Fritz was brilliant even as a student. The rest of his career—writing *The Intellectual Foundations of China*, several histories of China for Cambridge University Press, and just recently another book on Imperial China—was China-oriented. All his books stemmed from his love of China and the Chinese. I seemed to remember his asking once, "What other civilization is there?"

Fritz Mote was not very tall; he might even have been described as a little portly. His eyes? Were they green or grey? He had an air of ease and contentment with life. His voice was soft and measured and he laughed a lot, a warm, sympathetic laugh, often tossing his head back as he chuckled. He personified gentleness and intellectual modesty. His words were always very precise. He was often eloquent. Sometimes I thought he looked like a Chinese sage, or a Lohan, the kind you see in Chinese temples.

Fritz counselled me in most unusual ways. I remember especially when Jeannette Mirsky died in 1987; he spoke at her memorial service in Princeton. It was as if he were addressing me alone. He spoke of her trailblazing books on the history of exploration, including one on Chinese travelers that included a chapter on Xuanzang. For Jeannette had written about historical geography, and the history of exploration in the Arctic, Central Asia and China. In praising Jeannette for her creativity, he was also challenging me to follow her example.

Along with suggesting new sources, urging me to make a connection with UNESCO in Paris, or telling me about books in Chinese that I ought to have translated, Fritz described many incidental things about Xuanzang, the way you might tell a friend something about her ancestors.

Some years after this first meeting, and after my book had gone through many revisions, he wrote:

> It delights me that your friend Xuanzang is coming along so well. His indomitable spirit does not allow him to do otherwise. The additions and revisions of the material sound as if I will read quite a different piece of work when I see it and I am sure it grows in depth and interest as these developments occur.[31]

The most important change related to my discovery of *Mirror in the Shrine*[32] by Robert Rosenstone. I vividly remember looking at the books on the tables of the Corner Bookstore at 94th Street and Madison Avenue in New York, thumbing through the pages. I found it quite by accident. I was intrigued by the fact that Rosenstone could provide a multi-voiced narrative through the use of some of the techniques of the modern novel. Was it really possible to have several voices in a history book? I was fascinated with the way he wrote—so unlike any book I had ever read before. Rosenstone actually tells the reader that some of his sources are dull or impossible. He employs italics now and then to indicate a different voice.

I had been thinking of my book as a kind of cultural history, perhaps because my sources were so ancient—Xuanzang's report to the Emperor and his biographer's account are both from the seventh century. I didn't see clearly that most biographers have the same problem I was having. Think of the poetry of John Donne and consider Izaak Walton's biography of him. Think of what Gertrude Stein said about Picasso. So when I found *Mirror in the Shrine*, I began to wonder if I couldn't separate the dry history account from the dramatic stories of how Xuanzang nearly died of thirst crossing the desert, or how the pirates nearly burned him at the stake?

Could I do something like that, using italics for the pilgrim's biography and regular print for the principal narrative? I had been daunted by the problem of how to combine the pilgrim's dry and accurate report to the Tang Emperor with the dramatic stories his biographer told. What was worse, Xuanzang had evolved into the Chinese folk hero Tripitaka, who conquered all in order to bring Buddhist scriptures to China. This transformation from history to folklore made my task especially difficult. Like George Washington, he was and is best-known for these appealing folk stories. They overshadow everything else he did—his great work as a translator of Buddhist scriptures into Chinese, even his 10,000-mile journey to India and back.

Chalk and cheese? Apples and oranges? Not exactly, but the undertaking required two very different voices—a dry history voice and one that points to the long story-telling tradition about Xuanzang's exploits. They were good stories. By using poetic language and by putting them in italics, I could show the reader right away they were coming from a different source. I would try. I wanted to make Xuanzang as exciting to others as he was to me.

I always knew that I wanted to focus my book on interpreting his journey through art. Buddhist art gives meaning to Xuanzang's quest. This approach isn't so tidy, of course; it amounts to "hints followed by guesses."

I remember years ago in Quaker Meeting we were talking about Inner Landscapes that mean the most to us, the places we go to escape the tiresome and the discouraging. I was able to share Albert Camus's idea that "art springs from the attempt to discover the image, the place upon which the heart first opened." For me, this was my discovery at age sixteen of the Khmer Buddha sandstone head in the Seattle Art Museum. The sandstone head with the downcast eyes and elusive smile emitted such tranquility, such peace, and a kind of mystery: I wanted to penetrate, to understand.

This world was closed to me by World War II. Asia had become the enemy. Then through our Asian travels in the fifties and sixties, I rediscovered Buddhist art. So now my inner landscapes are the Kannon Buddha in Japan, and the beautiful Chinese cave art of Lungmen, Yungang or Dunhuang whose forms, feelings and spiritual purity are not unlike those of early Christian art. They are what move me, what may have led me to write about Xuanzang, the Buddhist monk.

I was always in danger of allowing my intellectual curiosity—the why of things—to overpower my feelings. One part of me knew how important feelings are, but I needed help in learning to tap them. My work with the Jungian analyst showed me how to be more aware of my dreams, of the unconcious, to ask myself how I felt, how Xuanzang felt—rather than establishing facts and exploring historical forces. Dr. Wallace helped show me that my feelings for Xuanzang, my sense of wonder, would propel me forward and lead to new insights that would make my writing better. She was right.

When I wrote to Friz Mote about my pictorial history, about using photographs for my book, he commented, "Photos about your subject (or are you his subject?) would be welcome." He concurred that diagrams of archaeological sites, plans, maps and other graphic material would enhance my book.

Since the early eighties, when Americans were first starting to be interested in the Silk Road, I had been collecting photographs for slide presentations, then for my article on the Northern Silk Road for *Archaeology*. I needed the permission of museums and publishers to use their images for both the article and the book I had finally decided to write. It took several years of tedium and complication to accumulate the requisite permissions, as well as a good-sized collection of images that I put in a blue plastic binder. I took the binder to the next Princeton-in-Asia dinner. Fritz looked at my portfolio of sixty pictures and suggested, in a very tactful way, that for people who didn't know the subject, it would be useful if the pictures had captions explaining what they were and where they were from.

Picture research was fun. What was in my portfolio? How did I choose certain pictures? Well, there were wall paintings of Xuanzang from Buddhist caves; the Buddha, Bodhisattvas; kings and queens Xuanzang had met; stone bas reliefs and site maps from monasteries; Buddhist temples and stupas; the monasteries themselves; the summit and a gorge in the Pamirs; a pagoda; a votive tablet; Buddhist scrolls. All Silk Road sites, scenes and artifacts related to the story I was telling.

For years I had also been collecting maps. One of my fattest files was labeled "Wonderful old maps of India, Central Asia and China." I sent some of the best ones to a young man named Phil Schwartzberg who was recommended to me by his father, the author of *The Historical Atlas of South Asia*. Phil was a very able cartographer who lived in Minneapolis. I talked to Phil many times on the phone; I got so familiar with his voice that I would recognize his nasal twang anywhere. We worked together for a year and more. (He would show me that Khotan was also Hotan and the Cherchen was also Quiemo.) At first I sent him maps I had found in Sweden that were made by Sven Hedin, the famous explorer; Aurel Stein's magnificent maps; maps of Younghusband and other explorers. Phil must have enjoyed seeing these maps, as well as the map in Thomas Watters's original translations of *Yuan*

Chwang's Travels in India, for it is a work of art. He himself produced gorgeous maps, which really give a sense of Xuanzang's 10,000-mile journey.

Earlier when Fritz Mote was approaching the Smithsonian Press about publication of my book, he wrote to me:

> I also said preposterous things about you. Hope you will forgive me. More important, I hope that what I have said will give you the opportunity to speak for yourself there. . . . Then my preposterous comments will no longer be of any significance. I will keep my fingers crossed. Your saint will be interceding for you. Anything could happen.[33]

For twenty years, Fritz was my mentor. We visited him in his home in the mountains of Colorado where he had retired. At that time he was working on his last book, *Imperial China: 900–1800*, 1,106 pages long with fine maps by Phil Schwartzberg, whom I had recommended to him. It was published before he died in March 2005.

I had finished the research. I had the style in which I wanted to present the material. I had the maps, photographs and charts that were needed to show where Xuanzang had been and what he saw. I had also completed the picture research that illuminated yet another part of that background. My agent, Carolyn Gilbert, felt that it was time to submit the book—still not finished—to publishers.

"Non-fiction publishers," she explained to me, "like to be involved in the way a book is put together." A publisher like W.W. Norton might want something heavy on narrative without much art, whereas Chronicle Books would go for fewer words, more pictures. Yale University Press would want footnotes, while Perseus Publishing would prefer endnotes. "Let's send out what you have and see what publishers have to say."

Then in 1992, I met Ellen Roberts. I had recently had lunch with Peggy Thomson, a much-published author, who mentioned that Ellen, too, had gone to Reed College, and recommended her highly.

Ellen was a lively woman with deep brown eyes. Her voice, her way of talking and laughing, her zest were magical. After Reed, she had worked as an acquisitions editor at St. Martin's, William Morrow and Prentice-Hall. She did a stint as Sales Manager at Columbia University Press; that led her to decide that the only part of publishing that interested her was working with writers. She described the company she founded to assist authors, Where Books Begin, as a well-baby clinic for new book projects.

Ellen and I saw each other every Monday morning in the Cornelia Otis Skinner room at the Cosmopolitan Club in New York. In this cozy library of theater memorabilia, just down the hall from the Coz's wonderful two-story library, we began to organize the material I had gathered, cutting away, refining, clarifying, occasionally embellishing, rewriting, hoping the whole book would someday emerge as Ben Booz described the emergence of a sculpture.

The mornings I liked best were when we were reaching out for incongruities, new juxtapositions and not just simple ironies, or trying to put together ideas that had never been put together before—in short, creating. Ebullient, funny, enormously capable— I reveled in her company and she enjoyed mine.

We worked together for four years. We added a glossary with a gazetteer. We accumulated rejection slips from twenty publishers that Carolyn had approached: the subject was too obscure. Where on earth was Central Asia anyway? A Chinese pilgrim with an unpronounceable name, walking somewhere in Asia during the Middle Ages, gathering religious relics and transporting Buddhist scriptures?

Then in June 1994, at a meeting of the Institute of Current World Affairs—a small and effective organization that sends Fellows to foreign countries for two years with the obligation to write one letter a month—Howard and I were talking to Doake Barnett, an Asian scholar. "Well, had you thought of Westview Press out in Colorado?" We hadn't, but Carolyn sent the manuscript off to them.

Susan McEachern at Westview liked it. She referred the manuscript to my old friend, Morris Rossabi, for an evaluation; in his report, he praised my book to the skies. Morris had been answering my questions about Central Asia for years. "Morris, what should I do? Is it worth while trying to translate Grousset's *Empires of the Steppes of Central Asia*?" Now, at last, I could say, "Morris, thank you."

Just to be sure Westview Press got to "yes," one snowy day before Christmas Howard and I rushed to Kennedy Airport to send off a huge poster about the book that Ellen and I had prepared. The poster folded down to 9" x 12", but once unfolded, it revealed sixteen color pictures as well as captions from the book to show how various elements came together under the umbrella of Xuanzang's life. I am sure this helped Susan to convince her board that they should accept my book, though she confessed later that the chief editor was color-blind and therefore couldn't truly appreciate the color photographs I had submitted.

My happiness at finding a publisher and receiving a contract was not unalloyed. The day the contract arrived was also the day that Carolyn Gilbert died of cancer. I was one of only a few people who knew that she was so afflicted.

Not long afterwards Ellen sent me this poem by Jan Morris.

> At the end of a sentence I will call for tea
> At the end of a paragraph bread and b.
> At the end of a page chip potatoes plus hake
> At the end of a chapter fillet steak.
> But ah! when I finish the ultimate line
> When I've brought to fulfillment the grand design
> When I look at the thing and it's mine, all mine
> Then it's oysters, my lovely, and cold white wine.[34]

When a new edition of *The Silk Road Journey with Xuanzang* came out in 2003, I dedicated it to Fritz Mote:
"Source of inspiration and unending support."

PART SEVEN
REUNIONS: SRI LANKA, JAPAN, AFGHANISTAN

Chapter 16

SAD RETURNINGS
TO SRI LANKA
1988

After a few weeks in India and Pakistan, where Howard was pursuing his political interests and I was haunting museums and stomping around archaeological sites, we returned to Sri Lanka for the first time since our departure from the Embassy in 1980. By this time Howard had retired from his many years of teaching and from running, with the close collaboration of Professor Ainslie Embree, the Southern Asian Institute at Columbia University. We were living in Riverdale, north of Manhattan.

So much had happened in Sri Lanka since we left. Even from America, we knew that the turning point had come in 1983 when, for four days, Colombo had been ruled by chaos. The incident igniting the flames was a botched funeral in Colombo for thirteen Sinhalese soldiers who had been killed by Tamil terrorists in Jaffna in the north. There had been a delay in flying in the bodies of the dead soldiers—enough time for Sinhalese chauvinists among the mourners to arouse the anger of the impatient crowd. Embittered Sinhalese mobs—some of them with lists of Tamil-owned properties, others with vehicles or trucks from government ministries—rampaged through Tamil neighborhoods in Colombo, killing several thousand innocent Tamil victims, smashing and burning hundreds of Tamil-owned factories, hotels and shops. Thousands of Tamils fled to India. The President had done nothing to control the violence, and finally, after four days of silence, he issued a statement that laid the blame on the victims. One could almost hear him say, "What could I do?" He didn't dare to use the police or the army against such widespread Sinhalese rage; he lost his nerve.

This provocation radicalized many hundreds of young Tamils in Colombo and in the North who hitherto had been sitting on the fence. They quickly became recruits to one of the four separatist organizations calling for Tamil Eelam, a separate Tamil state.

When we revisited Sri Lanka in 1988, we were shocked by the changes we saw. Our first home in Cinnamon Gardens had become the headquarters of the Army Reserve; the balconies had been enclosed and the garage enlarged. Young men with their would-be-beards stood on nearly every street corner with their Kalashnikov rifles. I went to see Spittel's Nursing Home, now the Wycherly School, where Jenny had been born. It is on a beautiful street with tall overarching trees, very much the same as it had always been.

I called on my old Buddhist tutor, Kheminda Thera. I remembered being told that he had tried to see me in the Joseph Fraser Nursing Home when I was recovering from a pulmonary embolism, so many years before. Alas, I had left the hospital the day before he came, but I was touched by his concern. I had written him from Bodh Gaya, to which he had replied, in his fine legible hand, with the Middle Length Sayings of the Lord Buddha. I looked forward to talking to him about the polarized politics of his country. He was eighty-four years old.

After we seated ourselves in the open verandah outside his room at the Vajirarama Temple, I asked him, "What has happened to your country?"

"Now it is like this . . . ," and he talked about the strong materialist forces of the previous eight years—TV, video. "These things increase man's desire, man's envy, and therefore the seeds of hatred." He went on to say that many Jaffna Tamils had been educated in British and American missionary schools. The Sinhalese too needed schools and education. They wanted jobs.

"Then?"

"Everything changes. All is suffering. Nothing lasts." (Buddhist phrases, I said to myself.)

"There are many forces that destroy," he continued. "They are all around us. It is for this reason that we must meditate on Buddha, on loving kindness."

I persisted, for I wanted a comprehensive story. "But why did all this trouble arise?"

"It is all in here," he said and went back to his bookshelves and came back with *The Middle Length Sayings*:

> And again monks, when sense pleasures are the cause, sense pleasures the provenance, sense pleasures the consequence, the very course of sense pleasures, kings dispute with kings, nobles dispute with nobles . . . householders dispute with householders, a mother disputes with her son. . . . Those who enter into quarrels, contentions, dispute, attack one another with their hands, and with stones and with sticks and with weapons, these suffer dying and pains like dying.[35]

Automatic rifles were much worse, I thought. However, I knew that there were many activist priests, unlike Kheminda Thera, who were in the forefront of the political struggle. These priests insisted that Sir Lanka be a Sinhalese Buddhist state wherein Tamils would exist by sufferance and not by right. I also remembered from our first stay in Sri Lanka in the 1950s that it was the Buddhist high priest, Buddha Mapitigama Rakita, who was known to be having an affair with the Minister of Health, and who was later also found guilty of conspiracy leading to the assassination of Prime Minister Bandaranaike.

We returned to Sri Lanka again in 2000. Powerful forces on the island had been at work in our absence this time and deserved to be explored. Prime among them was the success of the Tamil Tigers. What was happening? The Tamil Tigers were generally thought to have assassinated both Rajiv Gandhi, the Prime Minister of India, while he was campaigning in Madras in 1991, and President Premadasa of Sri Lanka in 1993. They carried cynanide capsules around their necks, vowing to kill themselves rather than be caught by the police or the army. The cynanide vial is deliberately exposed hanging on a cord around the neck. It is dear to LTTE (Liberation Tigers of Tamil Eelam) fighters, and there is even a song praising the taking of cyanide. Some of the Tamil Tiger innovations, such as the jacket apparatus worn by individual suicide bombers, are said to have been copied by Al Quaeda and other terrorist groups in Israel and Lebanon. In the early days some LTTE members trained with the Palestine Liberation Organization, and they still come in contact with terrorist organizations through the arms trade.

Before these assassinations, the LTTE had withstood the might of the Indian army, which came as a peace-keeping force and eventually occupied northern Sri Lanka with an army of an estimated 80,000 men. A humiliated Indian force left Sri Lanka in 1989; like the Vietnamese guerrillas, Prabhakaran and his guerrillas had shamed a major power in Asia.

People believed that suicide bombers took a last supper with their charismatic leader, Velupillai Prabhakaran, before they sacrificed their lives. He assured them of their place in history and told them that a hero's pillar would be erected for each martyr. Prabhakaran began organizing as early as 1976, hoping to found an independent Tamil state. Even before 1983, the Tamil Tigers had robbed banks and assassinated government officials and members of rival groups, but their first serious conflict with the Sri Lankan government was in 1983, when Tamil secessionists killed an army patrol. This marked the point of no return. They have been charged with 200 assassinations. Since that time 64,000 people have been killed in this civil war.

The Tiger leader Velupillai Prabhakaran, born November 26, 1954, was a ruthless self-taught military leader with a huge grievance against the Sri Lankan state. In one of his rare interviews, he spoke of his fascination with Napoleon and Alexander the Great. He was also influenced by the lives of Subhas Chandra Bose and Bhagat Singh, both of whom were involved in the struggle for independence in India. Valupillai Prabhakaran was a member of the Karaiyar caste in the Velvettithurai area on the northeast coast of Sri Lanka. Many of the Karaiyar caste are fishermen and are looked down upon by the privileged and better-educated Vellalas of Jaffna. His resentment against the higher caste helps to explain why he disposed of so many of the Jaffna leaders and their immediate followers in the early days of his struggle for power.

Prabhakaran's local origins gave him other advantages. He and his early followers hailed from a coastal town well-known for its fishing and sea-going tradition, which strengthened the Sea Tigers, the naval wing of the LTTE. This local community has long had trade and family ties with Singapore, where many Tamils, including Prabhakharan's father, had been born. Arms bought from international sources and shipped to Sri Lanka could be unloaded at night and ferried in smaller boats to the many beaches of the northeastern shore.

In reprisal for killings by Sri Lankan forces and for damage to the homes of Prabhakaran and other LTTE leaders, in 1985 the LTTE massacred 150 Buddhist pilgrims at Anuradhapura. One of the Tamil leaders of the Anuradhapura Massacre was killed the next year in a fierce gun battle. Although most of the LTTE were Hindus, there were also Tamil Catholics committed to Tamil nationalism. At the funeral of their leader, a Catholic priest known as Victor Fuseless delivered the eulogy, quoting the gospel according to St. John: "The seed shall not bring forth life unless it fall to the ground and die."

The most significant day on the Tamil Tigers' calender is November 27, when Prabhakaran delivers an annual oration in commemoration of the great heroes of the Tamil Tigers, and announces key slogans for the next year's struggle. An office of Great Heroes was set up in 1995, and care is given to "hero stones as sepulchres." These LTTE practices commemorating their heroes are reminiscent of the Northern Irish landscape, where new memorials to freedom fighters were being built all the time. The memorabilia and rites and even some dramatic performances carried a quality of sacredness for all who were devoted to Tamil Eelam and the LTTE.

Tiger fighters seemed to be drawn mostly from unemployed Tamil youths who faced economic and social discrimination. This is exactly what Punitham had been worried about. Agricultural workers who lost their livelihoods in the economic reforms of the 1970s were also recruited. The LTTE was estimated to have 8,000 to 10,000 combatants in Sri Lanka, among them a core of trained fighters. Nearly one third of the cadre were women. The LTTE raised money in the U.S., Britain, France, Norway, Germany, Sweden, and Canada, for buying weapons and producing propaganda. They maintained offices in forty capitals around the world, which target an estimated 450,000 Tamils who live outside Sri Lanka, and maintained a highly sophisticated communications network that enabled Prabhakaran to keep in touch with the world while living in a secret underground bunker in the jungle in the north of Sri Lanka.

Punitham, as a Tamil, had always worried about increased violence in Sri Lanka. I believe she thought of it in terms of Sinhalese versus Tamils. Then, on July 29, 1999, a Tamil activist killed her son, Neelan Tiruchelvam, who was a Tamil moderate. On the short drive from his home to his office, a suicide bomber on a motorcycle detonated the five-kilo bomb he was carrying. In the intensity of the blast, the car door caved in and Neelan's mutilated body was thrown against the opposite door. The security officer and the driver both survived. The assassin's remains were strewn across the road.

Why had Neelan been targeted? After having prepared his lectures at the Rockefeller Center in Bellagio, in Italy, he was about to go to the U.S. to teach at Harvard Law School. But instead, at the request of the President of Sri Lanka, Neelan returned to Colombo to help with promoting a hopeful legislative proposal in Parliament, a change in the constitution which would favor compromise agreements between the Tamil Tigers and the Sinhalese.

When we heard the news of Neelan's death, we knew that we must go back again to Sri Lanka. We were already making plans when Howard was invited to an international symposium in Neelan's honor. Howard had known Neelan for many years as a distinguished lawyer, a member of Parliament and a leading Sri Lankan moderate who had sought a constitutional solution to Sri Lanka's sixteen-year violent ethnic conflict. Howard had professional reasons for returning, but mine were personal. Even though I hadn't known Neelan very well, I had loved Punitham, and wanted to pay my respects to her family.

I could almost hear Punitham's voice saying, as she did in 1970: "I am terribly worried. I am afraid something awful will happen."

By this time in his career, Neelan was internationally known for his work in constitutional law and human rights. The symposium, held in Colombo in January 2000, brought together people from all over the world to honor Neelan. They discussed, among other subjects, ethnic violence, which has played such a role in Sri Lanka, particularly since the 1983 riots. Just a month before the symposium the LTTE had attempted to assassinate the President; she lost an eye in this attack. Security for the symposium was tight. Nothing happened.

The Prime Minister of India opened the session. Then the South African Judge Albie Sachs took the podium. He spoke about South Africa's effort to overcome its years of division. His calm, almost triumphant, bearing made me forget, and yet not forget, that he only had one arm. (I learned later that he also had only one eye. He had been the victim of a bomb attack during the period of explosive violence in South Africa.) He was so strong and serene that I didn't feel sadness about his arm. In his jail diary, he had described himself as having "a long thin face with high cheekbones, sad in repose and boyish when smiling." So he appeared to me as well.

Judge Sachs began:

"Judges don't usually speak in anecdotes and parables but this is what I am going to do. One day a man named Henry asked if he could see me in my chambers." And he went on to tell the story of

231

Henry, who was part of the group that had planted the bomb in his car. Henry had come to Judge Sachs's chambers for the encouragement he needed in order to go before the Truth Commission and confess what he had done.

Judge Sachs then launched into a discussion of what he called four kinds of law or truth: (1) microscopic truth, the kind lawyers often engaged in when they examine a case in excruciating detail; (2) judicial truth, using the law in its largest sense; (3) experiential truth—he cited Gandhi and his capacity to stand outside himself and look at his subjective experience in a truly objective way; and (4) dialogue-law or truth. "This is knowledge. But it is also 'acknowledgement' or acknowledging that you have done a terrible thing, publicly admitting, publicly describing and publicly asking for forgiveness. This is what we have been trying to establish with Bishop Tutu as the head of the Truth Commission."

The judge described the problems that he and other members of the Truth Commission faced—because the police had done terrible things with official encouragement during the apartheid years. The ANC (African National Congress) had done the same, murdering, mutilating, torturing people, and then getting away scot-free. Understandably, those same security forces had to be brought in so the South Africans could hold the elections that they were determined to have, as they needed to build a new and inclusive society.

In his quiet voice, Judge Sachs said, "It was at this stage, that to reconcile the competing considerations the proposal was made to grant an amnesty to the security forces, but not a blanket or general one. The right to amnesty would be based on each individual coming forward and acknowledging what he or she had done, and then getting indemnity to that extent. In this way the Truth Commission and the amnesty process were linked on an individualized basis. That turned out to be the foundation of the African Truth Commission and the basis for its unprecedented success."

After Judge Sachs had described the work of the Truth Commission with such understated elegance, he sat down. Then he got up again and said, "I forgot to tell you. After a heavy year with the Truth and Reconciliation Commission, I was at a reception late at night. I was tired. I felt someone pull at my sleeve. It was Henry. At first I didn't recognize him. Henry spoke: 'Remember, I came to . . .'" This man had summoned the courage to make his confession to the Truth Commission, and he wanted to shake Judge Sachs's hand and tell him so.[36]

Another judge from South Africa did not agree with Judge Sachs about the Truth Commission. Anyone could get up, tell a story and ask to be forgiven. That was too easy. Where was the evidence? But how else, I wondered, do you ever break the cycle of violence that has gripped both Sri Lanka and South Africa?

Punitham would have been pleased with what Judge Sachs had said. Neelan, who was very gentle like Judge Sachs, would have understood.

At the symposium I saw our old friend, Radhika Coomaraswami, who played a major role in organizing the gathering. She had forgotten how close I was to Punitham's family. She took me by the arm. "Neelan's love of the law came from his father and his love of South Asian culture came from his mother, an extraordinary woman who was involved in Tamil cultural affairs and social work."

I nodded and said, "I know," wanting to tell her that I had been Dushi's godmother. But before I could tell her, someone grabbed her arm and whisked her away. "Radikha, you've got to come . . ."

Even before then, Tamil violence had included new urban targets—the Central Bank in Colombo in 1996, where sixty were killed and 1,500 wounded; the Colombo World Trade Center in 1997. In a shocking incident, suicide bombers rammed into the Temple of the Tooth, Buddhism's holiest shrine in Sri Lanka, in 1998. Again in July 2000, they managed a dramatic suicide bombing in Sri Lanka's International Airport outside Colombo, destroying both men and planes. In 2001 suicide bombers blasted an oil tanker off Sri Lanka's coast.

The LTTE unilaterally declared a cease fire after September 11, 2001. It may be that the international crackdown on terrorist funds, a widespread disdain for suicide terrorism after the destruction of the World Trade Center, or the dwindling support for terror among many Tamils were among the causes. Their forces also were starting to include child soldiers, so perhaps Tamil resources were being depleted. Alas, while formally the cease-fire continued, in effect the war resumed.

*****

Howard met more people who were really impatient with the two Sinhalese political parties. But the Sinhalese political leaders seemed unable to unite against Prabhakaran, the unyielding leader of the Tamil Tigers. There was an eerie sense that "the war" was miles away in some other realm, instead of only 150 miles away in the north of the island. Over 300,000 Tamils and Sinhalese citizens had been displaced. Even though there were many military check points, for the moment, at least, they were casually manned. I wanted to visit Kheminda Thera, but I found that the Vajirarama temple area was blocked off in a high security zone. Very possibly Kheminda Thera was no longer alive.

Before we were to leave I asked to see the Embassy garden. I asked Susan Donnelly, wife of the Ambassador, if we might have a tour together. She was proud to show me the traveller's palms the gardeners had put in while we had been there. They were now over fifty feet tall! The Indian weeping willows were also doing well. The Flame-of-the-Forest tree with its sprays of scarlet branches, the gardenia hedge and the night-blooming cereus were all gone. But the vines with their variegated green and white leaves were now sixty, seventy feet tall. The exotic canon-ball tree, whose large, waxy cream and pink flowers grow right out of the trunk on long stalks, was flourishing. Someone cared, and it showed. And how seldom in life had I been able to see the fruit of our labors, my labors, and the labors of others as well.

*****

After the symposium I saw Janaki, Neelan's sister who, in 1989, had moved to Australia. She was one of the many thousands of Tamils who have emigrated since the troubles began.

234

As we said goodbye, Janaki shared the family news with us: Dushi, the baby I had bought back from the Hindu temple in the 1950s, was now a strapping fellow studying hotel management in Australia. He was outgoing like Punitham, she said. Janaki told me that Neelan had been born on the day of Mahatma Gandhi's assassination.

As we were leaving the island Howard showed me a newspaper clipping. Before he died, Neelan had told Parliament:

> We cannot glorify death whether in the battlefield or otherwise. We, on the other hand, must celebrate life, and are fiercely committed to protecting and securing the sanctity of life, which is the most fundamental value without which all other rights and freedoms become meaningless.[37]

Chapter 17

NEW HORIZONS IN JAPAN

It was a small notice in an academic journal that I just happened to see.[38] "'The Silk Road and the World of Xuanzang,' an exhibition sponsored by Japan's leading newspaper, the Asahi Shimbun group, will take place in three museums: Nara Prefectural Museum 6/12/99, Yamaguchi Prefectural Museum 8/20/99 and Tokyo Toritsu Museum 10/22/99." From that moment, I knew that I wanted to go to Japan.

I wrote to each of the three museums, and enclosed a copy of *Xuanzang: A Buddhist Pilgrim on the Silk Road*. In September, the Yamaguchi Prefectural Museum thanked me and graciously sent me a copy of the exhibition catalogue in return.

How could I find out more about it? I turned to Betty Lou Hummel.

"Betty Lou," I said, almost shouting into the phone, "there's this exhibition about Xuanzang in Japan. Why is it sponsored by a newspaper? Where can I learn more about it?"

Her response was almost instantaneous. "The person to consult is Ginny Anami. Her husband is in the foreign office in Tokyo.

She's American and she teaches Buddhist art at Temple University there. Why don't you write her?"

"Who is she? How did you know her?"

"When Art and I were stationed in Beijing, Ginny and I left our husbands behind and drove from Beijing to Yunnan by car. She knows both Japanese and Chinese. I've known her for years. She's a goldmine. Oh, and if you are seriously thinking of going to Japan, stay at International House, but you must write them immediately."

I did write to Ginny Anami. We ended up having a fascinating email correspondence, and even one long delightful trans-Pacific phone call. When I told her that we were hoping to go to Sri Lanka for the memorial symposium, and that we were thinking of coming home via Japan, she urged me to come.

"We should go to Nara together. I can take you there. There's a Xuanzang temple there called Yakushiji. His relics are there, and it is the leading temple of the Hosso Sect of Buddhism, which considers Xuanzang as one of its founders."

I had long been puzzled about why Japan always claimed to have a special relation to the Silk Road. Ginny's answer was that, in Japan, "the Silk Road boom was like finding their roots, their Buddhism, their music. And of course there was the romance of the unknown, the desert, the mountains . . . And NHK [Japan's leading TV station] brought it right to their doorsteps in a year-long series." Howard and I had seen one of NHK's six Silk Road programs in Citibank in Singapore in 1985. Later the series was shown in the United States and all over the world. Japan and Buddhism were intimately connected, but what was their link to Xuanzang, and how should I pronounce Yakushiji?

On our way to Colombo and Japan we planned a stopover in London to meet Shu Kassen, a Chinese woman whose *nom de plume* is Shu Shunyen. I had been emailing back and forth with her, for she was working on a book on Xuanzang. Judy Thomson, the wife of the British Ambassador to the United Nations, was the one who told her about my book. Shu is a Chinese film producer. Her husband is an economist whom she met while she was studying at Oxford. Our time together was very brief—lunch at their apartment in Headington. Her husband met us at the station and, on the way to their apartment, showed us the very churchyard where John Robinson, the inventor of the chronometer, was buried. Howard had just been reading about him in *Longitude*.[39] It worked out very well: Howard and Robert talked about economics, politics and life at Oxford. Shu served us rambutans, a seedy tropical fruit with a tough red skin, while she asked me questions about Xuanzang.

Shu was much younger than Robert. Like most Chinese, she was black-haired, with black eyes, and full of energy. She had studied English literature at Beijing University. Some time after our visit her book, *Ten Thousand Miles Without a Cloud*,[40] was published. The title refers to a Buddhist saying that refers to the search for a mind clear of doubts. Shu felt that this characterized Xuanzang's journey.

Shu had grown up during the Cultural Revolution. In her book she paints a vivid picture of her revolutionary parents and her aged grandmother, a devout Buddhist, who told Shu the Monkey story, which she loved. When her grandmother was a child her feet had been bound, as was the custom, so that in old age they were so painful that she used to soak them in very hot water at night, and Shu massaged them to help her go to sleep. Shu slept at the end of her grandmother's bed, head to toe, until she went away to college. She used to listen to the click of the beads as her grandmother prayed to the Buddha of Light, "Amitabha, Amitabha, Amitabha."

Everyone in Shu's family made fun of this superstitious old woman. But her rigidly Communist father ended his career a sadly disillusioned man, and her mother committed suicide. In the end, it was her devout grandmother (who had also lost seven children) who bore her pain and suffering better than anyone else. It was also her grandmother who compared Shu to Xuanzang. When Shu was granted a fellowship to Oxford, her grandmother told her about the Buddhist pilgrim who, just like Shu, went far away to another country to find the truth. *Can anyone tell me how this grandmother knew so much about Xuanzang? How was she able to make her imagination leap so far?*

At Oxford, Shu heard an Indian academic talk about Xuanzang's preservation of an important part of India's history.

After two years of intensive reading of Xuanzang, Shu spent a year following in Xuanzang's footsteps in China, India and Pakistan. As a Chinese, Shu was able to penetrate her own culture and follow Xuanzang in ways that I could not. Yet her desire to understand Xuanzang's ideas and feelings, his character and his worth, was similar to mine. Her profound feelings of devotion and piety when beholding the Buddha at Sarnath, her attempts to understand Yogachara Buddhism, struck a responsive chord in me. Shu also did something I have never done: she stayed in a Buddhist monastery for several months to try to understand Buddhism better. She did not become a Buddhist, but remained an observer, one who prefers to understand rather than to believe.

When we went to Japan on our way home from Colombo that January, we stayed at International House, as Betty Lou Hummel had suggested. Ginny Anami and many of her students came to hear me give a lecture on the Silk Road; there were so many questions afterwards that she and I had time only for a warm embrace.

When Ginny, Howard and I met again it was very early in the morning at the Tokyo station where the bullet train to Kyoto comes in. This high speed train would take us to Kyoto, then we would take another train for Nara, and finally a tiny train to a small village outside Nara.

A short woman with black hair, who conveyed a sense of warmth, high energy—it took me a while to realize how "high"—approached Howard and me. It was Ginny, who quickly hustled us onto the right train. Ginny knew the temple buildings at Yakushiji—there were seven of them—where one could see the Buddha's footprint, the temple treasures, the famous statues, relics and murals. She had many friends among the Buddhist clergy at Yakushiji.

Ginny told us part of her story as we rode the bullet train, at 180 miles an hour, on our way to Kyoto and Nara and the Yakushiji temple. Her face was animated. Ginny met her husband Korishege Anami (she always called him "Anami") when they were both studying Chinese in Taiwan. She had studied for her Master's degree at the East/West Center in Hawaii while Anami did graduate work at Harvard.

A native of New Orleans, a graduate of the University of California at Berkeley, Ginny had traveled around the world alone in the sixties. Once she had left Anami in Taiwan, not sure that it was right to commit herself to him. She got as far as Afghanistan and then made a U turn. Ostensibly it was to go back to Taiwan to improve her Chinese, but really it was to find out how serious she was about Anami.

"My father-in-law had been Minister of War at the end of the war, when Japan made peace. The Emperor selected him to announce Japan's defeat by the Allied Forces. So he did what he had to do. He took his sword and plunged it into his stomach. He committed ritual suicide. My mother-in-law wanted to commit suicide too, but she didn't. She eventually became a nun."

"But wasn't his *harakiri* about taking responsibility for the guilt of defeat, and to protect the Emperor?" Howard asked. Ginny continued almost without a pause.

"The Japanese have an expression," she said, "'Talking from the Stomach.' This is what my mother-in-law knew how to do." Ginny and Anami had come from Hawaii with a lei of tropical flowers and Anami had given it to his mother. So when Ginny met her for the first time, her Japanese mother-in-law was wearing the flowers around her neck. Her husband's Samurai armor, complete with mask and helmet, was there on the wall in the sitting room. Her mother-in-law took off the flower lei and hung it over the helmet on the wall, making us all relax immediately. (Was this a signal that love conquers all? I wondered.)

If Anami was to continue his career in the foreign service, Ginny would have to give up her American citizenship within six months of her marriage. Ginny went to the appropriate government building where she could become a Japanese citizen. She anticipated a ceremonial occasion, handshakes, flags, speeches of welcome. Ginny went to the proper office, waited in line. She was sent to a window, an official examined her documents, asked a few questions, picked up his chop, chop-chopped with the official stamp, and it was done. That was all. She was crestfallen. She had made a big decision, a huge commitment—and nothing had happened. Ginny came home and talked to her new mother-in-law, who sensed the situation immediately. The two of them drank cup after cup of sake until they were tight . . . far into the night. Just what Ginny needed.

Ginny's mother-in-law became a nun at Yakushiji temple, the one we were going to see. She had been persuaded by Abbot Gyoing, a distinguished Buddhist scholar. She had taken tonsure, which means shaving the head. "She took the one-hundred-day vows, which included fasting and no talking," said Ginny. "It was very difficult. Some monks try it now and can't do it. This was especially difficult for my mother-in-law because she loved to talk. When Anami was in school in Tokyo, he came out during vacations and used to do chores at the temple. He remembers shining the brass, and climbing up on the roof of the temple." In time, Ginny's mother-in-law was sent to a monastery in the Japanese alps in Nagoya.

At the train station Ginny introduced us to Junkei Yasuda, the wife of the abbot, sometimes called Bishop Yasuda, who was second in command at the temple. I wasn't prepared for the chic, vivacious woman with high cheekbones who greeted us when we arrived. Slim, almost Western-looking, black hair bobbed, Junkei had a cordial openness. She was a photographer. She also taught painting, and had had a show of her work in Beijing.

As we walked along a path from the railroad station, Junkei darted ahead of us snapping photographs now on one side, snap, snap; now the other, snap. Ahead of us were the temples and pagodas of Yakushiji. Howard began taking pictures too. So did Ginny. All this photography made for a very Japanese experience. We approached the bright red Middle Gate of a walled temple compound. Above us, we could see the East Pagoda with its bronze spire at least ten feet tall. Most of the buildings inside were white with green trim, with sweeping eaves and scarlet red doors They looked relatively new. Only the seventh-century Eastern Pagoda and the East building were old; no one had dared to apply bright fresh paint to their beams of brown yew wood.

We met Junkei's husband, Bishop Eyiin Yasuda, a powerful looking man with dark heavy eyebrows, black eyes and a non-committal demeanor. As we drank a welcome cup of tea, I noticed that his countenance was not a grand smiling one, like that of the Dali Lama. He seemed more worldly than spiritual. It was difficult to tell, though, for he spoke no English. He wore a black robe with an ample white scarf on his chest, upon which rested a gold chain; his feet were covered by immaculate white socks and white sandals.

I presented him a copy of *Xuanzang: A Buddhist Pilgrim on the Silk Road*. He lingered over some of the photographs in a way that made me dare to ask him a question. "How did you get interested in Asian archaeology?" I asked, as I sipped my tea.

Junkei translated for her husband. There had been an Afghan student at Nagoya University who took him to Afghanistan forty years before. Since then he and Junkei have traveled all over China, Central Asia, India and Pakistan while they were working on a four-volume book on the Silk Road. When later I looked at Junkei's photographs in their book, I saw that though she and I had visited many of the same places, she had been to the upper reaches of the Indus River, and to parts of Central Asia that I had never seen. Subsequently she gave me her book, as well as remarkable photographs of the Upper Indus River, which is truly "the land farthest out."

During our tour of the temple grounds, Junkei took pictures of the Abbot, Howard and me in front of the Main Hall, the one with the impressive Buddha Triad inside, and also in front of the unfinished Lecture Hall—called the Sutra Building for World Peace. She took us inside, where we were asked to donate tiles for the new roof. Ginny printed our names on two tiles. "Ginny Anami and Howard and Sally Wriggins, February 13, 2000."

I could hardly wait to see the temple known as Genjo Zanzoing, or Xuanzang Temple. Howard took many pictures of its scarlet doors, its interesting hexagon shape. Inside on the altar is a sculpture of Xuanzang. There were no incense sticks to light, so I just stood in front of the altar, thankful that I had been able to come so far to honor him. I still wished for a candle.

Ginny kept talking about a monk, Takada Koin. Sometimes she called him "the walkabout man." Yet it was hard to grasp the many facets of his extraordinary life and what a powerful influence he exerted in Buddhist affairs. I had forgotten about the Japanese monk who had walked around Pakistan with a small black box about eleven years earlier. He was none other than Takada Koin. (When the Japanese occupied Nanjing in 1942 they found the Xuanzang relics and sent them to Yakushiji temple, so these must have been the relics he was carrying.)

Takada Koin was also the abbot of Yakushiji temple, and the mover and shaker behind the restoration of many of its buildings. He was a key figure in persuading Ikuo Hirayama, a well-known Japanese painter, to help him in his Buddhist endeavors.

Buddhist clergy often ask Japanese painters to restore and renew their temples, for there has traditionally been a close relationship between Buddhism and Japanese art. As early as 1971, Ikuo Hirayama had been asked to oversee the design of the main hall at Yakushiji. It was around 1976 that Takada Koin launched a movement to build a special hall dedicated to Xuanzang where everyone could pay homage to his achievements. "You're an artist," he told Hirayama, "you can cooperate by doing the pictures." The painter's long association with the temple culminated in January, 2001 with a grand ceremony in which Hirayama put the final brushstroke on a project he had been working on for twenty years—monumental wall panels dedicated to Xuanzang and his Silk Road journey to India and back to China.

The panels represent events in a single day. They start with the Wild Goose Pagoda in the morning sun; the next panel is Gaochang and the Flaming Mountains in western China on the Northern Silk Road: then there is Jiayuguan Pass, the last outpost of the Great Wall; then Bamiyan Valley in Afghanistan, then the Deccan plateau in India; and finally, Nalanda Monastery by moonlight. There is a faint image in front of Nalanda which some say is Xuanzang—or is it the deceased former head of Yakushiji, Takada Koin, who with Hirayama dreamed up the idea of the murals? The ceiling is a dark blue sky with a moon: the floor is desert-colored tiles.

The formal opening for these huge murals—over six feet in height and 147 feet in total length—was broadcast on NHK, Japanese television. After Hirayama made his symbolic brushstroke, there were speeches and then, for some inexplicable reason, a glamorous opera singer sang "Ave Maria." Perhaps NHK felt that the chanting of monks would not hold a present-day Japanese audience. Hirayama's secretary wrote to me that during that first year an average of 70,000 people a day came to view the murals.

Hirayama's story is a moving one. He was fifteen and attending high school in Hiroshima when the atomic bomb was dropped. Although no physical symptoms appeared at the time, Hirayama was so traumatized that he could not talk about it for a long time. He took up painting as a career. Later, at the very time when he reached an impasse in his painting, medical tests showed a dramatic drop in his white blood cell count. Hirayama thought that he too was about to face death. But he yearned to paint at least one picture that would depict the horror of the atomic bombing and express a prayer for world peace. Rome was about to host the Olympics, and newspaper headlines were announcing that Tokyo had been selected as the next venue. One reporter suggested that the Olympic flames from Greece be carried to Japan along the ancient Silk Road. As though struck by revelation, Hirayama recalled the transmission of Buddhism and Xuanzang's epic search for truth. During this time of personal crisis when he thought he was going to die, he painted a picture of Xuanzang on his way back to China. Hirayama felt that this marked the beginning of his career as an artist. More important, he had found a theme that was to be the source of his physical and psychic well being—Buddhist imagery and the propagation of Buddhism to the East. He became, in short, a Silk Road painter.

Hirayama clearly identified with Xuanzang. In one of his many promotional books he mentioned that Xuanzang traveled for sixteen years and then spent nineteen years translating the Buddhist scriptures he brought back from India. In comparison, Hirayama indicated that he himself traveled on the Silk Road for twenty years and then spent twenty years working on his murals for the Yakushiji temple.

Hirayama was not only wealthy, but generous with his wealth. He received the Smithsonian's highest award for spearheading a drive to raise eleven million dollars for the Freer and Sackler Galleries of Asian art that are part of the Smithsonian Institution. By a curious irony, his first contact with the Smithsonian came at the time when the museum was planning an exhibition of the reassembled Enola Gay, the B-29 that dropped the atomic bomb on Hiroshima. A Japanese newspaper asked him to visit the museum and record his reactions. (Could he ever forget his own traumatic experience at Hiroshima?)

Hirayama had also been generous with his gifts to the British Museum and the Musée Guimet in Paris. In Japan itself, he established an Institute of Silk Road Studies at Kamakura which financed scholarly journals. As if this were not enough, Hirayama has crusaded for the preservation of international monuments such as Dunhuang, Bamiyan, and Angkor Wat. In time, he developed the concept of the Red Cross Spirit of Cultural Heritage, which served the need to rescue "wounded monuments." Hirayama was also a UNESCO Good Will Ambassador.

Before we left Japan, Ginny arranged for me to interview Hirayama in Tokyo. She acted as my interpreter. I had seen many pictures of him, but this spiffily dressed man with wavy gray hair has more the appearance of a wealthy international art collector than an artist. I asked him if his extensive philanthropic activities didn't interfere with his painting. His reply was succinct, his voice was soft. "They energize me," he said, his eyes twinkling behind his glasses.

Hirayama showed me with pride his UNESCO Good Will Ambassador pin. We talked a great deal about international cultural exchanges. His mind ranged freely on how he would like to study Mesopotamia and Syria, how it was that writing developed there, that Christianity had originated in that part of the world. He preferred to think of Japan as part of Asia and part of the world, not as an island nation. Ginny asked me to show him my book, which he examined with interest. "It is a new voice," she explained to him.

I posed the question of my doing an article on the Hirayama murals at Yakushiji, and he seemed responsive. This was published in *Orientations* magazine in 2002.[41]

After almost eighty trips on the Silk Road, Hirayama was still enthusiastic. I marveled at his enthusiasm. He was seventy years old, and gossip has it that his wife once said, "I am sick of going on the Silk Road."

Come to think of it, Howard is probably sick of the Silk Road too.

When we returned to America, I looked more closely at the books Junkei had given me. When we left Yakushiji temple and Junkei said goodbye, she presented me with many gifts, including books on the Silk Road, a small bag for carrying things, and even two boxes of sushi for the train ride back to Tokyo.

I was overwhelmed. So it was quite a while before I was able to examine the two books by Takada Koin. They were in Japanese, so I couldn't read them, but I was fascinated by the photographs of a monk in a black robe and very white socks, wearing sandals even on the roughest mountain paths. The walkabout man looked just like the Abbot of Yakushiji, carrying a small black box in his hands which must have contained Xuanzang's relics. As I turned the pages I recognized the cliffs of the Upper Indus River, ruins of the monasteries where I had been, and a Buddha chiseled in the rocks near Gilgit. This must have been his book about his pilgrimage to Gandharan Pakistan, published in 1988. In the second book, published in 1990, were photographs of the monk in black, before the little caves going up Vulture Peak mountain, the bas reliefs of Nalanda University, the bright flags on the Bo tree at Bodh Gaya—the record of his pilgrimage to India.

If only Takada Koin had been alive when we came to Yakushiji temple. What a lot we would have had to talk about. I wanted to know so much more about why he carried Xuanzang's relics, his working with Hirayama, so many things.

My *Xuanzang: A Buddhist Pilgrim on the Silk Road* finally came out in 1996.[42] I must have worked on it for about ten years. I was seventy-four years old when it was published. It was beautifully produced and I was pleased. My editor, Ellen Roberts, gave me a blank notebook, "On the Road with Xuanzang," to record "the secrets only lionized authors can tell." It had a picture of Fred Astaire and Ginger Rogers on the cover. A Tibetan monk came to my first book party and presented me with a white prayer scarf. When I put it around my shoulders, I felt it would be "all right"—that I had, so to speak, been blessed by him.

The book of my new friend Sun Shuyun, *Ten Thousand Miles Without a Cloud*, was published in 2003. She was the one who showed me that one's attitude toward the Chinese pilgrim—how one approaches Xuanzang—affects the questions one asks, the places one tries to explore, the personal traits one finds, the end result.

Chasing the Monk's Shadow, published in 2005, was written by a young Indian journalist, Mishi Saran.[43] She was born in Allahabad but left when she was ten. She became fascinated by China while she was studying at Wellesley. According to an article in the college's alumnae magazine, Saran thinks of herself as "an Indian girl with a Chinese craze, and Xuanzang as a Chinese monk with an Indian obsession."

There is also an Indian scholar, Dr. D. Devahuti, whom I met once in New Delhi in the eighties. She died in 1988 and her book, *The Unknown Hsuan-Tsang*, was published in 2001.[44] I remember going for a walk with her in the early cool of the morning in Lodhi Estates, a beautiful fifteenth-century Moghul garden with old tombs, near International House. We talked about the sweep of Xuanzang's life. Did he have a single unwavering purpose which never changed, or was he a very different person as a young man?

There are, of course, many Chinese and Japanese books on Xuanzang. However, I had the fun of being first in English, of working alone, writing about a subject that was not known in the West. I was pleased that, in the new edition, I was described as "the first woman and the first Westerner to travel extensively in the footsteps of Xuanzang." I have been well rewarded with translations into Chinese, Korean, Dutch, Italian, German, and Greek.

If I am tempted to flatter myself, I also take seriously the idea that there are still undiscovered treasures that remain to be found. I am not unmindful, as T. H. Barratt put it, "that the journey that started beneath my feet is yet longer and more marvelous" than I was able to convey.[45] Maybe in my next incarnation I can learn Chinese and Japanese, and go to some of the places that were not yet open to me when I was in Asia.

Chapter 18

AFGHANISTAN AND ITS SILK ROAD HERITAGE

We shall not cease from exploration
And the end of our exploring
Will be to arrive where we started
And know the place for the first time.[46]

W here and when did I become intrigued by Afghanistan? Where did the sparks become a flame? Was it when I learned that Xuanzang had described the giant Buddhas of Bamiyan? When I first explored that small Silk Road Museum in Kabul in 1969? When I first pored over maps of Aghanistan in the Embassy Residence in 1974 to see where Xuanzang had been?

Afghanistan was strategically placed to thrive from Silk Road caravans, which came from the Roman Empire in the West, China in the East, and India in the South. Bamiyan served as a monastic center as well as the hub of commercial activity. Buddhist monks first arrived here about the second century. Later they began to scoop out enormous alcoves in which they cut the core of the

gigantic Buddhas, shaping them with stucco and then painting and
gilding them. Because of the brilliance of the gilding, Xuanzang
thought that one of the Buddhas was made of bronze.

Xuanzang was the first to describe the Buddhas. The Chinese
pilgrim had reached Afghanistan from China in 630 C.E. after
years of travelling. His caravan had prevailed against blizzards,
mountain gods, and robbers. As he finally approached Bamiyan, an
oasis town in the center of a long valley separating the chain of the
Hindu Kush from that of the Koh-i-baba range, he glimpsed these
giant statues. The first sight of the valley of the Great Buddhas
must have made him gasp—immense cliffs of a soft pastel color,
and behind them indigo peaks dusted with snow, rising to a height
of 20,000 feet. He saw reddish cliffs in the cold, clear air; as he
came closer, he could make out two gigantic statues of the Buddha
standing in niches carved into the cliffs. Xuanzang writes:

> On the declivity of a hill to the north-east of the
> capital was a standing image of the Buddha made of
> stone, 140 or 150 feet high, of a brilliant golden
> color and resplendent with the ornamentation of
> precious substances. To the east of it was a
> Buddhist monastery built by a former king of the
> country. East of this was a standing image of
> Sakyamuni Buddha above 100 feet high, made of
> t'u-shih (bronze), the pieces of which had been cast
> separately and welded together into one figure.[47]

These two Buddhas, which face south, an orientation that
ensures the full benefit of the sun's warmth, were actually 175 feet
high and 125 feet high respectively.

Because of my new fascination with Xuanzang, I urged
Howard to think of returning to Afghanistan to see Bamiyan. We
had first tried to visit in 1974, but a blizzard in the mountains
prevented our going. Our second attempt was to be in May of
1979, when we planned to see the Buddhas with Spike Dubs, the
American Ambassador. While we were still in Sri Lanka, an
enthusiastic letter from Dubs reached us in Colombo, saying how

much he was looking forward to going to Bamiyan with us, and perhaps afterward to Mazar-i-Sharif. By the time Dubs's letter arrived, we already knew that he had been murdered in Kabul the week before. I still recall vividly the eerie feeling of receiving a letter from Spike a week after his death.

Dubs was stocky, an earthy, engaging guy. Howard had known him in the State Department when Spike had been Assistant Secretary for the Near East and South Asia. Howard felt he was both calm and wise in tough situations. Among other things, he had rescued Louis Dupree, a well-known American anthropologist whom the Russians were trying to imprison as a CIA agent. An expert in Soviet affairs, the Ambassador was President Carter's choice to represent America in Afghanistan as part of the U.S. "business as usual" approach to the Soviet presence there. The fact that Dubs spoke Russian may have been his undoing; perhaps they thought he knew too much.

A rebel group had kidnapped him and held him in a hotel in Kabul; apparently they thought this hostage might be useful in pressing the existing government to release one of their members. In this tense situation the Russians were advising the local police, who rushed the hotel; Dubs and all the kidnappers were killed. We were devastated, and, understandably, our trip to Bamiyan was cancelled.

Later in 1979, the Soviets did take over the Afghan government in an effort to prop up a Communist regime in Kabul. They occupied Afghanistan until they were defeated by the Mujaheddeen, the religious warriors who were financed and equipped by the United States and Saudi Arabia. A decade later, after a million and a half people had died, the Soviets withdrew. Unhappily, the Mujaheddeen continued to fight among themselves until a new group called the Taliban gradually gained control of the country and finally captured Kabul in 1996.

At first, many welcomed the arrival of the Taliban, who seemed to promise an end to the destruction wrought by the warring Mujaheddeen factions. In the beginning, Mullah Mohammed Omar, their narrowly educated leader, promised to protect Afghanistan's cultural heritage. But eventually Taliban hardliners, supported by Arab fighters loyal to the Saudi zealot Osama bin Laden, took over the government. Not long after, the Mullah agreed to the destruction of the Bamiyan Buddhas and all statues in different parts of the country. On March 23, 2001 the Taliban bombed the Buddhas of Bamiyan. Were they really aware of what they were doing? The giant Buddhas, the largest stone statues in the world, were among Asia's great archaeological treasures. In the end, the Taliban achieved something they had not intended—the weeks of shelling and the final demolition of the statues called the whole world's attention to Afghanistan's rich Buddhist past and the history of these stone sculptures; Afghanistan became "The Land of the Buddhas."

Xuanzang also mentions a third Buddha, 1000 feet long, in a supine position. One of the men forced to lay explosives to destroy the standing Buddhas is now organizing a substantial archaeological dig to find it. News stories in major American newspapers and magazines, as well as a television program sponsored by the National Geographic Society, have focused on the search for the Third Buddha.

Whenever Howard went to Afghanistan in the sixties for the State Department, he made a point of trying to talk to Louis Dupree and his wife Nancy. She and Louis were married in 1966 in a 19th-century palace in Kabul. She wore a blue velvet dress and an enameled gold belt, a gift from Louis that he said had belonged to an emir. Louis pledged, according to the requirements of a Muslim marriage ceremony, to compensate Nancy's family, should he ever leave her.

The guarantee was 10,000 Persian sheep.

The Duprees were devoted to Afghanistan and its people, traveling all over the country visiting small villages as well as excavation sites. In addition to making ethnographic films with her husband, Nancy Dupree also published many guides to the region, including the very ambitious *Historical Guide to Afghanistan.*[48]

The leader of the Taliban who ordered the shelling of the Buddhas reflected that if the Western world were not concerned about the one and a half million Afghans killed during their civil wars, why were we so concerned about their cultural heritage?

Nancy Dupree would argue that a nation that loses its heritage loses its soul. She started the Society for the Preservation of Afghanistan's Cultural Heritage (SPACH) and has been busy forwarding their work.

She was less sanguine about the museum, where an estimated seventy percent of the collection has been destroyed or looted. The staff of the museum did pack up a good number of pieces and stashed them in different places around Kabul, and the Tilla-tepe collection of 21,000 Bactrian gold objects (dating from the first century B.C.E. to the first century A.D.) was found intact in a sealed government vault in the Presidential Palace in April, 2003. But Nancy's field research revealed that plunder has taken place everywhere. Mujaheddeen units used pickaxes, bulldozers and even Land Rovers to ravage sites like Balkh, an ancient city that Alexander the Great made his headquarters from 329 to 327 B.C.E. Alas, this was also true of the extensive site of Ai Khanoum, the easternmost Greek city yet known.

The first time I went to the Kabul Museum—armed with Nancy's guidebook[49]—was on our round-the-world trip in 1969. I was entranced. It was cold, oh, so cold. We shivered in our overcoats and scarves, treading the icy floors of the unpretentious villa that housed the Kabul Museum collection. I wandered from room to room—the Begram room, the Bamiyan room, the Hadda room, the beguiling Fondukistan room—not knowing that these were the names of archaeological sites where the treasures were found. It was a rushed visit, and I only vaguely remember that there were also cases and cases of gold coins and rooms devoted to Prehistoric and Islamic art.

I stopped for a long time to look at the Buddha heads from Hadda, and was amazed by the small ugly faces of demons with grotesque eyes and pointed ears, that looked as though they had just come from French Gothic cathedrals. Yet these gargoyle-like objects dated from the first to the third centuries, a thousand years before their Gothic counterparts. Evelyn Ames, in her *Time Like Glass*, wonders: "Did some migratory wave bring their kind to Europe? Or do some forms tend to develop at different times in different parts of the world?"

I knew vaguely, very vaguely, about Bamiyan and Hadda, but the Begram ivories from India, carved on the lids of large boxes or coffins, were a true surprise. So were the Greek and Roman bronze statues of Hercules and Silenus, and a Greek horseman. And the elegant clay sculptures of a royal couple, and a Buddha and a Bodhisattva in the Fondukistan room, with their languid gracefulness, were like nothing I had ever seen before.

What were all these precious artifacts doing in Afghanistan? Why here? On that visit I missed many things, including the only known representation of the Lighthouse of Alexandria. At that time I had no conception, either, of Afghanistan as the half way point on the Silk Road, half way between Rome and Xian in China—or, for that matter, of Afghanistan as one of the most deeply land-locked countries in Asia. I had no idea of the volume of travel that took place in the ancient world. Unless we think of the Crusades, it is hard to conceive that so many monks, pilgrims and traders were once on the Silk Roads.

It was years before I came to realize these things, and to feel that the exquisite carved glass vase showing the Alexandrian Lighthouse, one of the Seven Wonders of the World, was a perfect symbol for the Silk Road in Afghanistan. The vase carries a representation of the Pharos, the Lighthouse. Standing on the Lighthouse is Poseidon, the Greek god of the sea, flanked by two Tritons. On the reverse side are depicted a galley with banks of oars, a merchant ship with a sail, and a small fishing boat.

Unlike any other museum that I know of, this modest villa contained a fabulous array of objects, none of which was acquired by purchase. For centuries these treasures had been buried in the earth in ancient temples, palaces and monasteries, until Délégation Archaeologique Française en Afghanistan (DAFA) began its archaeological digs in 1922. French teams working with Afghan researchers slowly uncovered their finds in Bactria, Begram, Hadda and Bamiyan, bringing Afghan history into the light.

And now it is gone—or most of it is. On May 12, 1993, as the Mujaheddeen factions fought each other, rockets slammed into the roof of the museum. As serious as the destruction of the Kabul Museum was, the looting for illegal sales on the international antiquities market has further diminished the museum's holdings. Looted artifacts passed from soldiers, guided by Pakistani and Afghani experts, to antique dealers in Kabul, Peshawar and Islamabad, to private art collectors around the world. A single Buddha statue might bring tens of thousands of dollars.

The war and the subsequent looting have destroyed a museum that was a repository of Afghanistan's history and culture, the most comprehensive record anywhere of civilizations that thrived along the ancient Silk Road. The collections spanned more than 50,000 years—from cave-dwelling tribes that lived along the Oxus River to early Hindu, Buddhist and Islamic dynasties, and on to Durrani kings who ruled Afghanistan before the current upheavals. But after all these losses, we still have the historical record, documentation of what has been, including Xuanzang's Report to the Tang Emperor on the Western Regions.

Several people have tried to catalogue the collection of ivories, statues, paintings, coins, gold, pottery, armaments and dress in the Kabul Museum. Among them is an old friend, Dr. Francine Tissot, whom I met in 1991 when I asked the head of the Musée Guimet if someone could show me the museum's pieces from Shotorok Monastery in Afghanistan. She is the author of several beautifully illustrated books on Gandharan art. I had been corresponding with her ever since. On our last overseas trip in 2001 (to Morocco) we stopped in Paris to see the Musée Guimet, which we had been unable to visit on recent travels because it had been closed for several years for restoration. Dr. Tissot was no longer on the staff of the museum but she asked us to tea in her apartment. A portly woman with wide grey eyes, she moved slowly around her living room. Something about the bemused expression on her face made me feel very much at home.

The occasion was nice for Howard, too, because he had lived in France several times and once spoke French fluently. He still spoke it with pleasure; he took on a new self, his eyebrows going up and down, he gestured with his hands with great gusto. He leaned forward. I have always loved to watch him when he speaks French. We found ourselves seated in front of a huge refectory table, heavy and dark, facing floor-to-ceiling bookcases. Their shelves were not for slim French novels; they were filled with large encyclopedic tomes. The drapes—heavier than curtains— were also dark, floor to ceiling. We sipped tea. We talked and talked, Howard and Dr. Tissot recalling the way things were shortly after World War II.

When I thanked her for helping me obtain the photographs of the Dipankara Buddha and the Lighthouse of Alexandria, Dr. Tissot told us that they didn't know where the glass vase was, The Lighthouse of Alexandria, the one that used to be in the Kabul Museum.

"But you know, someone dropped it when they were moving things around, in the 1980s."

We gasped.

"It shattered into thousands of pieces."

She paused. "But Mr. Popenoe of the DAFA (French Archaeological Delegation of Afghanistan) was able to restore it. It took a year, and he's written it up in *Asia Major*.

"I'll look it up."

Dr. Tissot and I talked about our love of Buddhist art; we discussed Japanese interest in Buddhism, the destruction of the Buddhas at Bamiyan, the marvelous museum in Kabul. As daylight turned to darkness, we all stayed in our seats. The magic of that afternoon stands on its own, but it would have been fun to know then, as I learned later, that Dr. Tissot had four children and, now, five grandchildren, just as I have three children and six grandchildren.

Born in Paris in 1917, Dr. Tissot had studied English at the Sorbonne. She began her career late in life, having been busy raising children for twenty years, as was I. In 1963, on a three-month holiday in Kashmir and Pakistan, she discovered Central Asian art. She concentrated on the Gandharan art of Pakistan and Afghanistan, earned another degree, and launched a distinguished career at the Musée Guimet.

It is presumptuous, I know, even to think of it, but I felt very close to this warm, attractive woman, as someone who had also begun a career and pursued it so late in life, as I had done. For Dr. Tissot our time together that day might have amounted to a very pleasant afternoon, but for me it was much more. Watching the day grow into night brought with it a sense of closure, and reminded me that I had had a very rich life and that I had accomplished what I had set out to do so many years ago—to make Xuanzang come alive and become known for the great man that he was.

Afterword

Howard and I can still go exploring. These spring days we make our excursions in the forests around our home in Hanover, New Hampshire. We search for trilliums, trailing arbutus, jack-in-the pulpits. I carry Howard's tripod and the stool for him to sit on. He carries a heavy camera case with several lenses that seems to have gotten heavier over the years. We walk slowly. The season for finding our treasures and taking photographs is very short. Soon the canopy of leaves in the forest will block out the sun and the wildflowers will be gone until next year.

> Come, thieving time, take what you must,
> Quickness to move, to hear, to see,
> When dust gathers near to dust,
> Such diminutions need must be,
> But leave, O leave, exempt from plunder,
> My sense of humor, curiosity, and wonder.[50]

In our bedroom at Kendal, a Quaker-inspired retirement community, hangs a student watercolor of two green pine trees with their dark trunks growing side by side. We bought it together at Eliot O'Hara's watercolor school at Goose Rocks Beach in Maine when Howard was courting me. It was as if we were trying out the feeling of owning something together. Each tree grows in its own direction, still the branches and leaves intertwine and play

261

with one another. I remember thinking to myself, "That is what I'd like our marriage to be about."

Ten years ago we celebrated our fiftieth wedding anniversary with our children and their children at Rudyard Kipling's house in nearby Brattleboro, Vermont. This very spacious Victorian house looks like a huge dark green ship riding on a wave. For two years Kipling and his American wife lived in this house, with its dark paneling, long hallways and colossal bathtubs with their wooden rims. It was here that he began to write *Kim*. Kipling once admitted, "There are only two places in the world where I want to live—Bombay and Brattleboro." In the study at the end of one of the long hallways, in exactly the spot where Kipling composed them, Howard read the *Just So Stories* aloud to our grandchildren. Will they remember where they first heard "How the Elephant Got Its Trunk"? Probably not, but we will remember. Given our many years in and out of Asia, it seemed just right.

To our children, Kipling was not only a great storyteller, but an old-fashioned defender of imperialism. When I was growing up in the thirties, the British Empire was very much alive, and much of my early awareness of things Asian was filtered through the knowledge of which European nation owned what part of the non-Western world.

That awareness of Asia came to me gradually. I remembered my older brothers taking a course in high school called "Pacific Rim"—I thought that sounded intriguing. My childhood friend Toto Ohata was Japanese/American. I knew a little about Asia from visiting the Asian Art Museum in Seattle, where I often stood fascinated by the mysterious smiles of the Khmer sandstone Buddhas. I knew about Northwest painters such as Morris Graves and Mark Tobey, whose inspiration was Asian.

I was eighteen when the exotic young Indian patriot came to our school to plead the case for Indian independence, followed a few months later by a middle-aged British army colonel defending imperialism. I could scarcely have imagined that the Indian would be a symbol of the future—my future—and point to my husband's career: for Howard's scholarship came to focus on the problems of newly independent countries. (India became independent in 1947 and Ceylon in 1948.) I recall our excitement about India's independence and how horrified we were by the massacres of Indians and Pakistanis that followed the partition of India. In the fifties we lived in a very British Ceylon while Howard researched his first book, *Dilemmas of a New Nation*. Bit by bit we became immersed in Asia, Howard in its politics and I in Asian religions. I tried to write about the firewalking that was carried on by Hindus and Buddhists alike.

So Asia came to be much on our minds. In Washington we knew many Sri Lankans, Indians and Pakistanis, old friends in government, diplomacy, journalism involved in Asia, from our time in Ceylon and in connection with Howard's responsibilities on the Policy Planning Council of the State Department. The men were all busy with their jobs, but there were few outlets for Asian women at the time.

So a group of us created what was later known as the Asian-American Forum. It still exists today, although the seminars are not quite as ambitious as they were when Sally Smith was bringing Asian and American participants together to discuss what constitutes progress. I came to know Indian journalists and very able Asian diplomatic wives. At our annual meeting, I got to stand in the receiving line with Faure Nehru, wife of the Indian Ambassador. (She was actually Hungarian, although few people knew it and she wore a sari with grace.) I remember watching her as she fingered a woman's necklace and complimented her on how stunning it was. Now that I think of it, quite apart from the stimulation of the seminars, I was gaining practical experience in diplomacy.

Our immersion in Asia deepened when Howard and I with two of our children traveled around the world. To prepare for his new job as Director of the Southern Asian Institute at Columbia, Howard wanted to visit scholars and universities in Europe and in Asia. We had the luxury of spending six months in India, Pakistan, Afghanistan, Nepal, Ceylon and Japan, as well as countries in Southeast Asia, even catching a glimpse of Communist China from the New Territories next to Hong Kong. My head was filled with images for a possible children's book about an exchange of ghosts between Asia and America, but I could never quite pull it off.

More enduring were memories of the cave paintings at Ajanta in India, the astonishing Silk Road Museum in Afghanistan, the vast temple area of Angkor Wat—an overview of Asian art and images that I would draw on for years to come. This immersion in Asia had also given me the experience of the physical backdrop of the Indian sub-continent, for in those days we flew in much smaller planes at lower altitudes and could see rising mountain ranges, the vast plains of India, the tropical forests. This sense of place enabled me to imagine the journey along the Silk Road made by the Chinese pilgrim, Xuanzang. This seventh-century traveler had seen the haunting Indian art in the Ajanta caves, as well as the site of ancient cities at Taxila—and now, so had I.

It was some time after we moved to Riverdale that I met Anne Goodrich, "an old China hand." She introduced me to *Monkey,* the first part of the Chinese epic *Journey to the West.* I retold the story of the mischievous Monkey, who acquired magic powers and created havoc in Heaven before setting out on a mythical journey with a monk. Because so few Americans seemed to know the Monkey story, I organized an exhibition, "The Nine Lives and Ancient Background of Monkey," at the New York Public Library.

In order to convey just how ancient the background of Monkey was, I included a copy of a fresco from the Dunhuang Caves in the Gobi desert, depicting Xuanzang the historical monk with his elephant—an elephant given to him by King Harsha; a greatly enlarged map showing his route from China to India, dated 630 C.E.; a picture of the Wild Goose Pagoda, the special temple that the Tang Emperor built to house the scriptures Xuanzang brought back from India. I also displayed the cover of Anthony Yu's book, *Journey to the West*, a full translation of the Monkey story that had just been published at the same time as my own book, *White Monkey King.*

Bit by bit, I got swept up in this fascinating history. I still found it astonishing that Xuanzang's journey had taken place between 629 and 645 C.E. Wasn't this a time when Europe was overrun by barbarians and England did not yet have a written history? When the story of King Arthur was just starting to become legend? Learning, scholarship and culture had ebbed from the

European continent and were just beginning to flow back. Yet on the other side of the world, a highly educated monk had taken a 10,000-mile journey to India to obtain the true Buddhist scriptures. He not only brought them back to China, along with intriguing artifacts, he also wrote an accurate report of the Western Region for the Emperor of the culturally rich and powerful Tang Empire.

I was smitten. I was not a scholar, that I knew, and I was poaching in new fields of Asian scholarship. Isaiah Berlin has noted that people are either foxes, who run around curious about everything, or hedgehogs, who dig deep in one place. I have known for a long time that I was a hedgehog and Howard was a fox. My furrow, the rich soil that I dug in—for about ten years, was it?—was Chinese history and culture in the seventh century. I was captivated by the Silk Road. I had always been fascinated by the literature of pilgrimage and Buddhist art as it developed in Asia. I didn't know how to put this passion into words, but Fritz Mote did: he said that I was "deeply stirred to understand the inescapable attraction of a powerful personality," that of the many-sided Xuanzang.

Xuanzang: A Buddhist Pilgrim on the Silk Road was published in 1996. It was an optimum time, for the Asian world was opening up to the West and people were fascinated by the Silk Road. The book did very well. It was translated into six languages and came out both in paperback and in a revised edition.

I have always admired the Indian ideas about the four stages of life: living with the family as a child; leading an austere life at the home of one's teacher as a student; returning to one's parental home as a householder with all the responsibilities of raising children; leaving home as a hermit in order to free the soul from material things. I thought of this not long ago when I received a letter from Himani Lal Khanna (a student of Howard's at Vassar who had accompanied me on a research trip to Mathura). She described the demolition of her family house near New Delhi. In its place are now three beautiful homes for Himani's children and grandchildren, "all independent and yet together."

For most American women, Anne Lindbergh's *Gift from the Sea,* with its vivid metaphors of the early stages of life, provides a more accessible model. She begins with a channeled whelk (which occupies the shell of a hermit crab) and a moonshell (symbol of solitude); then she describes a double-sunrise shell of love. She goes on to show the proliferation of children and possessions as an oyster shell, and finally describes shedding one's shell to go off alone as the paper nautilus. She is concerned with balancing life as a wife and mother with her work as a writer. She touches on widening circles of relationships and communications, just as I was trying to do long before email and cell phones.

Communication has been changing and continues to change. I feel almost antediluvian as I sift through old letters from Ceylon— those precious blue envelopes that unfold to reveal their messages on the inside; a telegram (remember?) announcing Jenny's birth in 1957; the 5" x 7" spiral notebooks I kept on my travels in the seventies, eighties and nineties; sixty years of letters from friends and family; email and print-outs from the Internet about recent events in Sri Lanka, Japan or Afghanistan. There are still shelves of books, fragile scrapbooks and slides. For many years Howard and I have written an annual Christmas letter which has been an invaluable source for the history I share in this memoir. I have also pored over novels, reference books and books of poems by my friends. Among them is *Dust on a Precipice* by Evelyn Ames, and this poem called "The Web: On finding an orb spider's web on a foggy morning."

Something keeps connecting
those of like heart and mind
whoever they are, however
many latitudes and longitudes apart:
they are joined. The threads, invisible
as air, quiver with life—
resilient strong—
like spider's gossamer that sags with dew—,
gets rain-pelted and yanked
by wind, yet doesn't tear.
Whatever it is weaves
us together, the web embraces
and surrounds the world.

Evvie was a member of the Lady Philosophers, that remarkable group of women in New York whose purpose was to discuss life's deeper meanings. I joined in the 1970s. Evvie was always generous with her gifts of discovery and meaning. Occasionally I had sought her advice in writing. I knew her as a poet and had read her books about Asia and Africa. Evvie and her husband Amyas spent a Christmas with us in Sri Lanka where we discovered that Amie was devoted to photography and took beautiful pictures. Howard had been a photographer many years before. Inspired by Amie, he has taken it up again. When Howard was planning a trip to Nairobi, Evvie introduced us to Bob Lowis, who had been their guide on African safaris. Bob was our guide too when we went to the Serengeti Plain where we were privileged to see the migration of the wildebeest.

After Evvie died, she gave me yet another gift, when we attended her services at St. John the Divine in New York. As part of the service we sang a Taizé chant, "Adoramus Te," which was my introduction to the extraordinary Taizé chanting. Later Howard and I went on to visit the Taizé community in France, where Brother Roger Schutz has set up a center for many young people of all nations to gather for worship. I find Taizé worship very congenial, especially since sometimes we Friends can get so absorbed in our social concerns that we forget all about adoration.

Ben Booz once declared that her "ascension music" would be Beethoven's *Triple Concerto*. I would opt for the joy and majesty of Bach.

Asia is still on my mind, and on Howard's mind as well. But we think about it in different ways. I didn't appreciate this difference until I began to write, and realized that I had learned about Ceylon and Sri Lanka from relationships with people: from my friend Punitham Tiruchelvam and from Kheminda Thera the Buddhist priest; about Burma and exploration from Jeanette Mirsky; about China from many friends, Anne Goodrich, Betty Lou Hummel, Ben Booz, Victor Mair and Fritz Mote; about Pakistan from Arthur and Betty Lou Hummel; about Japan from Ginny Anami; and about Afghanistan from Nancy Dupree. I also learned from Xuanzang, the Silk Road pilgrim who was the subject of my biography.

Why write one's life story? Marcia Davenport says that one has to be "in the late span of life" to write a true memoir. I don't know whether this is so, but it does seem to be a good time—I am in my mid-eighties—to tell stories, look for patterns and continuities, for the times when one's expectations were way off the mark, such as when I found myself in a hospital instead of going overseas with UNRRA. I thought for a brief time that I might not be able either to have children or to travel, and that I wouldn't live very long.

T.S. Eliot says in "Dry Salvages" that "we had the experience and missed the meaning." I am sure this happens. Can I see the shape, the contours of my life? Learn from the past? Try to assimilate what has happened after so many years in different countries in Europe and Asia? Or try to remember a time when so many countries were newly independent and we were so full of hope? Above all, can I provide a kind of historical record for our children and their children? There are many questions I wished I had asked my mother and father before they died. Especially one: I would love to have known what it was like to cross the country in 1906 when my father went west to San Francisco. I am sure he must have had wonderful stories.

In the early 1980s I wrote a "then and now" book about Ceylon and Sri Lanka. What was I like as a young mother and later as a diplomat's wife, what was Ceylon like in the 1950s, and what was Sri Lanka like two decades later? Although it was never published, I am glad I wrote it. A few years ago Ellen Roberts, my writing mentor, urged me to describe my journeys to Burma, Pakistan, China, India, Afghanistan and Japan as well. She encouraged me to discuss the experience of writing about Xuanzang along the Silk Road. I hadn't thought about trying to depict the intensive years when I was trying just to understand his *Report to the Tang Emperor*. And yet I have vivid memories of the early days, of being in the grip of something I couldn't quite define. I had to put together ancient and modern names of people and places. Since Yogachara Buddhism was the kind of Buddhism that attracted Xuanzang, I had to grasp its notoriously difficult concepts along with other esoteric Buddhist ideas. I had to become familiar with not only medieval Chinese language—which was daunting, even in translation—but also medieval thinking, in order to enter the whole world of Xuanzang.

While I was expanding my writing about my Asian experience, Ellen suddenly collapsed. I almost stopped writing. But she recovered, her doctor commenting, "A miracle is only a statistical deviation, but it is always nice to see one." Back at work on my memoir, she saw my life in a different light. The lonely trek of a Buddhist monk, she told me, paralleled my sojourn as an independent scholar. Xuanzang's brother gave him an unusual start in life, just as my family had with me. She urged me to explore my childhood and describe growing up in the energizing atmosphere of Seattle in the thirties. I relied almost entirely on childhood memories this time, and had fun doing it. Thus *Asia on my Mind* became a full autobiography, covering the entire chronology of my life.

Endnotes

[1] Dinesen, Isak, *Last Tales* (New York: Random House, 1957), 87.

[2] Sarathchandra, E. R., "Maname, Spirit of the Maheveli," in *The Sinhalese Folk Play and the Modern Stage* (Colombo: Ceylon University Press, 1953).

[3] Kipling, Rudyard, "In the Neolithic Age," in *Collected Verse* (New York: Doubleday Dora, 1926), 395.

[4] Tieck, William A., *Riverdale, Kingsbridge, Spuyten Duyvil: A Historical Epitome of the Northwest Bronx* (Old Tappan, N.J.: Fleming Revell Co., 1968), 111.

[5] Waley, Arthur, trans., *Monkey by Wu Cheng-en* (New York: Grove Press, 1943).

[6] Goodrich, Anne Swann, *The Peking Temple of the Eastern Peak* (Nagoya: Monumenta Serica, 1965), Monograph 15.

[7] Goodrich, Anne Swann, *Chinese Hells: The Peking Temple of Eighteen Hells and Chinese Conceptions of Hell* (St. Augustin: Monumenta Serica, 1981).

[8] Goodrich, Anne Swann, *Peking Paper Gods: A Look at Home Worship* (Nettetal: Steyler Verlag, 1991).

[9] Goodrich, Anne Swann, "Miao Feng Shan," *Asian Folklore Studies* 57(1998)1: 87-97.

[10] Forster, E. M., *Goldsworthy Lowes Dickinson* (New York: Harcourt Brace, 1934).

[11] Beal, Samuel, trans. *Si-yu-ki Buddhist Record of the Western World by Hiuen Tsiang*, 2 vols. (London, 1884; Reprint, Delhi: Oriental Books Reprint Corp.1969); and Watters, Thomas, trans. *On Yuan Chwang's Travels in India,* 2 vols. (London 1904-05; reprint, Delhi: Munshiram Manoharlal, 1961).

[12] Beal, Samuel, trans., *The Life of Hiuen-Tsiang, by Shaman Hwui Li* (London, 1884; reprint, Delhi: Munshiram Manoharlal, 1973).

[13] State Department Post Report 1977. Washington D.C.

[14] Millay, Edna St. Vincent, "Renascence," in *Renascence and Other Poems* (New York: Harper, 1917), 1.

[15] Ehara, Rev. N. R. M., Soma Thera, and Kheminda Thera, trans., *The Path of Freedom (Vimutti Magga)* (Kandy, Sri Lanka: Buddhist Publication Society, 1977) 164.

[16] Nanamoli Thera, trans., *Mindfulness of Breathing (Anapanasati)* [Buddhist texts from the Pali Canon and from the Pali Commentaries] (Kandy, Sri Lanka: Buddhist Publication Society, 1973).

[17] Ehara, Rev. N. R. M., Soma Thera, and Kheminda Thera, trans. from the Chinese, *The Arahant Upatissa, The Path of Freedom, translated into Chinese by Tipitaka Sanghapala of Funan* (Kandy, Sri Lanka: Buddhist Publication Society, 1977).

[18] *The Path of Freedom*, 104.

[19] *Mindfulness of Breathing*, 6.

[20] Woolf, Virginia, *Moments of being: unpublished autobiographical writings* (New York: Harcourt Brace Jovanovich, 1976), 79.

[21] Conze, Edward, ed. and tr., *Buddhist Scriptures* (Harmondsworth: Penguin, 1984), 148.

[22] Hartill, Lane, "When Life in a War Zone Tests US Families," *Christian Science Monitor*, Oct. 17, 2001, p. 18.

[23] Middleton, Nick, *Extremes Along the Silk Road* (London: John Murray, 2005), 29-30.

[24] The beginning of a chant from Taizé, an international ecumenical monastic community in southern France. *Chants from Taizé* (Taizé, France: Ateliers et Presses de Taizé, 1991).

[25] Wriggins, Sally Hovey, "A Monk's Journey to the Buddhist Holy Land," *Orientations* 10/10 (October 1979), 54-58.

[26] Yu, Anthony C., trans., *Journey to the West*, 4 vols. (Chicago: University of Chicago Press, 1977-83).

[27] Eliot, T. S., "Burnt Norton," in *Four Quartets* (New York: Harcourt Brace, 1943), 5.

[28] Kipling, Rudyard, *Kim* (Leipzig: Bernhard Tauchnitz, 1911), 11.

[29] Cahill, Thomas, *How the Irish Saved Civilization* (New York: Anchor, 1995), 262.

[30] Ben Booz to Sally Wriggins, personal letter, October 30, 1972.

[31] Fritz Mote to Sally Wriggins, personal letter, November 27, 1992.

[32] Rosenstone, Robert, *Mirror in the Shrine: American Encounters with Meiji Japan* (Cambridge: Harvard University Press, 1988).

[33] Fritz Mote to Sally Wriggins, personal letter, May 25, 1985.

[34] Jan Morris, in National Book League of Great Britain, ed. Gillian Vincent, *Writers' Favorite Recipes* (New York: St. Martin's Press, 1979), 2.

[35] I. B. Horner, trans., *Collection of Middle Length Sayings*, vol. 1 (London: Luzac, 1957).

[36] Speech Given by Honourable Albie Sachs, January 31, 2000, from Indian Center for Ethnic Studies Law and Society Trust.

[37] Speech in the Sri Lankan Parliament, June 15, 1999, by Dr. Neelan Tiruchelvam in opposition the re-imposition of the death penalty.

[38] Newsletter of The American Council for Southern Asian Art, Fall/Winter issue 1999, #52.

[39] Sobel, Dava, *Longitude: The True Story of a Lone Genius Who Solved the Greatest Scientific Problem of His Time* (New York: Walker, 1995).

[40] Sun Shuyun, *Ten Thousand Miles Without a Cloud* (London: Harper Collins, 2003).

[41] Wriggins, Sally Hovey, "Ikuo Hirayama, Artist and Advocate," *Orientations* 32:8 (October 2001): 88-93.

[42] Wriggins, Sally Hovey, *Xuanzang: A Buddhist Pilgrim on the Silk Road* (Boulder: Westview Press, 1996).

[43] Saran, Mishi, *Chasing the Monk's Shadow: A Journey in the Footsteps of Zuanzang* (London: Viking/Penguin, 2005).

[44] Devahuti, D., ed., *The Unknown Xuanzang* (New Delhi: Oxford University Press, 2001).

[45] Barratt, T. H., in *Journal of the Royal Asiatic Society* 7/2 (July 1997), 331.

[46] Eliot, T. S., "Little Gidding," in *Four Quartets* (New York: Harcourt, Brace, 1943), 39.

[47] Wriggins, *Xuanzang*, 44.

[48] Dupree, Nancy Hatch, *An Historical Guide to Afghanistan* (Afghan Air Authority, 1971).

[49] Dupree, Nancy Hatch, Louis Dupree, and A. A. Motamedi, *The National Museum Of Afghanistan: An Illustrated Guide* (The Afghan Tourist Organization & The Afghan Air Authority, 1974).

[50] Anonymous poem, from 93-year-old lady, given to her pastor in Washington church. Gathered on the Internet 7/9/06, at http://www.weeks-g.dircon.co.uk/page1.html.

Printed in the United States
207429BV00001B/358-375/P

9 781432 721800